American Poetry Contemporary Bibliography Series
General Editor: Lee Bartlett

Clayton Eshleman
A Descriptive Bibliography

by

Martha J. Sattler

American Poetry Contemporary Bibliography Series, No. 4

McFarland & Company, Inc., Publishers
Jefferson, North Carolina, and London

Frontispiece photo of Clayton Eshleman by Nina Subin.

British Library Cataloguing-in-Publication data available

Library of Congress Cataloguing-in-Publication Data

Sattler, Martha J., 1926–
  Clayton Eshleman : a descriptive bibliography.

  (American poetry contemporary bibliography series ;
no. 4)
  Includes index.
  1. Eshleman, Clayton — Bibliography. I. Title.
II. Series.
Z8272.44.S27 1988 [PS3555.S5] 016.811′54   88-42647

ISBN 0-89950-319-5 (lib. bdg.; 50# acid-free natural paper)

Printed in the United States of America.

McFarland Box 611 Jefferson NC 28640

For my husband, Ronald,
and my three daughters,
Carol, Nancy and Laura,
and my grandchildren,
Jennifer and Miles

Acknowledgments

I am grateful to many people who gave me encouragement and cheerfully helped me with information and advice. Foremost among them is Clayton Eshleman, without whom this bibliography would, of course, never have been written. His help and encouragement included the use of his personal library, suggestions about how to find publishers for information, and information on archival material in libraries. He has patiently answered many questions, some asked over and over again, looked over the final manuscript to make corrections, and graciously enhanced this work with an afterward.

One of Clayton's most valuable suggestions was that I contact Frank Walker at Fales Special Collections Library at New York University for a list of periodicals with Eshleman contributions. With this list, which I received in October of 1984, I was able to collect many of these magazines through bookdealers throughout the United States.

Although most of the books I have described are in my own library, I am also very grateful to the UCLA Research Library, as well as the Archive for New Poetry at the University of California–San Diego (UCSD) (Linda Claassen, director, and Jeff Wexler, archivist). Again, I must thank Frank Walker (and his assistant Russell James) who not only had a very well organized and preserved Eshleman archive, but was very helpful with assistance in my first use of the New York subway.

Joyce Vinge-Moore spent a day helping me run down magazines in the UCLA Research Library to verify their contents. Ralph Cook, who wrote *The City Lights Pocket Poets Series: A Descriptive Bibliography,* first explained to me how to go about compiling a bibliography.

Finally, it was Phillip Bevis of Arundel Press who undertook the exhausting job of going over the manuscript with me, correcting typos and misspelled words, and in some cases rearranging sentences so they make better sense. I am truly grateful for his intelligent editing. Of course, any errors or omissions are solely my responsibility.

I should also like to thank Michael Dovsky for the photographs of the books, broadsides, and magazines which illustrate this book.

Contents

Preface

The present volume attempts to record all books, pamphlets, and broadsides written, translated, or edited by Clayton Eshleman, as well as his periodical contributions and ephemera. This compilation includes all work published through 1987. Save for a few articles on the poet's work, one very elusive softcover edition, and a special printing mentioned by a publisher that only he seems to recall, I have examined all items.

Publication information for A and B sections includes date of publication, number of copies printed, and the original publication price whenever available. Signature collations are given only where there is more than one gathering. Black print on white or cream paper is understood unless other colors are mentioned, in which case both black and white are included with the other colors in the description. Measurements of bindings are in centimeters.

Titles of poems and essays vary in some publications. Many poem titles and first lines changed as they evolved through various printings, so that the poet may have published an initial version of a work which was revised in a later publication. Thus an essay titled, "An Open Letter to George Stanley, Concerning the State of Our Nation, the American Spiritual Body, Which I First Glimpsed in Peru" becomes "Who Is the Real Enemy of Poetry? An Open Letter to George Stanley." Further, translations of poems occasionally changed titles as well as first lines. Vallejo's first line, "It was Sunday in the clear ears of my burro...," has also been published as "It was Sunday in the fair ears of my burro...," "It was Sunday the pale ears of my burro...," and "It was Sunday in the clear ears of my jackass...," "It was Sunday in the bright ears of my jackass...." In every case I have given the poem as it appears in the publication. When a book title is a translation, the author's name is given as part of the title: *Cesar Vallejo: Spain Take This Cup from Me.* Accents are given as they appear in the publication.

Section A includes descriptions of books, pamphlets, and broadsides by Clayton Eshleman, as well as those translated by him. The initial heading of each entry identifies title, date of publication, and edition, followed by a quasi-facsimile transcription of the title page. Collation includes dimensions of item, as well as numbering or inferred numbering of each page. Dust jackets are described, followed by facts concerning publication, contents, and appropriate notes.

Section B presents anthologies in which Eshleman's work has appeared, though these entries are described in less detail than above. Section C lists periodical appearances: where a publication lacks date, "c." is used with my approximation in brackets.

Eshleman is the editor of important literary journals, one published while he was in college, one in the late 1960s and early 1970s, and one beginning in 1981 and continuing through the present. Further, he was the editor of a series of books, including first books of several important writers, as well as the editor of a poetry column in a Los Angeles weekly newspaper. All of these items are described in Section D.

Section E lists audio tapes in university archives, those available to the public, and a few from Eshleman's personal collection. Section F gathers miscellaneous material, including work in manuscript which has been mentioned in print, booksellers catalogues with essays by Eshleman, book titles which were contracted for but never published, odd items such as a T-shirt printed with a poem by Eshleman, and a picture book by Arthur Segunda with photographs of the Eshlemans and friends. The final section, G, lists criticism and reviews of Eshleman's work.

Chronology

1935   Born Indianapolis, Indiana, June 1.

1941   Family moves to new house at 4805 Boulevard Place. Attends PS #86; begins piano lessons.

1947   Transfers to PS #43 for junior high school; takes cartoon lessons at home in the evening; family car trip to Los Angeles.

1949   Enters Shortridge High School; active in track, football, and wrestling.

1951   Discovers jazz, attends "Jazz at the Philharmonic" concerts and through the mail purchases records by Bud Powell and Lennie Tristano; jams with the Montgomery Brothers at The Surf Club; varsity football; 3rd place in state-wide cartoon competition.

1953   Graduates high school, pledges Phi Delta Theta Fraternity and enters Indiana University as a Classical Music Major; lifeguard at Indianapolis Riviera Club; visits Los Angeles, studying jazz piano briefly with Richie Powell and Mary Paitch.

1954   Initiated into fraternity, drops out of music school, enters business school.

1956   Flunks out of business school; works as clerk in Block's Department Store in Bloomington; moves out of fraternity.

1957   Re-enters Indiana University as philosophy major; meets Jack Hirschman (who puts him in touch with Jerome Rothenberg, Robert Kelly, and David Antin), and Mary Ellen Solt (who puts him in touch with William Carlos Williams, Louis Zukofsky, Robert Creeley, and Cid Corman); courses in 20th-century American poetry and Creative Writing with Samuel Yellen and Josephine Piercy; first car trip to New York City; assistant editor of *Folio* magazine.

1958   Second place in campus philosophical essay contest for paper on Aristotle's Poetics and jazz; graduates with B.A. in Philosophy, mows lawns for a living, entering graduate school that fall as English literature major; numerous car trips to NYC, where he meets Paul Blackburn, Jackson Mac Low and Louis Zukofsky; friendship with Kelly and Rothenberg begins. Publishes first poem in *Folio.*

1959   Edits three issues of *Folio* after which magazine is suppressed by English Department; visits Williams, Allen Ginsberg, and Denise Levertov; works as cocktail pianist in Bloomington; hitchhikes to Mexico City; begins to read and translate Pablo Neruda and César Vallejo; participates in bilingual "Babel" reading series (reading translations of St. John Perse's *Eloges).*

1960   First reading of own poetry arranged by Blackburn at Metro Cafe, NYC; second trip to Mexico, living in Chapala, translating from Neruda's *Residencia en la Tierra;* friendship with William Paden and Ann McGarrell.

1961   Student teaching at Shortridge High School; M.A.T. in English literature; correspondence with Williams and Creeley; marries Barbara Novak; accepts instructorship with Far Eastern Division of University of Maryland; moves to Japan (teaching Composition and Literature in Tainan, Taiwan, and Tokyo); visited by Gary Snyder and Joanne Kyger.

1962   Teaching in Seoul and Inchon, Korea; leaves University of Maryland, moves to Kyoto. *Mexico & North; Residence on Earth* (translation of Neruda).

1963   Weekly conversations with Corman, Snyder and Will Petersen; translating Vallejo daily; studies William Blake, the *I Ching,* and world mythology; teaches English as Foreign Language at Matsushita Electric Company; begins "The Tsuruginomiya Regeneration" (500-page unpublished poem); correspondence with Blackburn, Thomas Merton, W.S. Merwin, Rothenberg and Kelly.

1964   Returns to Los Angeles, immigration class, by boat; visits the Hirschmans, returns to Bloomington; translates anthology of Latin American Poetry for OAS in Washington, D.C. (unpublished); completes third draft of translation of Vallejo's *Poemas humanos.*

1965   LSD with Daphne Marlatt; introduction to French wine and cheese by Denis Kelly; flies to Mexico City, buses to Panama City, flies to Lima, Peru; hired by North American and Peruvian Cultural Institute to edit bilingual literary review; meets Georgette Vallejo, Julio Ortega, Carlos Germán Belli, Maureen Ahern; visits Andes twice. *The Chavin Illumination.*

1966   Literary review *(Quena)* suppressed by NAPCI; birth of son Matthew Craig Eshleman; completes eighth draft of *Poemas humanos* with the help of Ahern; returns to Bloomington, then moves to

NYC, spending the summer at the Blackburns; separates from wife, moves into basement room at 10 Bank St.; dinners and readings with Neruda; friendship with Frank Samperi, Diane Wakoski, and Adrienne Winograd. *State of the Union* (translation of Aimé Césaire, with Denis Kelly); *Lachrymae Mateo.*

1967   Teaching in American Language Institute, NYU; founds and edits *Caterpillar* magazine; moves to 36 Greene St.; friendship with Nora Jaffe, Leon Golub, Nancy Spero, and Adrienne Rich; Reichian therapy with Dr. Sidney Handelman; Fales Library (NYU) begins yearly purchase of *Caterpillar* Archive. *Walks.*

1968   Active weekly as organizer and participant in "Angry Arts" protesting American war involvement in Vietnam; arrested and jailed for demonstration in St. Patrick's Cathedral; introduced to John Martin of Black Sparrow Press by Wakoski; readings with Robert Bly, Robert Duncan, Allen Ginsberg, Ed Sanders and others in Milwaukee and Seattle to raise money for draft resisters; in NYC organizes "Three Penny Poetry Reading," featuring Andrei Voznesensky; friendship with Carolee Schneemann, James Tenney, Michael Heller, Hugh Seidman, and Marie Benoit; meets Caryl Reiter at New Year's Eve party. *Human Poems* (translations of Vallejo); *Brother Stones* (with woodcuts by Paden); *Cantaloups and Splendor* (first Black Sparrow Press book).

1969   After brief involvement with Scientology, completes Reichian therapy; visits Los Angeles, meets John Martin, and raises money to keep *Caterpillar* going (now in its seventh issue); Poets in the Schools Program, NYC. *T'ai; The House of Okumura; The House of Ibuki; Indiana* (first full-length Black Sparrow Press book); *Yellow River Record; A Pitchblende.*

1970   Becomes full-time faculty member of the new California Institute of the Arts, Valencia; moves with wife Caryl to Sherman Oaks; death of mother; friendship with Stan Brakhage, Robin Blaser, and John and Barbara Martin.

1971   Teaches seminars on Blake, Reich, T.S. Eliot and Hart Crane at Cal Arts; directs reading series there, including Theodore Enslin, Kenneth Rexroth and Cid Corman; close association with Kelly (teaching at the California Institute of Technology); death of father. *Bearings; Altars; A Caterpillar Anthology* (material from issues 1–12).

1972   Teaches privately at home in Sherman Oaks; Poets in the Schools Program, LA; friendship with Oreste Pucciani, Joyce Vinje, and José Rubia and Eva Barcia; begins to translate Antonin Artaud; begins to retranslate Vallejo with Barcia; reshapes "The

Tsuruginomiya Regeneration" into "Coils." *The Sanjo Bridge.*

1973   Last issue of *Caterpillar* (#20), appears; sublets Parisian apartment of Albrto Cavalcanti; teaches "America A Prophecy" at the American College in Paris; meets Jacques Roubaud, Jean Daive, Claude Royet Journaud; Caryl Eshleman begins to function as the author's editor, commenting on each draft of a poem; working via the mail with Barcia on Vallejo revisions. *Coils; Human Wedding.*

1974   Rents apartment at Bouyssou farm outside Tursac; repeated visits to Upper Paleolithic decorated caves; visited by George Herms, Matthew Eshleman, and Peter Blegvad; returns to Los Angeles, renting the bottom of a duplex at 852 South Bedford St. *Aux Morts; Spain, Take This Cup from Me* (translations of Vallejo, with Barcia); *Letter to Andre Breton* (translations of Artaud); *Realignment* (with drawings by Nora Jaffe).

1975   Teaches privately in West Los Angeles; Fels Award for nonfiction prose. *Portrait of Francis Bacon; To Have Done with the Judgement of God* (translations of Artaud, with Norman Glass); *The Gull Wall.*

1976   Invited by State Department to lecture on American Literature at "The Summer Seminar," Frenstat, Czechoslovakia; begins correspondence with Eliot Weinberger; part-time teaching at UCLA. *Cogollo; Artraud the Momo* (translations of Artaud, with Glass); *The Woman Who Saw Through Paradise.*

1977   "Artist in the Community"; teaching fellowship from California Arts Council (carried out at Manual Arts High School, LA); working via the mail with Jan Benda on translations of Milan Exner; P.E.N. Translation Prize; begins to translate the collected poetry of Aimé Césaire with Annette Smith. *Grotesca; On Mules Sent from Chavin; Core Meander; The Gospel of Celine Arnauld.*

1978   Guggenheim Fellowship in Poetry; lives in England, France, and Germany (where he participates in Visiting Author Program, out of American Embassy in Bonn); first of five meetings with Aimé Césaire; friendship with Michel Deguy, Herbert and Margarit Graf, Karl and Gabrielle Möckl, Marwan and Karin Kassabachi. *Battles in Spain* (translations of Vallejo, with Barcia); *The Name Encanyoned River; What She Means; César Vallejo: The Complete Posthumous Poetry* (with Barcia).

1979   National Book Award in Translation for the Vallejo book; National Endowment for the Arts Poetry Fellowship; appointed Dreyfuss Poet in Residence and Lecturer in Creative Writing at Caltech. *A Note on Apprenticeship.*

1980   National Endowment for the Humanities "Summer Stipend" for research on Upper Paleolithic cave art; car accident and hos-

pitalization in the French Dordogne; second month-long partici-
pation in German Visiting Author Program; Visiting Lecturer
in Creative Writing at UCSD and UC-Riverside. *The Lich Gate;
Nights We Put the Rock Together; Our Lady of the Three-pronged Devil.*

1981   Regular book reviewer for *Los Angeles Times Sunday Book Review* (50
reviews between 1979 and 1986); National Endowment for the
Humanities Translation Fellowship for work on Césaire; Witter
Bynner Grant in Aid for work on Césaire; *Hades in Manganese*
finalist for *Los Angeles Times* Book Award; founds and begins to
edit *Sulfur* magazine at Cal-Tech; friendship with Leland
Hickman, Bob Peters, Bernard Bador, and Koki Iwamoto.
Foetus Graffiti.

1982   First of several travel articles co-written with Caryl Eshleman on
prehistory and food of the French Dordogne. *Antonin Artaud: Four
Texts* (translations of Artaud, with Glass).

1983   With Caryl Eshleman, leads first of two study tours of cave art in
the Dordogne; friendship with Arthur Secunda, Antonet
O'Toole, Joanne Leedom and Peter Ackerman; Magazine Panel
and Policy Committee Member, National Endowment for the
Arts; work on literary essays; edits poetry column for *L.A.
Weekly*, "Ill Fate and Abundant Wine." *Visions of the Fathers of
Lascaux; Fracture; Aimé Césaire: the Collected Poetry* (with Smith).

1984   Works with Frantisek Galan and Michael Heim on a translation
of Vladimir Holan's "A Night with Hamlet"; Director of Poets-
in-Residence Program at UCLA; third visit to Lascaux cave in
the Dordogne; moves *Sulfur* magazine (now in its 9th issue) to
UCLA Extension Writers Program. *Given Giving: Selected Poems
of Michel Deguy.*

1985   Visiting Lecturer in Creative Writing at UC–Santa Barbara; cor-
respondence with James Hillman, Clark Coolidge, Michael
Palmer, Rachel Blau DuPlessis; meets and is interviewed by the
Hungarian poet and translator, Gyula Kodolanyi; UCSD Ar-
chive for New Poetry purchases author's archive (1970–1985) and
Sulfur archive; attends seminar on psychology and alchemy by
Hillman. *Chanson* (translations of Artaud, with A. James
Arnold).

1986   Moves to Ypsilanti, Michigan, becoming a professor in the Eastern Michigan University English Department; writes 20,000-
word autobiography for Gale Research, and an extended essay
on poetic apprenticeship and curricula, "Novices" (unpublished);
directs dramatic readings of Artaud's "To Have Done with the
Judgement of God" at the Kerrytown Concert House, Ann Arbor; Traveling Fellowship from Soros Foundation, NYC, for

one month in Hungary. *The Name Encanyoned River: Selected Poems 1960–1985* (with an Introduction by Eliot Weinberger).

1987   Returns with Caryl Eshleman for the eighth time to French Dordogne; Cooper Fellow, Swarthmore College; Poet in Residence, Cranbrook Institute.

1988   Organizes and participates in *Sulfur Live: A National Symposium on Poetry and Poetics, at EMU; Sulfur,* now based at EMU, in its twenty second issue; receives indeterminate tenure at EMU; invited to International Poetry Symposium, Barcelona; with Gyula Kodolanyi cotranslates contemporary Hungarian poetry and prose for Sulfur; meets Arkadii Dragomoshčhenko and Susan Howe; National Endowment for the Arts Translation Fellowship to cotranslate with Annette Smith the rest of Césaire's poetry; Michigan Arts Council Summer Writer's Grant. *Antiphonal Swing: Selected Prose 1962–1987* (edited by Caryl Eshleman with an Introduction by Paul Christensen); *Conductors of the Pit: Major Works by Rimbaud, Vallejo, Cśaire, Artaud, and Holan.*

A. Books, Broadsides and Separate Publications

A1   Mexico & North   1962

MEXICO / & / NORTH / Ohne unsern wahren Platz zu kennen / handeln wir aus wirklichen [sic] Bezug. / — Rilke / CLAYTON / ESHLEMAN.

21 × 15cm.; 27 leaves; pp. [54]: p. [i] half-title; p. [ii] frontispiece [by William Paden]; p. [iii] title page as above; p. [iv] copyright page; p. [v] dedication; pp. [6–53] text; p. [54] blank.

[Rust colored rice paper wrappers, stabbed and bound Japanese style (reverse fold); printed in black:] MEXICO / & NORTH / CLAYTON / ESHLEMAN [top and lower edge trimmed; cream colored wove paper; on back inside cover:] Printed by Haku-o-do / Tel. (351) 5202, 9191. / Tokyo, Japan.

Publication: Published privately by Clayton Eshleman in Tokyo, Japan, in 1962. Printed by Haku-o-do in Tokyo, Japan. Cover design by Will Petersen. 500 copies, prices at c. $1.25 a copy.

Contains: "Evocation I, II," "Inheritance," "Red Shoes," "Las Brujas," "The Field," "Water-Song," "Etzatlan," "A Very Old Woman," "Are You Afraid?" "Caletilla Beach," "The Strong," "I Want to Live," "Un Poco Tomado," "Two Crossed," "The Hitch-Hiker," "La Mujer," "Dark Blood," "Bloomington: October," "The Spanish Lesson," "My Fiance As A Bear Timidly Trying to Disappear Behind A Stump," "Smoke," "Night Hawks," "The Minister As A Black Swan," "The Virgin Spring," "Little Song for A Departure," "Son of Lightning," "Prothalamion," "Fire!" "One Must Ask How Is Their Life."

[Note: Allen Ahearn: *Book Collecting: Book of First Books* (Rockville, Quill

A1. Mexico & North

& Brush, 4th edition, 1986, p. 88) cites "26 lettered copies." This is a part of
the first printing, which was lettered and signed by Eshleman, not on publication but several years later, when some copies which had been misplaced were
returned to the author. No priority, binding, or textural differences].

A2   Pablo Neruda: Residence on Earth   1962

[In outline:] RESIDENCE ON EARTH / [in black:] PABLO NERUDA /
translated by [in outline:] CLAYTON ESHLEMAN / [in black:] 1962

[A bilingual edition; original Spanish on versos, English on rectos].

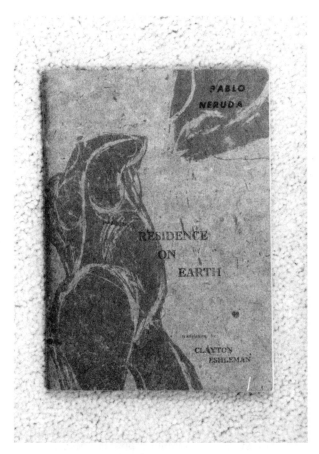

A2. Pablo Neruda: Residence on Earth

20.5 × 15cm.; 32 leaves; pp. [i–vii] [8–62] [63–64]: pp. [i] blank; p. [ii] AMBER HOUSE PRESS; p. [iii] title page as above; p. [iv] copyright page [states "first edition"] p. [v] dedication; p. [vi] blank; p. [vii] drawing by Will Petersen, divisional title; pp. [8–21] text; p. [22] blank; p. [23] drawing by Will Petersen, divisional title; p. [24–55] text; p. [56] blank; p. [57–62] essay by Clayton Eshleman; p. [63–64] blank.

[Brown Japanese mulberry paper backed with stiff green paper; super-imposed over red drawing of a torso, in black:] PABLO / NERUDA / [in outline:] RESIDENCE / ON / EARTH / [in black:] translations by / [in outline:] CLAYTON / ESHLEMAN [Back cover, in black:] Shimbi Printers / Kyoto / Japan [Printed on front inside cover:] distributed by / City Lights Books / 261 Columbus Avenue / San Francisco 11 [printed on back inside cover:] [acknowledgments.] COVER: drawn on stone by Will Petersen. [Paper: wove; all edges trim with the cover].

Publication: Printed and published by George Hitchcock of the Amber House Press in San Francisco in 1962 (with the exception of the cover which was printed by Shimbi Printers in Kyoto, Japan under the author's supervision). Although 300 copies were printed, approximately 120 were damaged in transit from San Francisco to Kyoto and thus the edition is about 180 copies, priced $1.50 a copy.

Contains: [Spanish titles — English verse] Pablo Neruda: from *Residencia En La Tierra 1* (1925–1931): "Unidad," "Sabor," "Ausencia De Joaquin," "Juntos Nosotros," "Arte Poetica," "Sonata Y Destrucciones," "Caballero Solo," "Ritual De Mis Piernas," "Tango Del Viudo." From *Residencia En La Tierra 2*(1931–1935): "Solo La Muerte," "Barcarola," "Walking Around," "Melancolia En Las Familias," "Maternidad," "Oda Con Un Lamento," "Materia Nupcial," "Agua Sexual," "Tres Cantos Materials," "Apogeo Del Apio," "Estatuto Del Vino," "Oda A Federico Garcia Lorca," "Alberto Rojas Jimenez Viene Volando," "Vuelve El Otono," "No Hay Olvido (Sonata)," [translated from the Spanish by Clayton Eshleman], Pecho De Pan, [an essay by Clayton Eshleman, an introduction presented as a postface].

A3   The Chavín Illumination   1965

THE CHAVÍN / ILLUMINATION / CLAYTON ESHLEMAN / LIMA [slash] 1965

20.6 × 11cm.; 8 leaves; pp. [16]: [i–ii] blank; p. [iii] title page as above; p. [iv] blank; pp. [5–12] text; p. [13] colophon; pp. [14–16] blank.

Loose cream dust jacket of Japanese paper; [paste-on label reads:] THE CHAVÍN / ILLUMINATION / CLAYTON ESHLEMAN [White wove paper (19.9cm. high) sewn in white thread (by Barbara Eshleman); fore-edge trim with cover]. [Note: there is an original watercolor by the author in each copy].

Publication: Printed in Lima, Peru (Ediciones de Rama Florida) in 1965 in an edition of 100 copies, no price; most of the originally distributed copies were given as gifts by the author. Colophon: THE CHAVÍN / ILLUMINATION / visión de Clayton / Eshleman, se acabó / de imprimir el 11 de / diciembre de 1965 en / el Taller de Artes / Gráficas ÍCARO, An- / tiguo Hotel Los Ánge- / les, casa letra I, Cha- / clacayo. La edición / consta de cien ejempla- / res nemerados de 001 / a 100, y ha sido impre- / sa en papel Pluma por / el autor y Javier / Sologuren. / EJEMPLAR / [number stamped in black] / [Author's signature].

Contains: "Chavín Sunset 6: 27–7:30 Oct 27, 1965"

[Note: The Chavín Illumination is a section of a longer work: *On Mules Sent From Chavin: A Journal and Poems (1965–66).* (see A45), some of which was first published in *Some/thing* #5, Summer 1968. (C114).]

A4   The Crocus Bud   1965

[Cover title:] THE CROCUS BUD / My legs are sleeping before me: Barbara / in Japanese, *bara* a rose in ¾ time. / Sing it out, song. / "as if she were looking over your shoulder" / — but then, ah, we should speak! [a black and white photograph of an unidentified young woman is above title; on the right ⅓ of the page is a thin ruled rectangle within which is:] the / camels / hump: / 4, a poem by / [below the lower rule of the rectangle:] clayton eshleman [printed parallel to the upper left rule and outside the rectangle:] masca

28 × 21.7cm.; 4 mimeographed leaves (printed on rectos only) unnumbered; stapled once at top left; wove paper.

Publication: Published by Richard Morris in Reno, Nevada in 1965, in an edition of 300 copies. Mailed to subscribers of *Camels Coming* magazine at no extra cost. *Camels Hump* was a poetry newsletter edited by Richard Morris, and these 8 poems comprise the whole 4th issue.

Contains: Untitled: "Oh! She goes over to it — a crocus...," untitled: "First flower...," "As She Sleeps," "After Rimbaud," "The Aborigine," "We Must Love One Another or Die," untitled: "I picked a caterpillar from a leaf...," untitled: "By the leaf a shrine...."

[Notes: These poems are dated Kyoto 1963 — Bloomington 1964 at the end of the last poem. An earlier version of these poems appeared in *El Corno Emplumado,* #7 July 1963. (see: C31)].

A5   Aime Cesaire: State of the Union   1966

STATE OF THE UNION / AIME CESAIRE / Translated from the French by / Clayton Eshleman & Denis Kelly / CATERPILLAR 1966

21.7 × 14cm.; 22 leaves; pp. [i–iv] [5–44]: [i] title page as above; p. [ii] copyright and acknowledgments; pp. [iii–iv] blank. pp. [4–42] text; p. [43] colophon; p. [44] blank.

[Stiff pea-green wrappers; red tape covering the spine and extending 1.7cm. front and back to cover two staples. Front cover in black:] STATE OF THE UNION / AIME CESAIRE [Back cover, centered in black:] CATER-PILLAR 1966 (paper: wove; all edges trim with the cover].

Publication: Printed by Clayton Eshleman, on mimeograph, in Bloomington, Indiana in the summer of 1966 in an edition of 100 copies, priced at $1.00 a copy. Colophon: STATE OF THE UNION is the first CATERPILLAR, / a series of publications edited by Clayton Eshleman. The / Cesaire poems were translated from: / *Les arems miraculeuses,* Gallimard, Paris, 1947. / *Cadastre,* Editions du Seuil, Paris, 1961. / *Ferrements,* Editions du Seuil, Paris, 1960. / Bloomington, Indiana / 1966

Contains: Aime Cesaire: "First Problem," "Night Tam Tam," "Magic," "Word of the Oricous," "The law is Naked," "Lure," "Between Other Massacres," "The Griffin," "Recovery," "Mississippi," "Blues for Rain," "Threads of Lightning," "Votive Offering for a Shipwreck," "Tornado," "Interlude," "The Wheel," "Sun and Water," "Stages of Perturbation," "Barbarous," "Antipode," "Silent Crossings," "For Ina," "Beat It Night Dog," "Fangs," "Bucolic," "At the Tomb of Paul Eluard," "State of the Union," "Africa." [Translated from the French by Clayton Eshleman and Denis Kelly].

A6   Lachrymae Mateo   1966

(a) *first edition:*

[On light blue-green paper:] LACHRYMAE MATEO / 3 poems for Christmas 1966 / CLAYTON ESHLEMAN / Caterpillar III

28 × 21.5cm.; 6 leaves; [printed on rectos only]: p. [i] title page; pp. [3–9] text; p. [11] colophon.

Dark blue construction paper wrappers; maroon cloth tape covering the spine and extending 5cm. front and back to cover three staples. [Front cover, in block letters:] LACHRYMAE MATEO / CLAYTON ESHLEMAN [paper wove; all edges trim with the cover].

Publication: Published by Clayton Eshleman in New York, in 1966 as CATERPILLAR III. Colophon: LACHRYMAE MATEO is the third *Caterpillar,* a series of / publications edited by Clayton Eshleman. 100 copies of / this book were mimeoed in New York City, December, 1966. / Copies may be obtained through The Asphodel Bookshop, 465 / The Arcade,

Cleveland 44114, Ohio, or The Phoenix Bookshop, / 18 Cornelia, NYC. All rights belong to the author. [100 copies, priced at $1.00 a copy].

Contains: "Holding Duncan's Hand," untitled: "The night in the Okumura House . . . ," "Lachrymae Mateo."

(b.) *Second edition (1966 and 1967):*

Same as above except: title-page printed on white paper.

7 leaves; [printed on rectos only]: p. [i] title; pp. [3–11] text; p. [13] colophon; p. [14] blank.

[Printed on brown construction paper wrappers, with three exposed staples, in block stencilled letters:] LACH / RYM / AE M [letter "M" is solid black] / AETO / [in solid black letters:] ESHLEMAN [Printed on back cover in block stencilled letters:] CATERPILLAR / [centered horizontally is the CATERPILLAR GLYPH; a small napalmed Vietnamese child] / [in block stencilled letters:] III [all edges trim with cover].

Colophon: LACHRYMAE MATEO is the third *Caterpillar,* a series of / publications edited by Clayton Eshleman. The edition consists / of 300 copies, 100 [sic] which were mimeoed & 200 of which were / multilithed, New York City, December 1966 & February 1967. / Copies may be obtained thru The Asphodel Bookshop, 306 / Superior Avenue, Cleveland, Ohio, or The Phoenix Book / Store, 18 Cornelia, NYC. All rights belong to the author. / [also lists four other Caterpillar publications; a statement about "The Caterpillar Glyph":] The Caterpillar / Glyph is a small napalmed Vietnamese child. Until the / end of the war this black caterpillar. [200 copies, priced at $1.00 a copy].

[Notes: The extra leaf is necessary because the title poem now takes up two pages instead of one as in the first edition due to different spacing of multilithed pages. Some minor changes to text: "A woman of which Duncan sang" changed to: "A woman of whom Duncan sang." In this edition poem dates are emended to include the year: 1966. "Holding Duncan's Hand" was later changed to "Sensing Duncan" at the request of Robert Duncan. see A13, C88, C125].

A7   Translations from the Spanish   1967

QUARK I / Translations from the Spanish / by Clayton Eshleman / & Cid Corman / Copyright © 1967 by Clayton Eshleman / Cover by Walt McNamara

28 × 21.6cm.; 15 mimeographed leaves stapled three times on left; printed on rectos only; pp. [i–iii] [5–27] [29]: p. [i] title page as above; p. [iii] divisional title; pp. [5–27] text; p. [29] publisher's advertisement.

[White wrappers; on black ground, in white:] Q / [on white ground, in black:] UARK I / Translations from the Spanish / [a black and white ink drawing intersected by a thin "Y" shaped black rule; below, to the right of the "y".] by / CID CORMAN / & / CLAYTON ESHLEMAN / 25 [signed on left of "Y" stem:] McNamara [Paper: wove; all edges trim with cover].

Publication: Published by Richard Morris of *Camels Coming* magazine, P.O. Box 8161, University Staion, Reno, Nevada in 1967, as a poetry newsletter that was mailed, gratis, to subscribers of *Camels Coming* in an issue of about 800 copies.

Contains: Seven Poems by César Vallejo: "I Am Going to Speak of Hope," "The Soul That Suffered from Being Its Body," "The Starving Man's Rack," untitled: "Another touch of calm, comrade . . . ," untitled: "A man is watching a woman, . . . ," "Height & Hair," "Old Asses Thinking." [Translated from the Spanish by Clayton Eshleman]. Two Poems by José Hierro: "Fé De Vida," untitled poem: "Wherever you are, and how. . . ." [Translated from the Spanish by Clayton Eshleman and Cid Corman].

[Note: The "Working title" of *Translations from the Spanish* was called *César Vallejo: Seven Poems.]*

A8   Walks   1967

WALKS / Clayton Eshleman / *Caterpillar* / X / [a print of a small napalmed Vietnamese child].
31.5 × 21.3cm.; 27 leaves; pp. [i–iv] pp. 1–47 [48–50]: p. [i] title page as

above; p. [ii] blank; p. [iii] dedication; p. [iv] blank; pp. 1–47 text; p. [48] blank; p. [49] colophon plus advertisement for Caterpillar publications; p. [50] blank.

Four bindings, no priority as follows:

a. [Black cloth tape over black matboard covers, perfect bound; a white paste-on label on front cover reads, in lavender:] WALKS / CLAYTON / ESHLEMAN [Paper: wove; all edges trim with cover].

b. Same as above except: yellow cloth tape backstrip.

c. Same as above except: red cloth tape backstrip.

d. Same as above except: One of 26 copies, lettered and signed by the poet.

[Note: The color of the tape backstrip used on WALKS was "extremely arbitrary" according to the author and publisher.]

Publication: Published by Clayton Eshleman in New York, in 1967 as *Caterpillar* X, in an edition of 300 copies, priced at $3.00 a copy. Colophon: WALKS by Clayton Eshleman is the 10th *Caterpillar,* a series / of publications edited by the author. This book, in an edition / of 300 numbered copies was multilithed & handbound in NYC, / in the year of the Burnt Child. Copies can be purchased thru / Asphodel Bookshop, 306 Superior Ave, Cleveland, Ohio, or in / NYC at the Phoenix, 18 Cornelia Street. Price: $3. With *Cat-/erpillar* X, that particular tree has been stripped, & these / books will become (in upper case) CATERPILLAR magazine, / to come forth quarterly for 3 years, beginning October 1967. / However, there will be an occasional *Caterpillar Book.* [a list of the 10 *Caterpillar* publications follows. Below this list:] The *Caterpillar Glyph* is a small napalmed / Vietnamese child. Until the end of the war this black caterpillar.

Contains: "Fire Burial," "Walk I," "Walk II," untitled: "Over candles at the Director's house...," "Walk III," "Walk IV," "Walk V," "Walk VI," "Walk VII," "The Herrera Warehouse," "Letter to César Calvo Concerning the Inauguration of A Monument to César Vallejo," untitled: "This son who's appeared to us...," untitled: "She is delivered...," "Walk VIII," untitled: "Matthew a caterpillar...," "Mrs. Vallejo," "Evelyn," "Walk IX," "Walk X," untitled: "God as a postage stamp...," "For Carlos Germán Belli."

A9   Cesar Vallejo: Poemas Humanos/Human Poems   1968

a. *First edition:*

[Double spread title page; on verso, on black ground, in white:] Poemas Humanos / [portrait of Cesar Vallejo, taken in Paris by an unidentified

A9d. César Vallejo: Poemas Humanos/Human Poems

photographer; on recto:] Human Poems / by César Vallejo / Translated by
Clayton Eshleman / Grove Press, Inc., New York

[A bilingual edition; original Spanish on versos, English on rectos].

20.8 × 14.5cm.; 176 leaves; pp. [i–iv] v–xxvi [1]–326: p. [1] half title, pp.
[ii–iii] title pages as above; p. [iv] copyright page [states "First Printing"]; pp.
v–xviii translator's foreword; p. [xix] divisional title; pp. xx–xxv contents,
[Spanish titles on versos, English translations on rectos]; pp. [xxvi] blank; p.
[1] divisional title; pp. 2–326 text. White endpapers.

[Black cloth covered boards; spine reading at top, side to side, in gilt;] César
/ Vallejo / [thin rule] / [reading top to bottom:] Poemas Humanos / Human
Poems [lower spine reading side to side;[Grove / Press [Paper: white wove;
all edges trimmed. False headbands].

Dust jacket designed by Kuhlman Associates, as follows: [glossy white paper;
on spine on black ground, reading top to bottom, in white:] Poemas
Humanos [a dark green slash; in light green:] Human Poems [in dark green:]
by César Vallejo [reading side to side in light green:] GP — 475 / GROVE /

PRESS [front cover on black ground, in white:] Poemas Humanos / [in light green:] Human Poems / [in dark green:] by César Vallejo / a bilingual edition / translated by / Clayton Eshleman / [a bust of Vallejo in blue based on a photograph by Juan Larrea. On back in Black:] "César Vallejo is the greatest catholic poet / since Dante—by catholic I mean universal." / [in blue:]— Thomas Merton / [a portrait of Vallejo by Juan Larra] / [in green:] GROVE PRESS, INC., 80 University Place, New York, N.Y. 10003 [On inside front cover, in light green:] $8.50 / GP-475 / [in black:] Poemas Humanos / Human Poems / by César Vallejo / translated by Clayton Eshleman / [blue rule] / [unsigned statement on Vallejo and Eshleman and this translation, continued on back flap below, in blue:] (continued from front flap) / [continued statement] [light green rule] / [brief biographical statement on Vallejo] / [light green rule] / [brief biographical statement on Eshleman] / [light green rule] / Photos by Juan Larrea / Jacket design: Kuhlman Associates

First printing, of approximately 2,000 copies, priced at $8.50 a copy.

b. *Second printing:*

[First Evergreen edition], (1969), same as above except: 20.3 × 13.6cm.; [verso of title page:] First Evergreen Edition, 1969 / First Printing [sewn signatures, glued in glossy white paper wrappers; spine printing same as dust jacket spine except, now reading from side to side in white:] [publisher's device] / E-512 / GROVE / PRESS [Front cover same as dust jacket except: the line cut bust of Vallejo is printed in black and white and in lower right hand corner parallel to fore-edge reading bottom to top, in white:] [publisher's device] EVERGREEN E-512 $2.95 [back cover: on white ground in black:] AN EVERRGREEN BOOK—(E-512) $2.95 / Poemas Humans [slash] Human Poems / [in light green:] by César Vallejo / [in darker green:] Translated by Clayton Eshleman / [light green rule] / [in black, blurb by Robert Duncan] / [blue rule] / [in black, blurb by John Knoepfle, The Nation] / [light green rule] / [in black, blurb from Library Journal] / [blue rule] / [in black, blurb from Publishers Weekly] / [light green rule] / [in black:] GROVE PRESS, INC., 80 University Place, New York, N.Y. 10003 / Cover photograph: Juan Larrea [Paper wove; white endpapers; all edges trim].

Published in an edition of approximately 7,000 or 8,000 copies, prices at $2.95 a copy.

c. *Second printing, second issue:*

Same as above except: not sewn signatures, [verso of title page:] First Evergreen Edition, 1969 / Second printing [the price on front and back cover now reads:] $3.45 [there is a number added to lower right back cover:] 394–17317–1

d. *First English edition:*

Same as a. except: [lacks frontispiece portrait; single title page reads, in black:] Poemas Humanos / Human Poems / [rule] / César Vallejo / Translated by Clayton Eshleman / [publisher's device] / Jonathan Cape Thirty Bedford Square London.

[22.1 × 15.3cm.; same collation as above; copyright page reads:] First published in Great Britain 1969 [light brown cloth over tan paper boards; in gilt on spine, reading bottom to top:] [publisher's device] Poemas Humanos [slash] Human Poems César Vallejo [Paper: wove; white endpapers; all edges trim, top edge stained red].

Dust jacket, as follws: [a wraparound illustration of Gustave Doré's "The Severed Head of Bertrand de Born Speaks," from Dante's *Inferno,* (lower right and center section only) covering front, spine, and back: black figures on orange ground; on spine reading bottom to top, in white:] [publisher's device] Poemas Humanos [slash] Human Poems Cesar Vallejo [front cover in white:] Poemas Humanos [slash] Human Poems / César Vallejo / A bilingual edition translated by Clayton Eshleman [inside front flap;] [promotional material on César Vallejo and Clayton Eshleman] / [in lower right corner:] 555. Net in U.K. only [inside back flap:] [César Vallejo biographical material] / SBN 224 61648 x / Jacket design by Leigh Taylor / © Jonathan Cape Ltd, 1969

Publication: Published by Jonathan Cape in London in 1969. Printed in Great Britain by Lowe and Brydone on paper made by John Dickinson & Co. ltd. Bound by A.W. Bain & Co. Ltd, London. 1,250 copies, priced at "555. Net in U.K. only."

Contains: Translator's Foreword. César Vallejo: (The Undated Poems: 1923 (?) 1937): "Loin of the Scriptures," "Common Sense," "Hat, Overcoat, Gloves," "Height and Hair," "I'm Laughing," "Violence of the Hours," "The Starving Man's Rack," untitled: "The miners came out of the mine . . . ," untitled: "It's here today I greet, I fix on my collar and live . . . ," "Angelic Greeting," untitled: "Ultimately, without that good repetitive aroma . . . ," "Epistle to the Pedestrians," untitled: "Today I'd really like to be happy . . . ," untitled: "Considering coldly, impartially . . . ," "Gleb," untitled: "Longing quits, tail to the air . . . ," untitled: "A woman with peaceful breasts . . ." "The most perilous moment in life," untitled: " — No one lives in the house anymore . . . ," untitled: "Between pain and pleasure three children mediate . . . ," untitled: "And if after so many words . . . ," untitled: "The moment the tennis player magisterially serves . . . ," untitled: "Checked on a stone . . . ," untitled: "Until the day it returns, from this stone...," untitled: "But before all this good luck...," "Paris, October 1936," untitled: "Exists a man mutilated...," "Old Asses Thinking," untitled: "It was Sunday in the fair ears of my burro...," untitled: "From disturbance to disturbance...," "Tuberous Spring," untitled: "And don't tell me anything...," untitled: "Four simultaneous...." "Bone Catalogue," "I Am Going to Speak of Hope," untitled: "The windows have been shaken...," "Black Stone on a White Stone," untitled: "Life, this life...," untitled: "Today I like life much less...," "Discovery of Life," "Telluric and Magnetic," untitled: "Sweetness through heartic sweetness..." (The dated Poems 4 September—December, 1937): untitled: "Heat, tired I go with my gold to where...," untitled: "A pillar supporting solace...," "Poem to Be Read and Sung," untitled: "Brooding on life, brooding...," untitled: "The accent hangs from my shoe...," untitled: "The point of the man...," untitled: "O bottle without wine! O wine that widowed from this bottle...," untitled: "He is running, walking, fleeing...," untitled: "Finally, a mountain...," untitled: "My chest wants and doesn't want its color...," untitled: "This happened between two eyelids...," untitled: "I stayed on to warm up the ink in which I drown...," untitled: "Peace, wasp, wad, rivercourse...," untitled' "Starved with pain, solomonic, proper...," untitled: "Well? The pallid metalloid heals you...," untitled: "Of pure heat I'm freezing...," untitled: "Confidence in glasses, not in the eye...," "Earthquake," untitled: "Mocked, acclimatized to good, morbid, urent...," untitled: "Alfonso, I see you watching me...," "Stumble Between Two Stars," "Farewell Remembering A Goodbye," untitled: "Chances are, I'm another; walking, at dawn, another who marches...," "The Book of Nature," "Wedding March," untitled: "Hear your mass, your kite, listen to them; don't moan...," untitled: "I have a terrible fear of being an animal...," untitled: "The anger that breaks man into children...," "Intensity and Height," "Guitar," untitled: "What does it matter that I whip myself with the line...," "Anniversary," "Pantheon," "Two Anxious Children," untitled: "A man is watching a woman...," "The Nine Monsters," untitled: "A man walks by with a loaf of bread on his shoulder...," untitled: "There comes over me days a feeling so abundant, political...," untitled: "Today a splinter has entered her...," "The Soul That Suffered From Being Its Body," "Palms and Guitars," "Yokes," untitled: "The one who will come just passed...," untitled: "Let the millionaire walk naked, barebacked...," untitled: "If the evil one came with a throne on his shoulder...," untitled: "Contrary to those mountain birds...," untitled: "The fact is the place where I put on my...," untitled: "Something identifies you...," untitled: "In sum, to express my life...," untitled: "Another touch of calm, comrade...," "The Wretched of the Earth," "Sermon on Death," untitled: "Whatever may be the cause I have to defend..." (Translated from the Spanish by Clayton Eshleman).

A10   Cantaloups & Splendor   1968

[Printer's device: in black, double rule of stars] / [On lime ground, in black:] CANTALOUPS / [printer's device as above] / [on lime ground:] & SPLENDOR / [printer's device as above] / clayton eshleman / [printer's device: in black, single rule of stars] / Black Sparrow Press [dot] Los Angeles [dot] 1968 / [printer's device: single rule as above].

29.2 × 20cm.; 12 leaves; pp. [i–iv] 5–18 [19–24]: pp. [i–ii] blank; p. [iii] title page as above; p. [iv] copyright page; pp. 5–18 text; pp. [19–20] blank; p. [21] colophon; pp. [22–24] blank. Maroon endpapers.

Two bindings, no priority as follows:
a. [Multicolored (red, magenta, pink, green, yellow, blue) cloth spine over lime paper covered boards; on spine, a white paper label reading in black top to bottom:] CANTALOUPS AND SPLENDOR [single dot] Clayton Eshleman [Front cover printed in black: publisher's device] / [printer's device: double rule of stars] / [on orange ground] CANTALOUPS / [printer's device as above] / [on magenta ground:] & SPLENDOR / [printer's device as above] / clayton eshleman [Hand sewn, in black thread by Barbara Martin. Paper: Watermark:] PASTELLE USA STRATHMORE [lower edges uncut]. 90 signed copies, of which 75 copies (numbered 1–75) were for sale, priced at $12.00 a copy, and 15 copies (1 each marked "Author's Copy," "Publisher's Copy," "Printer's Copy," "Binder's Copy" and 11 numbered and marked "Presentation Copy,") not for sale. Handbound in boards by Earle Grey.

b. Same as above except: 28.5 × 19cm.; paper covers hand sewn (by Barbara Martin) with black thread through to spine. Maroon, free endpapers. 259 signed copies, of which 250 copies (numbered 76–325) were for sale, priced at $7.00 a copy, and 9 copies (numbered and marked "Review Copy") not for sale.

Publication: Published by John Martin of the Black Sparrow Press in Los Angeles September 3, 1968. Printed by Noel Ypung in Santa Barbara August 1968. Colophon: [publisher's device] / Printed August 1968 in Santa Barbara by Noel Young for / the Black Sparrow Press. Design by Barbara Martin. / This edition is limited to 250 numbered copies / sewn in wrappers & 75 numbered / copies handbound in boards / by Earle Gray, all / copies signed by / the author. / This is copy No. [number of copy written in red ink].

Contains: "Glyph on the 9th Maximus, " "New Guinea," "The Bell-Shrine," "The Dedication," "Cantaloups & Splendor."

[Note: Cloth bound copies include an extra paper spine label, laid in loose].

A11   Brother Stones   1968

[In blue and purple:] BROTHER / STONES / [in blue:] CLAYTON ESHLEMAN [superimposed over:] POET [in lavender] / [in blue:] WILLIAM PADEN [superimposed over:] PRINTMAKER [in lavender / [in blue and purple:] KYOTO 1968 / A CATERPILLAR BOOK

19.5 × 16.3cm.; 19 loose leaves including 6 woodblocks in color; printed on rectos only: p. [1] title page as above; pp. [2–18] text and illustrations; p. [19] colophon signed and numbered by poet and printmaker; each woodblock numbered, titled and signed by the artist in pencil.

Loose leaves laid in a "chitsu" (a four leaf fold-over box covered with blue linen, lined with gampi paper, fastened with two plastic pegs on the fore-edge). [The paper spine label of kizuki-kozo, reads:] BROTHER / STONES [centered with and adjacent to the latter is:] ESHLEMAN [slash] PADEN [On the front cover is a label of kizuki-kozo paper with:] BROTHER / STONES [Contents printed on Jun-kozo]. [See note.]

Publication: Published privately by William Paden in 1968 in Kyoto, Japan, and by Clayton Eshleman in New York City as a Caterpillar Book, out of series (not numbered) in an edition of 250 copies, priced at $15.00 a copy. Colophon: BROTHER STONES / A Caterpillar Book / Clayton Eshleman–Poet / William Paden–Printmaker / Copy Number_____ [hand numbered in ink] of a limited edition of 250. / The woodcuts are printed on *kizuki-kōzo sarashi,* / a Japanese mulberry paper. All the cutting and / printing was done by the artist in Kyoto, 1967–68. / The poems are printed on *jun-kōzo* by the Genichido / Print Co., Kyoto, 1968. / The *chitsu* (case) was made by K. Asada.

Contains: POEMS: "Han-Shan Variations," untitled: "In the upper corner of a deserted bell-shrine...," "American Hunger," "Ancient Idol," untitled: "Seeing in her arms...," "Brother Stones," "For Kelly," "The Burden," "Black Gorilla," "The Earth," "Flowers." WOODBLOCKS: "Fields," "Sundown," "River," "Hills," "Storm," "Flowers."

[Note: The Japanese "jun" as in jun-kōzo and "ki" as in kizuki means "pure," both are echizen hosho, made of 100% kōzo fibers that come from the white

inner bark of the paper mulberry plant, kōzo. The six woodcuts ranging from seven to ten colors each, were printed using silver magnolia blocks.]

A12   The House of Okumura   **1969**

THE HOUSE OF OKUMURA / by Clayton Eshleman / Weed [slash] flower Press / Toronto Canada / March—1969

21.7 × 16.5cm. 20 leaves; pp. [i–ii] [1–4] 5–37 [38]: p. [i] half title; p. [ii] blank; p. [1] title as above; p. [2] copyright page; p. [3] half title; p. [4] blank; pp. 5–37 text; p. [38] colophon.

Stiff black construction paper cover, folding 8.5cm. over white free endpapers and glued to the spine. Leaves stapled twice from spine to center. [Front cover: a design of black squares (black on black hand-printed serigraph design by Barbara Caruso) vertically on right from top to bottom:] THE HOUSE OF OKUMURA / CLAYTON ESHLEMAN [Paper, watermark:] Gestetner made in Canada [all edges trim]. Cover paper: Mayfair.

Publication: Published by Nelson Ball of the Weed [slash] Flower Press in Toronto, Canada in March, 1969 in an edition of 500 copies, priced at $2.00 a copy. Colophon: This book was designed by Nelson Ball and printed in a / limited edition of 500 copies by Weed [slash] flower Press. / Cover designed and printed by Barbara Caruso. / Weed [slash] flower Press, 756A Bathurst St., Toronto, Canada.

Contains: "The House of Okumura I," "The House of Okumura II," "The House of Okumura III." "The House of Okumura IV," "The House of Okumura V," "The House of Okumura VI: A Tale," "The House of Okumura VII: Commentary," "The House of Okumura VIII: Vision," "The House of Okumura IX: Vision," "The House of Okumura X," "The House of Okumura XI," "The House of Okumura XII," "The House of Okumura XIII," "The House of Okumura XIV," "The House of Okumura XV," "The House of Okumura XVI."

A13   Indiana   **1969**

[In black:] Poems / By / Clayton / Eshleman / [in red:] INDIANA / [in black:] Black / Sparrow / Press / Los Angeles / 1969

24.5 × 16.7cm.; 92 leaves; 1–23⁴; pp. [i–x] 11–178 [179–184]]: p. [i] blank; p. [ii] advertisements; p. [iii] title page as above; p. [iv] copyright page; p. [v] dedication; p. [vi] poem quote; pp. [vii–viii] table of contents; p. [ix] date; p. [x] blank; pp. [182–184] blank. Red endpapers.

Three bindings, no priority as follows:

a. [Red leather spine over yellow paper covered boards; on spine, a yellow paper label reading from top to bottom in black:] CLAYTON ESHLEMAN [single dot] INDIANA [Front cover: a photograph of wind god/demon from Sanjusangendo, Kyoto, Japan, selected by the author] / [in red:] INDIANA / CLAYTON ESHLEMAN [Back cover: portrait of the author from a photography taken by Susan Wiley, below this is a brief biography of the poet]. Paper: wove; top edge cut, fore-edge and bottom edge uncut. False headband. Unprinted acetate dust jacket. Lettered and signed; an extra leaf is bound in before title page with a holograph poem by the author. Hand-bound in boards, by Earle Gray. 30 signed copies, each with a holograph poem by the poet on a separate leaf bound in as a frontispiece, of which 26 copies (lettered A–Z) were for sale, priced at $25.00 a copy, and 4 copies (1 each marked "Author's Copy," "Publisher's Copy," "Printer's Copy," and a "File Copy") not for sale. All copies have the same holograph poem.

b. Same as a. except: multicolored (red, gold, black and white) cloth spine; lacks extra leaf. 257 signed copies, of which 250 copies (numbered 1–250) were for sale, priced at $15.00 a copy, and 7 copies (5 marked "For Presentation," and 1 marked "Binder's Copy" and a "File Copy") not for sale.

c. Same as above except: 23.7 × 15cm.; glued in paper wrappers, [Printed on the spine, reading from top to bottom in black:] CLAYTON ESHLEMAN [single dot] INDIANA Black Sparrow Press. [Red, free endpapers]. 1000 copies, priced at $4.50 a copy.

Publication: Published by John Martin of the Black Sparrow Press in Los Angeles July 15, 1969. Printed by Noel Young in Santa Barbara June 1969. Colophon: [Publisher's device] / Printed June 1969 in Santa Barbara by / Noel Young for the Black Sparrow Press. / Design by Barbara Martin. This edition / is limited to 1000 copies in paper / wrappers; 250 hardcover copies numbered / & signed by the poet; & 26 lettered / copies handbound in boards by / Earle Gray, signed & with a holograph / poem by the poet.

Contains: 1963–1965: "The Crocus Bud," "The Book of Yorunomado," "Barbara Sick," "One Morning," "The Library," "Sungate," "Ibuki Masuko," "Hand," "The Stones of Sanjusangendo," "Nestual Investigations," "The

White Tiger." 1966: "Walk I," "Walk III," "Walk VII," "Letter to César Calvo Concerning the Inauguration of a Monument to César Vallejo," "Walk VIII," untitled: "Matthew a caterpillar . . . ," "Walk IX," "Walk X," "Sensing Duncan I," "The Matisse 1914 Colligure," "Bud Powell 1925–1966," "Washington Square Park," "Theseus Ariadne," "The 1802 Blake Butts Letter Variation," untitled: "Rocks angering dirt . . . ," "The Burden," "Flowers," "For Kelly," "For Carlos Germán Belli," "Sensing Duncan II," untitled: "The night in the Okumura house . . . ," "Lachrymae Mateo." 1967: "Black Gorilla," "The Yellow Garment," "New Guinea," "The Bank," "The Creek," "Bear Field," "Cantaloups & Splendour." 1968: "The Black Hat," "Lilacs & Roses," "Hymn 2," "Hymn 3," "Hymn 5," "Sensing Duncan III," "Sensing Duncan IV," "Diagonal," "The Bedford Vision," "Blood," "Night Entering Vala August Intensity Raga," "Sunday Afternoon," "Soutine."

[Notes: There is a red chinese character (chi) at the end of the poem "Blood" on page 155. The poems in *Indiana* were originally assembled under the title "The American Vita Nuova" by Eshleman in 1968 and then disassembled in order to make the present book. A promotional flyer 21.6 × 13.9cm.; yellow card stock; prints the epigraph poem from the book under a newly supplied title: "Indianapolis" as follows: [in red:] INDIANA / [in black:] CLAYTON ESHLEMAN / [in red: ornamental rule] / [in black: poem, book promotional material and biography of the poet] / Indiana is published in two editions: / Wrappers: $4.50 Signed cloth edition: $15 / [in red: ornamental rule] / [in black: publisher's device] BLACK SPARROW PRESS / P.O. Box 25603 [dot] Los Angeles, California 90025].

A14   T'ai   1969

[In black:] Clayton Eshleman: / [in red: Chinese character "T'ai" (meaning peace)] / [in black:] THE SANS SOUCI PRESS / Cambridge, Massachusetts

20.7 × 16cm.; 20 leaves; 1–5⁴; pp. [i–viii] 9–35 [36–40]: pp. [i–ii] blank; p. [iii] half title; p. [iv] blank; p. [v] title page as above; p. [vi] copyright page; pp. 9–35 text; p. [36] blank; p. [37] colophon; p. [38] Printed at the Ferguson Press / Cambridge, Massachusetts pp. [39–40] blank. [Tan endpapers].

Lavender paper covered boards; [on spine, in gilt reading from top to bottom:] T'AI CLAYTON ESHLEMAN San Souci Press [Front cover: Chinese character "T'ai" stamped in blind]. Paper: [watermark:] Warren's Olde Style; [all edges trim]. Glassine dust jacket.

Publication: Published by William Young of the San Souci Press in Cambridge, Massachusetts, in 1969 in an edition of 99 copies [see note] priced at $15.00 a copy. Printed by William Ferguson of the Ferguson Press in Cambridge, Massachusetts. Colophon: This first edition of T'AI / is limited to ninety-nine copies / numbered and signed by the author. / Published by William Young at / the Sans Souci Press. / No. [hand numbered in ink].

[Note: Approximately 130 copies were printed and bound with a colophon leaf signed by the poet, according to the printer, and given to the publisher, William Young (now deceased). I have seen a copy lettered "E," so it is possible that 26 copies were lettered by the publisher. A book dealer also reports having a copy with "out of series" printed on the colophon. None of these copies were known to the author.]

Contains: "T'ai."

A15   A Pitchblende   1969

[in grey:] A PITCH— / BLENDE / [in black:] CLAYTON ESHLEMAN / MAYA QUARTO THREE

25.2 × 19.1cm.; 6 leaves: p. [i] half title; p. [ii] blank; p. [iii] title page as above; p. [iv] copyright page; pp. [5–11] text; p. [12] colophon.

Two bindings, no priority as follows:
a. [Grey-brown wrappers; 6 leaves; handsewn with cream colored thread through to the spine; on cover, on paper label, in grey:] A PITCH— / BLENDE / [in black:] CLAYTON ESHLEMAN [Paper: laid, watermark:] Curtis Rag. [All edges trimmed]. 250 copies priced at $2.25 a copy.

b. Same as above except: 26 × 20cm.; light grey wrappers; printed on Tovil in Fabriano wrappers numbered and signed by the poet. Untrimmed edges. 50 copies priced at $7.50 a copy.

Publication: Published by Jack Shoemaker and David Meltzer in the summer of 1969 as part of a series called "Maya Quarto" which included thirteen "Quartos"; *A Pitchblende* was the third in this series.

Printed by Clifford Burke at the Cranium Press, in San Francisco in 1969. Colophon: [hand printed in black ink:] MÁYÁ / [in black print:] Quarto Three was hand set in / Clarendon types and printed by / Clifford Burke at Cranium Press, / San Francisco. Two hundred / fifty copies are on Curtis papers. / Fifty copies are on Tocil in Fab- / riano wrappers and are numbered / and signed by the poet. August 1969.

Contains: "San Felipe," "Walk 12," "Walk 14."

A16   The House of Ibuki   1969

THE HOUSE OF IBUKI: A POEM / by Clayton Eshleman / NEW YORK CITY 14 March–30 Sept. 1967 / SUMAC PRESS

19.4 × 12.4cm.; 26 leaves; 1^2, $2-4^8$; pp. [i-vi] 7–49 [50–52]: p. [i] title page as above; p. [ii] copyright and acknowledgments; p. [iii] contents; p. [iv] blank; p. [v] calligraphy by Hidetaka Ohno [reading "ibukinouchi" which means "house of ibuki" in Japanese]; p. [vi] blank; pp. 7–49 text; pp. [50–51] blank; p. [52] colophon. Red endpapers.

Two bindings, no priority as follows:
a. [Black cloth covered boards; spine reading from top to bottom in gilt:] THE HOUSE OF IBUKI ESHLEMAN SUMAC PRESS [Front cover in gilt:] Clayton Eshleman / [short rule] / THE HOUSE OF IBUKI [Paper: wove; all edges trimmed]. 126 copies 26 hand letterd and 100 hand numbered signed by the author priced at $7.50 a copy.

b. Same as above except: glued in white paper wrappers, all edges trim; [printed on black spine reading from top to bottom in white:] THE HOUSE OF IBUKI ESHLEMAN SUMAC PRESS [Front cover on black ground, a photograph of Head of Medusa by Bernini] / [in red:] THE / HOUSE OF IBUKI [on right below the photograph, in white:] CLAYTON / ESHLEMAN [Back cover on white ground, upper left corner:] $1.95 / [a portrait of the author from a photograph by Susan Wiley, below this is a brief biography of the poet]. 1,000 copies priced at $1.95 a copy.

Publication: Published by Dan Gerber of the Sumac Press in Fremont, Michigan in October 1969. Printed by Sequoia Press in Kalamazo, Michigan in September 1969. Designed by Raymnd Hoagland. Colophon: [number or letter of copy inked in on hardbound copies and signed below colophon] / This edition consists of / 1000 soft cover copies and / 100 numbered and / 26 lettered hardbound copies. / All lettered copies / have been signed by the poet.

Contains: "Ibuki Masuko," "Morning Working," "Afternoon Out: i," "Afternoon Out: ii," "Afternoon Out: iii," "Public Bath," "Night: i," "Night: ii,"

"The Insistence," "The Bell Shrine," "Barbara's Tree," "Tsuruginomiya," "Glyph on the 9th Maximus," "The Dedication," "New Guinea: i. The Leg," "New Guinea: ii Becoming Serious."

A17   Yellow River Record   1969

YELLOW RIVER RECORD / CLAYTON ESHLEMAN / a BIG VENUS publication

22.2 × 18.2cm.; 8 leaves; pp. [i–ii] [3–12] [13–16]: p. [i] title page as above; p. [ii] letter from poet to publishers dated 26 July 1969; pp. [3–12] text; pp. [13–14] blank; p. [15] lists publisher and distributor, copyright 1969; p. [16] Printers: Roy & Erica Eden.

Stiff yellow wrappers; 8 leaves of heavy white paper stapled twice through to spine; cover extends 1.1cm. over fore-edge and about .5cm. over top and bottom edges of inside leaves. [Front cover:] YELLOW / RIVER / CLAYTON ESHLEMAN [Paper wove; all edges trim].

Publication: Published by Nick Kimberley of Big Venus Press in London, England in 1969, the third in a series. Nick Kimberley also edited *Big Venus* magazine. Printed by Roy and Erica Eden. 300 copies, priced at $.50 a copy.

Contains: "The Yellow River Record."

A18   The Wand   1970

50.2 or 50.7 × 24.8cm.; single leaf.

Issued on nine different papers (no priority) as follows:

a. On patterned wallpaper as follows: [silver ground with a pattern of 3 shades of blue print, in magenta:] THE WAND / [first 6 lines] [in purple-black: lines 7–30] / (how I read "Aquarius"— / Clayton Eshleman. / Oct. 1970 Sherman Oaks / [wavy black rule] / Printed by Noel Young in Santa Barbara, December 1970, 50 signed copies [On the reverse side, reading bottom to top, in black:] Allure / WALL FASHIONS / by SUNWORTHY [run number of the wall paper may show on back].

b. Same as above except: printed on gilt, yellow and orange patterned wallpaper.

c. Same as above except: printed in black only, on white, gilt and black patterned wallpaper.

d. Same color printing as a. except: printed on a different patterned white and yellow wallpaper.

e. Same color printing as a. except: printed on a different patterned gilt and red wallpaper.

f. Same color printing as a. except: printed on white, red, pink, orange and black flower patterned wallpaper.

g. Same as f. except: printed on white, brown and black flower patterned wallpaper.

h. Same as a. except printed on purple construction paper. The reverse side is blank.

i. Same as a. except: printed on red construction paper. [In magenta: title and first 6 lines; the rest of printing is in black.

[Note: The printing on the reverse of the wallpaper may be partial or absent on some runs of the paper].

Publication: Printed by Noel Young in Santa Barbara December, 1970, in an edition of 250 copies. 200 copies priced at about $2.50 a copy. 50 numbered copies were signed by the poet, priced at about $10.00 a copy (according to the printer).

Contains: "The Wand."

A19   The Bridge at the Mayan Pass   1971

35.2 × 7.4cm.; [top and bottom measurements may vary, the top trimmed wider than the bottom; 7.5cm. at the top & 7.2cm. at the bottom; another copy was cut off at bottom line to measure 34.6cm. so exact measurements are rather arbitrary;] a single leaf printed on one side.

[On cream, in brown, a poem of 20 stanzas dated:] 8–12 December 1970 [signed above the date]. Paper: heavyweight Basingwerk.

Publication: This broadside poem, which sometimes sells as a separate item as described above, was originally published as part of a student quarterly "magazine" by Peace Press [students of California Institute of the Arts in Valencia] called: *The Box* (see B9). Printed by Western Screen Printers of Sun Valley, California. All work was copyrighted 1971 in the name of its author. There were an unknown number of copies printed.

Contains: "The Bridge at the Mayan Pass" which is the first section of the complete poem, printed in *Coils* (see A24).

A20   Altars   1971

[In purple:] clayton / eshleman / [in red:] ALTARS / [in purple:] black / sparrow / press / los / angeles / 1971

24.2 × 16.1cm.; 62 leaves; $1-7^8$; 8^4; 9^2; pp. [i–viii] 9–120 [121–124]: p. [i] blank; p. [ii] advertisements; p. [iii] title page as above; p. [iv] copyright and acknowledgments; p. [v] dedication; p. [vi] blank; p. [vii] contents; p. [viii] blank; pp. 9–120 text; p. [121] colophon; p. [122] biographical notes by the poet; p. [123] portrait of the author from a photograph by Ben Lifson with continuation of biographical notes below; p. [124] blank. Purple endpapers.

Four bindings, no priority as follows:
a. [Red and white patterned cloth spine over red paper covered boards; on spine, red paper label reading from top to bottom:] ALTARS [dot] Clayton Eshleman [Front cover, in purple:] clayton eshleman / ALTARS / [photograph of an Aztec sculpture or bas relief, in black (selected by Robert Kelly)]. [Paper: wove; all edges trim. False headband. Unprinted acetate dust jacket]. signed; an extra leaf is bound in before title-page with an original holograph poem or statement by the author; handbound in boards by Earle Gray. 34 copies, of which 26 copies (lettered from A–Z) were for sale, priced at $25.00 a copy. 8 copies (1 each marked "Author's Copy," "Publisher's Copy," "Printer's Copy," "Binder's Copy," and a "File Copy," and 3 marked "Author's Presentation Copy") not for sale.

b. Same as a. except: spine bound in purple and white patterned cloth; lacks extra leaf. 201 copies, of which 200 copies (numbered from 1–200) were for sale, priced at $15.00 and a "File Copy," not for sale.

c. Same as above except: 23.3 × 15.3cm.; glued in paper wrappers; [in purple, printed on the spine reading from top to bottom:] ALTARS [dot] Clayton Eshleman BLACK SPARROW PRESS [Purple, front and back, free end-paper.] 990 copies priced at $4.00 a copy.

d. First edition, second issue: same as c. except bound in darker red wrappers. Published June 24, 1971. The printer ran short of the medium red covers and bound up this number of copies in the darker stock. 40 copies at the same price as above.

Publication: Published by John Martin of the Black Sparrow Press in Los Angeles, California, June 24, 1971. Printed by Noel Young in Santa Barbara, California, May 1971. Colophon: [Publisher's device] / Printed May 1971 in Santa Barbara / for the Black Sparrow Press by Noel Young. / Design by Barbara Martin. This edition is / limited to 1000 copies in paper wrappers; / 200 hardcover copies numbered & signed by the / poet; & 26 lettered copies hand-bound in / boards by Earle Gray, signed & with an / original holograph poem by the poet.

Contains: Untitled: "We sat on the beach . . . ." "An Ode to Autumn," "Altars," "The Pyramid," "The Plum," "The Mountain," "The Cusp," "The Stan Brakhage Altar Stone," "The Gates of Capricorn," "The Nuclear Sutra," "The Wand," "The Dissolution," untitled: "Rasputin . . . ," "Ode to Reich," "Lustral Waters from the Spring of Aries," untitled: "It comes in rushes . . . ," "A Soliloquy for Tom Meyer," "The Meadow," "Cid & William," "Brothers," "The Tourbillions," "Visions of the Sons of Cancer," untitled: "What is the work . . . ," "Claws," A Commentary.

[Notes: There is a red heart printed on page 98 before the untitled poem "What is the work . . ." This poem is indicated in the table of contents by a heart in outline. *Altars* is a "daily composed book length poem written over a period September 1969 until 1970 and reworked intermittently until published in 1971 . . . on the theme of regeneration using astrological month-symbols and the Chinese oracle the I Ching as a combined source-framework" [the author]. A promotional flyer prints part of a poem from the book with a comment by the author; as follows: 19 × 12.6cm.; red card stock; [in black: the photograph used on the book cover; superimposed in blue:] CLAYTON ESHLEMAN / ALTARS / [in black: biographical comment by the author] / [last section of "An Ode to Autumn": "Waters stored in the earth . . ."] / Wrappers: $4.00 Signed cloth edition: $15.00 / [Publisher's device] BLACK SPARROW PRESS / P.O. BOX 25603 / LOS ANGELES, CALIFORNIA 90025. [Printed in an edition of approximately 1000 copies].

A21   Bearings   1971

[On black rectangular ground, a green and white photograph of Tlazolteotl-Ixcuina (Aztec goddess of childbirth giving birth to the maize god); below photograph, outside rectangle, in dark green:] CLAYTON ESHLEMAN / BEARINGS / Capricorn Press Santa Barbara 1971

22.9 x 16cm.; 14 leaves; 1^8, 2^4, 3^2; pp. [i-iv] 5-22 [23-28]: p. [i] description and location of original "childbirth goddess" used in photograph on cover; p. [ii] advertisement; p. [iii] title page as above; p. [iv] copyright page; pp. 5-22 text; pp. [23-24] blank; p. [25] colophon; p. [26] blank; p. [27] autobiographical statement; p. [28] blank. Blue-grey endpapers.

Two bindings, no priority as follows:
a. [White paper covered boards, printed on spine:] BEARINGS [slash] ESHLEMAN CAPRICORN PRESS [front cover on black ground, a black and white photograph of childbirth goddess giving birth to the Maize god, below on green ground:] CLAYTON ESHLEMAN / BEARINGS [Paper: cream wove; all edges trim]. 100 copies handbound and hand numbered, priced at $6.50 a copy.

b. Same as above except: 22.3 x 15.2cm.; glued in paper covers, un-numbered. Pea-green, tan, or gold endpapers [arbitrary selection]. 900 copies priced at $2.00 a copy.

Publication: Published and printed by Noel Young at the Capricorn press in Santa Barbara, California in 1971. Colophon: [Publisher's device] / Edition limited to 1000 copies designed & printed / by Noel Young in Santa Barbara, / with 100 copies handbound / and numbered. / [number inked in].

Contains: An essay addressed to today's young, on the relationship of the sexual to the creative life.

[Note: Bearings at one point was xeroxed from typescript and distributed by the author to a few friends with a different title: *A Bringing of Rilke into My Own Road and Thought.* It was first published as described above].

A22   One of the Oldest Dreams   1972

16.5 x 10cm.; single leaf printed on both sides.

[On tan, with short side up, in grey: a wood engraving of a bird with a sun below it's beak] / [in grey, a 6 line poem] / Clayton Eshleman / (12 March

1971) [on verso, with long side up, on left side, in grey:] wood engraving by
Ann Mikolowski [bisecting the card, bottom to top:] THE ALTERNATIVE
PRESS DETROIT [Paper: Teton].

Publication: Published by Ken Mikolowski of The Alternative Press in Detroit,
Michigan in early 1972, in an edition of 500 copies. Hand set and printed by
Ken Mikolowski on an old 1904 Chandler letter press, November 1971. De-
signed by Ann Mikolowski.

Contains: Untitled 6 line poem beginning: "One of the oldest dreams. . ."

[Note: This postcard was part of an envelope issue from the Alternative Press
under the general title of "Art Poetry Melodrama" which consists of printed
work of various poets, artists, photographers, etc., all issued together in a
grey clasp envelope quarterly to subscribers. The postcard was not sold
seperately although the poet was given some for his own use]. (See B11)

A23   The Sanjo Bridge   1972

[Cover title:] [inside red decorative rule and solid rule frame, in black:]
SPARROW 2 / [publisher's device in black at center of red ornamental leaf
rule] / [in black:] "LIVING, I WANT TO DEPART TO WHERE I AM"—
D.H. LAWRENCE / [red thick over thin rule] / [in black:] THE SANJO
BRIDGE / by / Clayton Eshleman / SPARROW will appear monthly. It will
print poetry, fiction, / essays, criticism, commentaries, & reviews. Each issue
will / present the work of a single author. The poet is prophet. / BLACK
SPARROW PRESS: November 1972 [Back cover, inside red decorative rule
and solid rule frame, in black:] CURRENT PUBLICATIONS / [a list of 5
publications follows] / [inside black rule frame:] Sparrow is printed for the
Black Sparrow Press / by Noel Young. [Below frame, on left:] Black Sparrow
Press / P.O. Box 25603 / Los Angeles, California 90025 [in large print to
right:] 50¢

23.6 × 15.5cm.; 8 leaves, stapled twice through to spine; pp. [ii] [3–15]: p. [ii]
copyright page; pp. [3–15] text. [Paper: sub. 55 natural book].

Publication: Published by John Martin of the Black Sparrow Press in Los
Angeles, California as *Sparrow 2,* November 13, 1972. Printed by Noel Young
in Santa Barbara, California November 1972 in a first edition of 750 copies,
priced at $.50 a copy. There was a second printing of 525 copies. States
"second printing" on copyright page. There was a third printing of 563 copies.
States "third printing" on the copyright page.

Contains: Essay on being a poet: ". . . where does art begin and entertainment end?"

[Note: Later printings have a black decorative rule frame and black ornamental leaf rule on cover instead of the red decorative rule frame of the first printing. *Sparrow 2* was also bound in cloth covered boards with *Sparrow 1–12;* see B15].

A24   Coils   1973

[Orange wavy rule] / [in red:] CLAYTON / ESHLEMAN / [3 orange wavy rules] / [in green:] COILS / [2 orange wavy rules] / [in green:] 1973 / BLACK SPARROW PRESS / Los Angeles

24.3 x 16.4cm.; 76 leaves; 1^2, 2–10^8, 11^2; pp. [i–x] 11–147 [148–152]: p. [i] blank; p. [ii] advertisement; p. [iii] title page as above; p. [iv] copyright and acknowledgments; p. [v] dedication; p. [vi] blank; p. [vii] contents; p. [viii] [I Sing the Body Electric]; p. [ix] I; p. [x] introductory essay by the poet; pp. 11–147 text; p. [148] blank; p. [149] colophon; p. [150] blank; p. [151] portrait of the author from a photograph taken by Caryl Eshleman, below this is a brief biography of the poet; p. [152] blank. [Red endpapers].

Three bindings, no priority as follows:
a. [Machine-embroidered magenta and orange cloth spine over cream paper covered boards; on spine, a cream paper label reading from top to bottom, in green:] COILS Clayton Eshleman [Front cover, inside three ovoid wavy shapes (red, pink, orange) in green:] COILS / by / CLAYTON / ESHLE-MAN [Paper: wove; all edges trim. False headband. Unprinted acetate dust jacket]. Lettered & signed; an extra leaf is bound in between pp. [iv-v] with an original holograph poem by the author. Handbound in boards by Earle Gray. 38 copies, of which 26 copies (lettered from A–Z) were for sale, priced at $25.00 a copy, 12 cpies (1 each marked "Author's Copy, "Publisher's Copy," "Printer's Copy," "Binder's Copy," 2 marked Presentation Copy," and 5 marked "Author's Presentation Copy" and a "File Copy,") not for sale. The holograph poem in the Binder's Copy and in one of the Presentation Copies was written on the first recto in the book rather than bound in on an additional leaf.

b. Same as above except: spine bound in green cloth; lacks extra leaf. 201 signed copies of which 200 copies (numbered 1–200) were for sale, priced at $15.00 a copy; one "File Copy" not for sale.

c. Same as above except: 23.5 × 15.5cm.; glued in paper wrappers; [in green, printed on the spine reading from top to bottom:] [ornament] COILS [ornament] Clayton Eshleman [ornament] Black Sparrow Press [Red free endpapers]. 1491 copies, priced at $4.00 a copy.

[Note: One unsigned copy bound in full red leather was presented to the author. It contains the author's corrections to the "Acknowledgments" (ie. line 6: "Gnosis, 1961" corrected to "1969"; line 15: "in tish" corrected to "trenches" and now signed in black: unnumbered).]

Publication: Published by John Martin of the Black Sparrow Press in Los Angeles, California, 16 March 1973. Printed by Noel Young in Santa Barbara in February, 1973. Colophon: [Publisher's device] / Printed February 1973 in Santa Barbara for / the Black Sparrow Press by Noel Young. / Design by Barbara Martin. This edition / is published in paper wrappers; there / are 200 hardcover copies numbered & signed / by the poet; & 26 lettered copies / handbound in boards by Earle Gray, / signed & with an original holograph / poem by the poet.

Contains: Introduction to Section I, "Webbs of Entry," "Trenches," Introduction to Section II, "The Left Hand of Gericault," "Neimonjima," "Divine Aid," Introduction to Section III, "The House of Okumura I," "The House of Okumura II," "The House of Okumura III," "The House of Okumura IV," "The House of Okumura V," "The House of Okumura VI: A Tale," "The House of Okumura VII: A Commentary," Introduction to Section IV, "T'ai," "Letter From New Platz," "The Bloodstone," Introduction to Section V, "Origin," "Mokpo," Introduction to Section VI, "The Golden String," "The Overcoats of Eden," "Botticelli Childhood Conjunction," "The Baptism of Desire," "The Bridge at the Mayan Pass," Introduction to Section VII, "Brief Hymn to the Body Electric," "The Octopus Delivery," "The Physical Traveler," "Coils."

[Notes: "Tsuruginomiya Regeneration," a very long poem (approximately 350 pages) manuscript, was transformed into a much shorter poem and published here as "Coils." Many parts of "Tsuruginomiya Regeneration" appeared in magazines, under this title. A promotional broadside: 35.6 × 25.5cm.; (light weight yellow paper) prints a complete poem from the book entitled "The Physical Traveler" and a statement by Gary Snyder; as follows: [inside a red wavy rule frame in red:] COILS / [in black:] A NEW BOOK OF POEMS BY / [in red:] CLAYTON ESHLEMAN / [in black:] [printer's device] / THE PHYSICAL TRAVELER / [poem of eighteen stanzas, in two columns] / [statement by Gary Snyder] / WRAPPERS. $4 SIGNED CLOTH EDITION: $15 / [outside red rule frame, in black:] BLACK SPARROW

PRESS [slash] P.O. Box 25603 [slash] LOS ANGELES, CA. 90025 / [publisher's device] / BROADSIDE [Slash] FLYER NO. 5 [100 copies were numbered and signed by the author. This is #5 in a series of Black Sparrow broadside flyers].

A25   The Last Judgement   1973

64.8 × 48cm.; a single leaf printed on one side.

[Laid out in three columns divided by vertical blue decorative rules, as follows:] [first column, with a blue decorative initial letter "T"; in black:] [44 lines of poem] [centered above middle column, in blue with blue decorative device on each side:] CLAYTON ESHLEMAN / The Last Judgement / FOR CARYL / her thirty-first birthday, for the end of her pain / [in black:] [35 lines of poem] [third column, in black:] [44 lines of poem] / Sherman Oaks, 21 March 1973 [verso, lower left, in black:] [publisher's device] / Printed by Saul & / Lillian Marks at the / Plantin Press, Los Angeles [Paper: deckle edge manilla wove].

Publication: Privately published in April 1973 by the poet as a birthday present for his wife, Caryl. Printed by Saul Marks at the Plantin Press in an issue of 100 copies hand numbered and signed by the poet, priced at $12.00 a copy.

Contains: "The Last Judgement."

A26   Human Wedding   1973

[In black:] CLAYTON ESHLEMAN / [within a blue diamond of type ornaments, in black:] Human / Wedding / [below blue diamond, in black:] Los Angeles Black Sparrow Press 1973

21.5 × 15.5cm.; 10 leaves; 1¹⁰; pp. [i–vi] [1–7] [8–14]: p. [i–iv] blank; p. [v] title page as above; p. [vi] copyright page; pp. 1–7 text; p. [8] blank; p. [9] colophon: pp. [10–14] blank. White, front and back, pastedowns.

Three bindings, no priority as follows:
a. Blue, red and gilt marbled paper covered boards, [white paper label on cover:] [within blue ornamental frame in blue:] HUMAN / WEDDING [sewn in red thread]. Paper: watermark; Curtis Rag. All edges trimmed. 35 signed copies, of which 26 copies (lettered A–Z) were for sale, priced at

A25. The Last Judgement

$25.00 a copy, and 9 copies (1 eachmarked "Author's Copy," "Diane [Wakoski]'s Copy," "Michael [Watterlond]'s Copy," "Publisher's Copy," "Printer's Copy," "Binder's Copy," and "File Copy" and 2 numbered and marked "Presentation Copy") not for sale.

b. Same as above except: 21.5 × 15.1cm.; 8 leaves (one blank leaf front and back lacking). Green, red and gilt marbled wrappers. Copies are hand numbered 1–98.

c. Same as above except: blue, red and gilt marbled wrappers of a different pattern from a. Copies are hand numbered 99–200.

242 signed copies of which 200 copies (numbered 1–200) were for sale, priced at $10.00 a copy; and 42 copies not for sale as follows: 2 (one in each binding) marked "File Copy," and 40 (in green marbled wrappers) divided between the author and Diane Wakoski.

Publication: Published by John Martin of the Black Sparrow Press of Los Angeles, California April 20, 1973. Printed by Saul & Lillian Marks at the Plantin Press, Los Angeles, California. Colophon: [Publisher's device] / Published to celebrate the marriage / of Diane Wakoski & Michael Watterlond. / Designed & printed for the Black Sparrow Press / by Saul & Lillian Marks at the Plantin Press, / Los Angeles. The edition is limited to / 226 numbered & lettered copies / signed by the author.

A26. Human Wedding

Contains: "Human Wedding."

A27   Aux Morts   1974

[Cover title same as SPARROW 2 except:] SPARROW 18 [title and date which read:] Aux Morts / by / Clayton Eshleman / BLACK SPARROW PRESS : MARCH 1974 [Back cover same as *Sparrow 2* except a list of 9 current publications].

23.7 × 15.6cm.; 8 leaves, stapled twice through to spine; pp. [ii] [3–15]: p. [ii] copyright page; pp. [3–15] text. [Paper: sub. 55 natural book].

Publication: Published by John Martin of the Black Sparrow Press in Los Angeles, California as *Sparrow 18,* March 18, 1974. Printed by Noel Young in Santa Barbara, California March 1974 in a first edition of 934 copies, priced at $.50 a copy. There was a second printing of 540 copies.

Contains: "Keeping the Flies from My Mother's Head," "Aconite," "Chaim Soutine," "At the Tomb of Soutine," "At the Tomb of Vallejo."

[Note: Sparrow 18 was also bound in cloth covered boards: *Sparrow 13–24;* see B18].

A28   Realignment   1974

[In red:] REALIGNMENT / poems & / an essay by / CLAYTON / ESHLEMAN / drawings by / NORA / JAFFE / TREACLE / PRESS / 1974

23.4 × 18.4cm.; 26 leaves; 1^{10}, 2^8, 3^8; pp. [i–vi] [7–50] [51–52]: pp. [i–ii] blank; p. [iii] title page as above; p. [iv] copyright page and colophon [states "First Edition;" pp. [v–vi] blank; p. [7] poem; p. [8] blank; p. [9] drawing; p. [10] blank; p. [11] poem; p. [12] blank; p. [13] drawing; p. [14] blank; pp. [15–16] poem; p. [17] drawing; p. [18] blank; p. [19] poem; p. [20] blank; p. [21] drawing; p. [22] blank; p. [23] poem; p. [24] blank; p. [25] drawing; p. [26] blank; p. [27] poem; p. [28] blank; p. [29] drawing; p. [30] blank; pp. [31–34] poem; p. [35] drawing; p. [36] blank; pp. [37–42] poem-essay; p. [43] drawing; p. [44] blank; p. [45] poem; p. [46] blank; p. [47] drawing; p. [48] blank; pp. [49–50] poem; pp. [51–52] blank. Beige thistle-type endpapers.

Two bindings, no priority as follows:
a. [Red cloth over boards, stamped on spine top to bottom, in gilt:] REALIGNMENT ESHLEMAN & JAFFE TREACLE PRESS [Paper: laid, Warren's [slash] Olde Style].

[Dust jacket: (.5cm. shorter than the book in most copies) grey paper, on spine top to bottom, in blue:] REALIGNMENT ESHLEMAN & JAFFE TREACLE PRESS [On cover in blue:] REALIGNMENT / CLAYTON / ESHLEMAN / NORA / JAFFE [on right, in red: drawing by Nora Jaffe]. 20 copies signed by the author and artist, priced at $8.00 a copy.

b. Same as above except: 22.8 × 18.cm.; paper wrappers, blue endpapers. Cover, reproducing dust jacket, glued to blue endpaper at spine and folded over 10.5cm. at fore-edge; free endpaper with fore-edge rough cut front and back. 430 copies, priced at $2.50 a copy.

A28. Realignment

Publication: Published by Bruce McPherson at the Treacle Press in Providence, Rhode Island, September 15, 1974. Colophon: [on copyright page] Printed offset and letterpress / in Providence, Rhode Island / during August & September / in editions of 430 paperbound trade / and 20 clothbound deluxe copies / signed by the author / and artist. / This is number _____. [hand numbered in ink].

Contains: "My Deadness Abandoned for Caryl Reiter," "Entry," "To the Creative Spirit," "Credo," "Winding It into a Ball," "Reduction," "Sugar," "Adhesive Love," "4705," "Realignment." With 9 black and white ink drawings by Nora Jaffe.

[Notes: There were 2 or 3 additional copies quarter bound in red leather with marble paper boards, stamped in gilt on spine according to the publisher.

Neither the artist nor the author remember these and I have not seen a copy. A promotional broadside flyer, 27.5 × 21cm. was printed in two editions as follows:

a. Typographical with poem, "My Deadliness (sic) Abandoned for Caryl Reiter," giving as publication date August 30, 1974.

b. Cover drawing reproduced with poem, "My Deadness Abandoned for Caryl Reiter" (note spelling change) giving as publication date September 15, 1974. These flyers were reproduced via corner store offset on white paper in an edition of approximately 500 copies].

A29   Antonin Artaud: Letter to André Breton   1974

[Cover same as SPARROW 2 except:] SPARROW 23 [title and date which read:] Letter to André Breton / by / Antonin Artaud / Translated by Clayton Eshleman / BLACK SPARROW PRESS : AUGUST 1974 [back cover: lists 9 current publications; printer credit deleted].

23.7 × 15cm.; 8 leaves, stapled twice through to spine; pp. [ii] [3–15]: p. [ii] copyright page; pp. [3–15] text. [Paper: sub. 55 natural book].

Publication: Published by John Martin of the Black Sparrow Press in Los Angeles, California as *Sparrow 23,* July 26, 1974. Printed by Graham Mackintosh in Santa Barbara, California July, 1974 in a first edition of 995 copies, priced at $.50 a copy. There is a second printing of 560 copies; a third printing of 526 copies.

Contains: Antonin Artaud: Letter to André Breton. dated: "About the 28th of February, 1947"; (translated from the French by Clayton Eshleman).

[Note: Sparrow 23 was also bound in cloth covered boards: *Sparrow 13*–24; see B18].

A30   César Vallejo: Spain, Take This Cup from Me   1974

[Double spread title page; on verso:] España, / Aparta de mí este Cáliz [on recto:] Spain, / Take This Cup from Me / by César Vallejo / Translated by Clayton Eshleman / and José Rubia Barcia / Grove Press, Inc., New York

[A bilingual Edition; original Spanish on versos, English on rectos]

20.9 × 14cm.; 48 leaves; 1–6⁸; pp. [i–v] vi–xiii [xiv] [1] 2–77 [78–82]: p. [i] half title; p. [ii–iii] title pages as above: p. [iv] copyright page, [states: "First Printing"]; p. [v] blank; p. vi Indice; p. vii Contents; p. [viii] blank; pp. ix–xiii "César Against Vallejo," (an introduction by Clayton Eshleman) p. [xiv] blank; p. [1] divisional title; pp. 2–77 text; pp. [78–82] blank. White endpapers.

Two editions, no priority as follows:
a. [Black cloth covered boards; spine reading from top to bottom, in red;] César Vallejo [in gilt:] SPAIN, TAKE THIS CUP FROM ME [reading side to side:] GROVE / PRESS [Paper: wove; all edges trim].

Dust jacket: [spine: on yellow ground, reading top to bottom, in black:] Spain, Take This Cup From Me [in red:] César Vallejo [reading side to side, in black:] GP-752 / GROVE / Press [Front cover, on yellow ground, in black:] Spain, / Take This Cup / From Me / [thin black rule] / by César Vallejo / [in red an abstract head and arm (from drawing by Picasso of "Weeping Woman" occasioned by the Spanish Civil War, selected by Clayton Eshleman) [in upper right corner above thin black rule and parallel to book title, in black:] a bilingual edition / translated from the Spanish / by Clayton Eshleman and / José Rubia Barcia [Back cover, on yellow ground: a black and white portrait of César Vallejo from a photograph taken by Juan Larrea] / César Vallejo / GROVE PRESS, INC., 53 East 11th Street, New York, N.Y. 10003 0-394-49263-3 [on right of photograph, reading bottom to top:] Photo: Juan Larrea [Front inside flap, on white ground in black:] GP-752 $10.00 / Spain, / Take This Cup / From Me / [thin black rule] / by César Vallejo / a bilingual edition / translated from the Spanish / by Clayton Eshleman and / José Rubia Barcia / [thick black rule] / [biographical notes on César Vallejo] / [thick black rule] / [back flap, on white ground:] [thick black rule] / [continuation and conclusion from front flap] / [thick black rule] / Cover Design: Kenneth R. Deardoff. 3,000 copies, priced at $10.00 a copy.

b. According to archival records, at the George Arents Research Library, at Syracuse University, Syracuse, N.Y., there was a simultaneous Evergreen edition in wrappers. *Book Review Digest* (1975 edition) lists (page 1297) a wrapper edition at $2.95 a copy. I have been unable to locate a copy.

Publication: Published by Grove Press, December 12, 1974 in New York City.

Contains: "César Against Vallejo," [an introductory essay by Clayton Eshleman]; César Vallejo: "Hymn to the Volunteers for the Republic,"

untitled: "Man from Estremadura...," untitled: "Then, retreating from
Talavera...," untitled: "But from here, later...," untitled: "In Madrid, in
Bilbao, in Santander...," untitled: "Málaga without father nor mother...,"
untitled: "He used to write with his big finger in the air...," untitled: "The
beggars fight for Spain...," "Spanish Image of Death," "Cortege After the
Capture of Bilbao," untitled: "For several days the air, companions...," un-
titled: "Back here...," "Short Prayer for a Dead Loyalist Hero," "Winter
During the Battle for Teruel," untitled: "I looked at the corpse, at its visible
swift order...," "Mass," "Funeral Drumroll for the Ruins of Durango,"
"Spain, Take This Cup from Me," untitled: "Beware, Spain, of your own
Spain...," (Translated and with notes by Clayton Eshleman and José Rubia
Barcia).

A31   Portrait of Francis Bacon   1975

[On yellow, in black:] PORTRAIT OF / FRANCIS BACON / BY /
CLAYTON ESHLEMAN / Rivelin Press Publications, / 157 Sharrow Vale
Road / [underlined in black rule:] Sheffield S11 8ZA

25.4 × 20.3cm.; 11 leaves; pp. [i–ii] 3–11: p. [i] title page as above; [printed
on rectos only]; p. [ii] acknowledgement and copyright; pp. 3–11 text.

[Stiff pink covers with three staples vertically on the left; printed in black:]
PORTRAIT / OF / FRANCIS / BACON / [thin rule] / CLAYTON /
ESHLEMAN [Back cover, underlined in black:] portrait of francis bacon /
[in black:] clayton eshleman / [colophon] / [four small dots] / [brief biography
of poet] / [six small dots] / [advertisements] / [underlined in black rule:] ISBN
0 904524 05 1 [on far right, same line:] Rivelin Press / portrait of francis bacon
[far right:] 157 Sharrow Vale Road / [underlined in black:] Sheffield S11 8ZA
/ [in black:] PRICE 20p [Paper: yellow wove; all edges trim with cover].

Publication: Published by David Tipron of the Rivelin Press, June 1975 in
Sheffield, England. Colophon: An edition of 250 copies, published by Rivelin
Press, June / 1975, and obtainable from the address below. The first 25 /
copies are numbered and signed by the author. 250 copies, priced at 20p a
copy.

Contains: "Portrait of Francis Bacon."

[Note: Some copies show address of publisher changed in holograph from 157
Sharrow Vale Road to 5 Ashgate Close, according to Herb Yellin in his
Eshleman check-list published in Bruccoli and Clark: *First Printings of American
Authors* (Detroit, Gale Research, 1977). I have not seen such a copy].

A32. The Gull Wall

A32   The Gull Wall   1975

[In black:] Clayton Eshleman / [in red:] THE / GULL / WALL / [in black:] Los Angeles / Black Sparrow Press / 1975

23.6 × 16cm.; 58 leaves; 1^2, $2-3^{16}$, 4^8, 5^{16}; pp. [i-xii] 13-111 [112-116]]: p. [i] blank; p. [ii] advertisement; p. [iii] title page as above; p. [iv] copyright and acknowledgements; p. [v] dedication; p. [vi] blank; p. [vii] table of contents; p. [viii] blank; p. [ix] quotations; p. [x] blank; p. [xi] I.; p. [xii] blank; pp. 13-111 text; p. [112] blank; p. [113] colophon; p. [114] blank; p. [115] portrait of the author from a photograph taken by Caryl Eshleman, below this is a brief biography of the poet; p. [116] blank. Gold endpapers.

Three bindings, no priority as follows:
a. [Red, gold, tan and blue leaf patterned cloth spine over yellow paper covered boards; on spine, a yellow paper label reading top to bottom, in red:] THE GULL WALL [in black:] Clayton Eshleman [Front cover, in red:] THE / GULL / WALL / [in black:] clayton eshleman [superimposed over an image, in gold of a chimere from the Second Gallery of Notre Dame in Paris, (selected by Clayton Eshleman)]. Paper: wove; all edges trim. False headband. Unprinted acetate dust jacket. Lettered and signed; an extra leaf is bound in between pp. [iv-v] with an original holograph poem by the author. Handbound in boards by Earle Gray. 37 copies, of which 26 copies

lettered A–Z) were for sale, priced at $30.00 a copy. 11 copies (one each marked "Author's Copy," "Publisher's Copy," "Printer's Copy," "Binder's Copy," and a "File Copy," and 6 marked "Author's Presentation Copy") not for sale.

b. Red cloth spine, lacks extra leaf. 201 signed copies of which 200 copies (numbered 1–200 were for sale, priced at $15.00 a copy, one "File Copy" not for sale.

c. Same as above except 22.7 × 14.7cm.; glued in paper wrappers: [on spine reading from top to bottom in red:] THE GULL WALL [in black:] Clayton Eshleman [in red:] Black Sparrow Press [Gold, front and back, free endpaper]. 1502 copies, priced at $4.00 a copy.

Publication: Published by John Martin of the Black Sparrow Press in Los Angeles, California, September 3, 1975. Printed by Noel Young in Santa Barbara, California and Edwards Brothers in Ann Arbor, Michigan, July 1975. Colophon: [Publisher's device] / Printed July 1975 in Santa Barbara & Ann Arbor for the Black Sparrow / Press by Noel Young & Edwards Brothers Inc. Typography by Graham / Mackintosh. Design by Barbara Martin. This edition is published in / paper wrappers; there are 200 hardcover copies number & signed by / the author; & 26 lettered copies handbound in boards by Earle Gray each / with an original holograph poem by Clayton Eshleman. [Hand lettered or hand numbered].

Contains: "To the Creative Spirit," "Reduction," "Entry," "Gargoyles," "Aconite," "Sugar," "Puberty," "Bud Powell," "50 Men for a 41 Kill Per Hour," "Study for a Self-Portrait at 12 Years Old," "4705," "Realignment," "Rotunda," "Creation," "The Gull Wall," "Baby Rhubarb," "Adhesive Love," "Portrait of Vincent Van Gogh," "Portrait of Charlie Parker," "Portrait of Chaim Soutine," "Portrait of Paul Celan," The 9 Poems of Metro Vavin, [the poems included with this essay are: "In Paris," "A Woman in the Subway," "A Change of Heart," "Meeting An American Poet," "My Neighborhood 1964," "What I Believe," "1943," "Thinking About Love," "A Poem About My Destiny"]; "Portrait of Antonin Artaud," "Portrait of T.R.," "Portrait of Hart Crane," [after Arthur Rimbaud:] "Le Bateau Ivre," "At the Tomb of Vallejo," "My Gargoyle," "A Visit from Paul Blackburn," "Collage to the Body Electric," "My Jackal Henchman," untitled: "Leon Golub working on a painting...," "Portrait of Francis Bacon," "Germanic Halo," "The Ronin Cock."

[Notes: "The 9 Poems of Metro Vavin" were written by Clayton Eshleman. The persona of Metro Vavin was conceived by Eshleman, (see appendix A). The Black Sparrow Press promotional catalogue: "Forthcoming Titles" January–August 1975 (21.5 × 14cm., in black and purple) announces the publication of *The Gull Wall* and 8 books by other authors. It prints (on page 8 of 12 pages) the first 6 lines of "Paul Celan" from *The Gull Wall].*

A33   Antonin Artaud: 1975
        To Have Done with the Judgment of God

[Cover same as SPARROW 23 Except:] SPARROW 34 [title and date which
read:] To Have Done With / The Judgment of God / by / Antonin Artaud
/ translated by / Clayton Eshleman & Norman Glass / BLACK SPARROW
PRESS : July 1975 [Back cover lists 8 current publications; price changed to:]
$1

23.7 × 15.5cm.; 12 leaves, stapled twice through to spine; pp. [ii] [3–23]: p.
[ii] copyright page; pp. [3–23] text. [Paper: sub. 55 natural book].

Publication: Published by John Martin of the Black Sparrow Press in Los
Angeles, California as *Sparrow 34,* July 23, 1975. Printed by Graham Mackintosh in Santa Barbara, California July 1975 in a first edition of 1545 copies,
priced at $1.00 a copy.

Contains: Antonin Artaud: untitled: "kré Everything puc te. . .," untitled
poem: "I learned yesterday. . .," "Tutuguri," "The Search for Fecality," "To
Raise the Question of. . .," "Conclusion," "Note," (translated from the French
by Clayton Eshleman and Norman Glass).

[Note: Sparrow 34 was also bound in cloth covered boards: *Sparrow 25–36;* see:
B22].

A34   The Woman Who Saw Through Paradise   1976

[Cover title, in black:] TANSEY 2 / [in green, a design inside rectangle] /
[in black:] [double rule] / [double rule] / THE WOMAN WHO SAW
THROUGH PARADISE / by / CLAYTON ESHLEMAN

21.6 × 14cm.; 4 leaves; pp. [i] [1–8]: p. [i] [verso of front cover] copyright
page; pp. [1–8] text.

Front cover as above; back cover, inside green ornamental rectangle: colophon, brief biography, and credits. Stapled twice through to cover; all edges
trim with cover. Paper: wove.

Publication: Published and printed by John Moritz of the Tansy Press in
Lawrence, Kansas in October, 1976, in an edition of 350 copies, to be given

gratis at a poetry reading; later sold for $.50 a copy. Colophon: THE WOMAN WHO SAW THROUGH PARADISE was prepared / especially for Clayton Eshleman's reading at Kansas University, Oc- / tober 21, 1976.

Contains: "The Woman Who Saw Through Paradise," "Alleluia Choruses."

[Note: The cover design is a collaboration between Lee Chapman and John Moritz. Tansy 2 was part of a series of publications [17 in all] published occasionally by John Moritz, devoted to the work of a single artist].

A35   Still — Life, with Fraternity   1976

41.7 × 26.5; single leaf, printed on one side.

STILL — LIFE, WITH FRATERNITY / for Ted Grieder / [rule] / [73 line poem] / - Clayton Eshleman / 1976 / SUA Poetry Hour announces a reading by Clayton Eshleman on October 21st at 8:00pm in the Pine Room of the Kansas Union / A COTTONWOOD REVIEW PUBLICATION [signed above poet's printed name]. Paper: Cream, 60 pound vellum.

Publication: Printed by John Moritz for Cottonwood Review Press in October, 1976, in an issue of 200 copies to be given gratis at the reading given by Clayton Eshleman at the University of Kansas, October 21, 1976.

Contains: "Still-Life, With Fraternity"

A36   Antonin Artaud: Artaud the Mômo   1976

[Cover same as SPARROW 34 except:] SPARROW 47 [title and date which read:] Artaud the Momo / by / Antonin Artaud / translated by / Clayton Eshleman & Norman Glass / BLACK SPARROW PRESS : AUGUST 1976 [Back cover (below the list of 8 current publications) changed to:] Black Sparrow Press / P.O. Box 3993 / Santa Barbara, California 93105 [in large print to right:] $1.00

23.7 × 15.6cm.; 12 leaves, stapled twice through to spine; pp. [ii] [3–23]: p. [ii] half-tone of a self-portrait sketch by Antonin Artaud and copyright; pp. [3–23] text [printed in black and red]. [Paper: sub. 55 natural book].

Publication: Published by John Martin of the Black Sparrow Press in Santa Barbara, California as *Sparrow 47,* August 24, 1976. Printed by Graham

Mackintosh in Santa Barbara, August 1976 in a first edition of 1527 copies, priced at $1.00 a copy.

Contains: Note by Clayton Eshleman; Antonin Artaud: "The Return of Artaud, the Mômo," "Mother Center and Pussy Boss," "Insult to the Unconditioned," "The Execration of the Father—Mother," "Madness and Black Magic," (translated from the French by Clayton Eshleman and Norman Glass).

[Note: Sparrow 47 was also bound in cloth covered boards: *Sparrow 37–48;* (see B23)].

A37   Cogollo   1976

COGOLLO / Clayton Eshleman / 1976 / ROXBURY POETRY ENTER-PRISES. / Newton, Massachusetts.

21.6 × 14cm.; 14 leaves; pp. [i–vi] [7–27] [28]: p. [i] blank; p. [ii] advertisement; p. [iii] title page as above; p. [iv] copyright and acknowledgement; p. [v] no hay pirámide escrita, sin cogollo / —César Vallejo p. [vi] blank; pp. [7–27] text; p. [28] colophon.

Stiff wrappers; [Horizontal line of type ornament] / COGOLLO / [Chinese characters meaning "Cogollo" or important and fundimental] / clayton eshleman / [horizontal line of type ornament]. [Stapled twice through to the spine; paper: wove; all edges trim with the cover].

Publication: Published by Peter Ganick of Roxbury Poetry Enterprises, Newton, Massachusetts, in April 1976. Printed by Paul Chremka in Abington, Massachusetts, April 1976. Colophon: Photo-offset April 1976 for Roxbury / Poetry Enterprises in Cambridge, / Massachusetts by Gnomon Copy. Cover / design by Caryl Eshleman. Cover / printed by Paul Chremka in Abington, / Massachusetts. This edition is / published in paper wrappers; there / are three hundred and fifty copies.

Contains: "Eternity," "Tree Textures Along the Taconic," untitled: "Making love to you this morning your 8 year...," untitled: "There is something in him...," "What to Call It," "A Climacteric," "Ira," "The Dragon Rat Tail," "Daily," "The Cogollo," "Chrysanthemum Lake" (sic.).

[Note: Because of the author's dissatisfaction with the significant typographical and editing errors in the text, this book was withdrawn].

A38   Core Meander   1977

[Cover same as SPARROW 47 except:] SPARROW 57 [title and date, which read:] Core Meander / by / Clayton Eshleman / BLACK SPARROW PRESS : JUNE 1977 [Back cover same as SPARROW 34 except lists 9 current publications, the price is changed to:] 75c.

23.7 × 15.6cm.; 8 leaves, stapled twice through to spine; pp. [ii] [3–15]: p. [ii] copyright page; pp. [3–15] text. [Paper: sub. 55 natural book].

Publication: Published by John Martin of the Black Sparrow Press in Santa Barbara, California as *Sparrow 57,* June 2, 1977. Printed by Graham Mackintosh in Santa Barbara, California in a first edition of 1230 copies, priced at $.75 a copy.

Contains: "Core Meander," untitled: "'Play vanilla,' Lester Young is said...," "Still-Life, with African Violets," "After the Second Death," "Om Hollow," "Variations Done for John Digby."

[Note: Sparrow 57 was also bound in cloth covered boards: *Sparrow 49–60;* (see B26).

A39   For Mark Kritzer   1977

29 × 21.6cm.; single leaf printed on one side.

[On blue, within a blue single rule frame with a vertical single rule on right and left inside, in blue:] FOR MARK KRITZER [in upper right corner, an outline of a bird in flight above two trees] / [22 line poem] / Clayton Eshleman / Designed and printed in Northridge during the summer of 1977 for the celebration of Sheldon and Joy Kritzer. The edition consists of 200 numbered copies. This is number _____ [hand numbered in ink] [Paper: watermark: "LINWEAVE TEXTRA"; the bottom edge is uncut].

Publication: Published by Herb Yellin in Northridge, California in the summer of 1977 for the celebration of the bar mitzva of Mark Kritzer. Printed in an edition of 230 unsigned copies: 200 copies [numbered 1–200] and 26 copies lettered A–Z, and 4 copies without number or letter for: "author," "printer," "Sheldon and Joy Kritzer."

Contains: "For Mark Kritzer."

[Note: These broadsides were given to the guests who attended the bar mitzva of Mark Kritzer and were signed upon request by the poet, who was in attendance].

A40   Grotesca   1977

[On tan in black:] NEW LONDON PRIDE PRESENTS / GROTESCA / BY CLAYTON ESHLEMAN / EXCLUSIVE MIMEOGRAPH MASTERPIECES 977

27.6 × 20.7cm; 29 leaves; pp. [1-4] 5-38 [39-43]: p. [1] blank leaf of tan card stock p. [2] blank on recto, printed on verso: advertisements; p. [3] title page as above, blank on verso; p. [4] copyright and acknowledgements, blank on verso; p. 5 dedication, blank on verso; p. [6] blank leaf; p. 7 contents, blank on verso; p. [8] blank leaf; pp. 9-38 text; [leaf 6 and leaf 8 are blank and unnumbered but seem to have been counted in the pagination. All other pages in the text [9-38] are numbered on the versos and counted in the pagination only if they are also printed with the continuation of a poem from the recto]. p. [39] blank; p. [40] colophon; p. [41] blank; p. [42-43] blank leaf of tan card stock.

[Glued in glossy white art board wrappers, reading top to bottom, in black:] NEW LONDON PRIDE EDITIONS GROTESCA CLAYTON ESHLEMAN [Front cover, printed in black gothic type letters:] GROTESCA / [photograph of a collage by Caryl Eshleman of the poet's torso with a pillow in the shape of two lips covering the lower portion, across which is printed in white:] CLAYTON ESHLEMAN [On back cover in black:] [publisher's device] / NEW LONDON PRIDE EDITIONS [Paper: Mimeographic; lithographic for title page. All edges trim with cover].

Publication: Published by Allen Fisher of New London Pride in London, England in 1977. Printed by Allen Fisher at Spanner Studio in London in 1977, in an edition of 255 wrappered copies, 25 of which were lettered A-Y and signed by the author, original price not known. Designed by Allen Fisher with the front cover designed by Caryl Eshleman. Colophon: This Exclusive Mimeograph Masterpiece published in / July 1977 in an edition of 280 copies by NEW / LONDON PRIDE 97 Kingsley Flats Old Kent Road SE1 5NL. / 25 copies have been signed by the Author and lettered / A-Y. / NEW LONDON PRIDE are distributed in North America by / Truck Distribution Service 1141 James Avenue / Saint Paul Minnesota 55105 USA. / This is part of New London Pride's second series.

Contains: "Study for a Portrait of Robert Duncan," "Study for a Portrait of Norman Glass," "Study of a Shadow," "Portrait of Diane Wakoski," "A Climacteric," "Ira," "The Dragon Rat Tail," "Dummies," "Still-Life, with Manson," "Still-Life, with Fraternity," "Study for a Portrait of Hans Bellmer," "The Red Snow," (ascribed to "Metro Vavin"), "1945," "The Wood of Isis."

[Note: Grotesca was part of a series of books known as "Exclusive Mimeograph Masterpieces" edited by Allen Fisher in London, England].

A41 New Poems and Translations by Clayton Eshleman 1977

[Cover title, on tan in black:] OASIS 19 / [thin rule] / NEW POEMS AND TRANSLATIONS BY CLAYTON ESHLEMAN / [thin rule] / [in green: portrait of the author from photograph by Caryl Eshleman] / [thin black rule]

20.6 × 14.5cm.; 20 leaves stapled twice; pp. [i–ii] 3–39 [40]: p. [i] title of publication and table of contents; p. [ii] copyright page; pp. 3–39 text; p. [40] advertisements.

[Stiff tan wrappers; cover glued near spine to inner first and last leaf; on spine in black:] OASIS [thin black rule] 19 [thin black rule] On cover in black:] OASIS 19 / [thin black rule] / NEW POEMS AND TRANSLATIONS BY CLAYTON ESHLEMAN / [thin black rule] / [in green: a line cut head of the author from a photography by Caryl Eshleman] / [thin black rule] [On back cover, in black:] New Poems and Translations / by Clayton Eshleman. / [thin black rule] / [thin black rule] / with José Rubia Barcia: / from PAYROLL OF BONES / by Cesar Vallejo. / With Norman Glass: / from THE THEATRE OF CRUELTY / BY Antonin Artaud. / Nine Recent Poems / by Clayton Eshleman. / [in green:] COVER: from a photo / by Caryl Eshleman. / 50p [slash] $1.50 / ISSN 0029-7410 / [thin black rule]. [Note: The three black rules on front cover continue across the spine to the back cover.] Paper: bond, wove; cover: buff card stock, all edges trim with cover.

Publication: Published by Oasis Books, 12 Stevenage Road, London SW6 6ES, UK., as Oasis 19, October 19, 1977. Printed by Oasis Books October 12, 1977 in an edition of 500 copies, priced at 50p in UK and $1.50 in U.S. Edited by Ian Robinson & Antony Lopez. Designed by Ian Robinson.

Contains: Note by Clayton Eshleman, from: *Payroll of Bones By César Vallejo:* "Height and Hair," untitled: "We probably already were of a compassionate age, when my father . . . ," untitled: "It was Sunday in the bright ears of my jackass . . . ," untitled: "Life, this life . . . ," untitled: "Today I would like to be happy willingly . . . ," untitled: "Finally, without that good continuous aroma . . . ," "Telluric and Magnetic," "The Thinking Old Asses," (translated from the Spanish by Clayton Eshleman and José Rubia Barcia); Note by Clayton Eshleman and Norman Glass; Antonin Artaud: "The Theatre of Cruelty," "2 Post Scriptums," "Open Letter to the Reverend Father Laval," (translated from the French by Clayton Eshleman and Norman Glass); Note by Clayton Eshleman, Nine Recent Poems by Clayton Eshleman: "The Green Apple Photo," "For Milena Vodickova," "Czech Sunset," "For Jan Benda," "Old Jewish Cemetery," "At the Tomb of Abigdor Kara," "Les

Fleches De Prague," "Charles Bridge, Cantata," untitled: "This Doktor Ur-banova...," "Charles Bridge, Wednesday Morning."

A42   Rancid Moonlight Hotel   1977

35.6 × 13.3cm.; single vertical leaf folding to form 3 panels; recto and verso; p. [i] title; p. [ii] blank; p. [iii–v] poem; p. [vi] colophon

[On lime, in black forming an "L" shape:] M / O / O / NLIGHT / HOTEL / HOTEL / HOTEL [on the right, within the "L": a black circle with a lime crescent moon; within this circle on the crescent, in black:] r [on the black moon in lime:] ancid [below on lower half inch of pp. [iii–v] but showing as part of a title:] CLAYTON ESHLEMAN 1977 [On back, reading from short side to short side:] Colophon. [Paper: lime, wove].

Publication: Published by The University of Connecticut Library in Storrs, Connecticut on October 27, 1977. Printed by University Publications, University of Connecticut on October 20, 1977, in an edition of 250 copies, issued gratis at the reading at the Wilber Cross Library. Colophon: Issued in an addition of 250 copies on the occasion of a reading by the poet at The / University of Connecticut Library, October 27, 1977. © 1977 by Clayton / Eshleman. Design by Colette M. Butterick.

Contains: "Rancid Moonlight Hotel."

A43   The Gospel of Celine Arnauld   1977

[On yellow, in green:] THE / GOSPEL / OF / CELENE ARNAULD / [in black:] by Clayton Eshleman / Printed at TUUMBA PRESS / as Tuumba 12 / November 1977

22.8 × 14.5cm.; 12 leaves stapled twice through to the spine: pp. [i–ii] blank; p. [iii] title page as above; p. [iv] copyright page; p. [v] half title; p. [vi] blank; pp. [7–19] text; p. [20] blank; pp. [21–22] note on the text.; p. [23] colophon; p. [24] blank.

[On stiff tan wrappers, in green:] [ornamental rule] / [in black:] TUUMBA 12 / THE / GOSPEL / OF / CELENE ARNAULD / by Clayton Eshleman / [in green:] [ornamental device]. [On back cover in black:] $2.00 / Subscription: $6 series / Individual copy: $2 / TUUMBA PRESS / 2639 Russell Street / Berkeley, California 94705 [on lower right corner in black:] [publisher's device] [Paper: yellow strathmore pastelle].

Publication: Published by Lyn Hejinian of the Tuumba Press as *Tuumba 12,* in Berkeley, California, November 1, 1977. Printed in Berkeley, California by Lyn Hejinian, October 1977, in an edition of 425 wrappered copies, priced at $2.00 a copy. Colophon: THE GOSPEL OF CELINE ARNAULD was / designed and printed at Tuumba Press by Lyn / Hejinian. Of an edition of 425 this is No. [hand numbered in green ink].

Contains: "The Gospel of Celine Arnauld," and "A Note on the Text," by Clayton Eshleman.

[Note: This is not a translation, but rather, a serial poem written in the spirit of Celine Arnauld, who is transformed and released from her own work, in Eshleman's vision. (see Appendix A)].

A44   The Name Encanyoned River   1977

[Inside brown rectangular rule, in black:] THE NAME ENCANYONED RIVER / CLAYTON ESHLEMAN / [red printer's device] / [below rectangular rule, centered in black:] The Woodbine Press / MCMLXXVII

16 × 12.2cm.; 22 leaves; 1^{10}, 2^{12}; pp. [i–viii] 1–29 [30–36]: pp. [i–ii] blank; p. [iii] title page as above; p. [iv] copyright page; p. [v] Note by author (with title in red); p. [vi] blank; p. [vii] half title; p. [viii] blank; pp. 1–29 text; p. [30] colophon; p. [31] number and signature of author; pp. [32–34] blank; p. [35] errata; p. [36] blank. Verticle brown line on left margin of text. Red endpapers.

Two bindings, no priority as follows:
a. [Brown cloth covered boards; on spine reading top to bottom in gilt:] THE NAME ENCANYONED RIVER C. ESHLEMAN [Paper: 70 lb. Ticonderoga laid Sandstone. All edges trimmed].

[Dust jacket on spine in black:] The Name Encanyoned River [Front cover, in magenta:] CLAYTON ESHLEMAN / [in black: drawing by Nora Jaffe] / [in magenta:] THE NAME / ENCANYONED RIVER [100 signed copies, (numbered 1–100), priced at $8.00 a copy. 26 lettered copies, signed, are hors commerce].

b. Same as above except: 15 × 11.4cm.; pp. [31–32] blank; p. [33] errata; pp. [34–36] blank. Glued in stiff paper wrappers. [On spine in black, reading top to bottom:] The Name Encanyoned River [dot] Clayton Eshleman [dot] The Woodbine Press [Front cover same as dust jacket in a. except lacks the author's name, title printed in red instead of magenta; [on back cover in black:] Cover Drawing: Nora Jaffe / Typography: Paul Woodbine [far left within a circle:] Printed / in / U.S.A. [to the right:] 4.00. [400 hand numbered copies (numbered 101–400), priced at $4.00 a copy].

Publication: Published and printed by Paul Woodbine of the Woodbine Press in Riverside, R.I. October 1, 1977. Colophon: This book was handset in 12 pt. Weiss Roman foundry type / and printed directly from the type. / The paper is 70 lb. Ticonderoga Laid Sandstone. / The typesetting and presswork were performed by Paul Woodbine. / The typography is by Paul Woodbine. / Of 400 paperbound copies and 100 smyth-sewn cloth- / bound copies this is number (hand numbered in black ink in paperbound copies).

Contains: "The Name Encanyoned River."

[Notes: The Woodbine editor, Bruce McPherson recalls that there were 4 copies in quater-bound red leather with marbled paper boards. The author and artist do not recall such a binding, and I have not seen a copy. A publicity flyer, 37.5 × 12.3, folded in center to form 2 leaves, printed on white in blue, brown and black, quotes part of a poem from the book and a quote from *Library Journal* about the author].

A45   On Mules Sent from Chavin   1977

ON MULES SENT FROM CHAVIN / A Journal and Poems (1965–66) / Clayton Eshleman / Galloping Dog Press / Swansea, U.K. 1977.

22.9 × 15.1cm.; 36 leaves; 1-2^8, 3-4^{10}; pp. [i-vi] 7-70, [71-72]: p. [i] blank; p. [ii] advertisements; p. [iii] title page as above; p. [iv] copyright page; p. [v] table of contents; p. [vi] blank; pp. 7-70 text; p. [71] colophon; p. [72] blank. White endpapers.

Two bindings, no priority as follows:
a. [Tan cloth over boards, spine reading top to bottom in black:] eshleman [device] on mules sent from chavin [Paper: laid; watermark:] Abby Mills Greenfield [All edges trimmed]. 26 copies lettered A-Z and signed by the author, priced at 4.50 UK and $10.00 US a copy.

b. Same as above except: 22.1 × 14.3cm.; glued in stiff black glossy wrappers; [on spine reading bottom to top, in white:] [publisher's device] on mules sent from chavin [dot] eshleman [Front cover: a portrait of the author seated on a mule by an anonymous photographer; on right, in white:] ON / MULES / SENT / FROM / CHAVIN / [on left in white:] CLAYTON / ESHLEMAN [700 copies, priced at £1.50 UK and $3.50 US a copy].

Publication: Published by Galloping Dog Press, Swansea, West Glamorgan, United Kingdom in winter 1977–78. Printed by the Arc Press, Todmorden, Lancs. U.K. Colophon: Edition of 726, of which 26 copies are hardbound, lettered A–Z, and / signed by the author. / Printed by the Arc Press, Todmorden, Lancs. U.K. / [signed and lettered in black ink, in hardbound issue]. Cover design for softcover edition by Caryl Eshleman.

Contains: Preface by Clayton Eshleman, "Descent from Huancayo," "On Mules Sent from Chavin," "A Vision of Tsuruginomiya," "The Formation of Mercy."

A46   For Cheryl Lynn Wallach   1978

33 × 25.2cm.; single leaf printed on one side.

[Black ornamental leaf rule] / [in red:] for Cheryl Lynn Wallach / [in black: a 31 line poem] / Clayton Eshleman / [black ornamental leaf rule] / This broadside was designed and printed / by Herb Yellin during the summer of 1978 / for the celebration of Merv and Marlene Wallach. / The edition consists of 200 numbered copies. / This is number / [hand numbered in red ink]. [Paper: creme textured wove].

Publication: Printed by Herb Yellin in Northridge, California in the summer of 1978 for the celebration of the bat mitzva of Cheryl Lynn Wallach, in an edition of 230 copies: 200 copies [numbered 1–200], 26 copies [lettered A–Z] and 4 special copies for: "author," "designer," "printer," and "Cheryl Lynn Wallach."

Contains: "For Cheryl Lynn Wallach."

[Note: These broadsides were given to the guests who attended the bat mitzva of Cheryl Lynn Wallach and were signed upon request by the poet, who was in attendance].

A47   **Cesar Vallejo: Battles in Spain:**   1978
Five Unpublished Poems

[Cover same as *Sparrow 47* except:] SPARROW 65 [title and date which read:] Battles in Spain / Five Unpublished Poems / by / César Vallejo / Translated by / Clayton Eshleman & José Rubia Barcia / BLACK SPARROW PRESS : FEBRUARY 1978 [Back cover lists 8 current publications, price reads:] 75¢.

23.7 × 6cm.; 8 leaves, stapled twice through to spine; pp. [ii–iii] [4–15]: p. [ii] copyright page with Note by translator Clayton Eshleman; p. [iii] continuation and conclusion of Note; pp. [4–15] text. [Paper: sub. 55 natural book].

Publication: Published by John Martin of the Black Sparrow Press in Santa Barbara, California as *Sparrow 65,* February 15, 1978. Printed by Graham Mackintosh in Santa Barbara in a first edition of 1200 copies, priced at $.75 a copy.

Contains: Note by Clayton Eshleman; César Vallejo: "Trilce," untitled: "We probably already were of a compassionate age...," untitled: "There she goes! Call her...," from: "Battles in Spain": [eight Roman numeraled poems (I–VIII), untitled:] "Under your foot I hear the smoke of the human wolf...," "The bony darkness presses on...," "Loss of Toledo...," "From here, from this point...," "The cemeteries were bombed...," "He used to write with his big finger in the air...," "The beggars fight for Spain...," "Beware, Spain, of your own Spain..." "Funereal Hymn for the Ruins of Durango." (translated from the Spanish by Clayton Eshleman and José Rubia Barcia).

[*Note: Sparrow 65* was also bound in cloth covered boards: *Sparrow 61–72*; (see B28).]

A48   **What She Means**   1978

[Within light blue ornamental outer frame and red single rule inner frame, in dark blue:] CLAYTON / ESHLEMAN / [in purple:] WHAT / SHE / MEANS / [in dark blue:] BLACK SPARROW PRESS / SANTA BARBARA / 1978

A48. What She Means

23.6 × 16cm.; 100 leaves; 1^2, $2-3^{16}$, 4^2, $5-8^{16}$; pp. [i–xii] 13–194 [195–200]: p. [i] advertisement; p. [ii] blank; p. [iii] title page as above; p. [iv] copyright and acknowledgments; p. [v] dedication; p. [vi] blank; p. [vii–viii] table of contents; p. [ix–x] preface by Clayton Eshleman; [xi] half title; p. [xii] blank; pp. 13–194 text; p. [195] colophon; p. [196] blank; p. [197] portrait of the author from a photograph taken by Al Vandenberg, below is a brief biography of the poet; p. [198–200] blank. Dark blue endpapers.

Three bindings, no priority as follows:
a. [Violet, pink, red and purple leaf patterned cloth spine over light blue paper covered boards; on spine, a light blue paper label reading from top to bottom, in red:] Clayton Eshleman [in purple:] WHAT SHE MEANS [Front cover, within a dark blue ornamental outer frame and red single rule inner frame, a light blue ornamental frame and a single red rule frame, in purple:] WHAT / SHE / MEANS / [within a light blue ornamental frame and a red single rule inner frame, in dark blue:] CLAYTON / ESHLEMAN [Paper: wove; all edges trim. False headband. Unprinted acetate dust jacket; lettered and signed; an extra leaf is bound in between pages [iv–v] with an original holograph poem by the author. Hand bound in boards by Earle

Gray. 43 copies, of which 26 copies [lettered from A–Z] were for sale, priced at $30.00 a copy. 17 copies (1 each marked "Author's Copy," "Publisher's Copy," "Printer's Copy," "Binder's Copy," "File Copy," and "Proofreader's Copy"; and 11 marked "Author's Presentation Copy") not for sale.

b. Dark blue cloth; lacks extra leaf. 201 signed copies of which 200 copies (numbered 1–200) were for sale, priced at $15.00 a copy, one "File Copy" not for sale.

c. Same as above except: 22.8 × 14.9cm.; glued in paper wrappers; [on spine, reading from top to bottom in red:] Clayton Eshleman [in purple:] WHAT SHE MEANS [in red:] BLACK SPARROW PRESS [Dark blue endpaper]. 1793 copies, priced at $4.50 a copy.

Publication: Published by John Martin of the Black Sparrow Press in Santa Barbara, California, August 18, 1978. Printed by Graham Mackintosh and Earle Gray in Santa Barbara and Edwards Brothers in Ann Arbor, Michigan July 1978. Colophon: [Publisher's device] / Printed July 1978 in Santa Barbara & Ann Arbor / for the Black Sparrow Press by Mackintosh and Young / & Edwards Brothers Inc. Design by Barbara Martin. / This edition is published in paper wrappers; there / are 200 hardcover copies numbered & signed by the / author; & 26 lettered copies have have [sic.] been handbound / in boards by Earle Gray each containing an original / holograph poem by the author.

Contains: Preface, by Clayton Eshleman, untitled: "To tense, then bound...," "Study for a Portrait of Norman Glass," "Study of a Shadow," "Eternity," "32 Variations on Shiki's 'furukabe no sumi ni ugokazu harami gumo'," "Portrait of Diane Wakoski," "Poem Copied from Text Written in a Dream," "The Sandstone Gate," "The Woman Who Saw Through Paradise," "The Male Will," "Variations Done for Gary Snyder," "Ixcuina," "Saturday Evening," "A Climacteric," "Ira," "The Dragon Rat Tail," "Daily," "Dummies," "Assassin," "Still-Life, with Manson," "Still-Life, with Fraternity," "Study for a Portrait of Hans Bellmer," "The Cogollo," "Chrysanthemum Lane," "Alleluia Choruses," "And Now?" "Scorpion Hopscotch," "The Spider Bride," "Barter," "1945," "The Green Apple Photo," "Old Jewish Cemetery," "At the Tomb of Abigdor Karo," untitled: "This Doktor Urbanova...," "Charles Bridge, Wednesday Morning," "August, Senex," untitled: "So

much feeling about September . . . ," untitled: "'For your father,' she said . . . ,"
untitled: "Here for the breath of . . . ," "Archai," "For Jan Benda," "Jalapa,"
"The Wood of Isis," "Core Meander," "For Milena Vodickova," "Hearing
Betty Carter," "After the Second Death," "Foo to the Infinite," "Still-Life, with
African Violets," "The Name Encanyoned River," "Satanas," "Joseph,"
"Variations Done for John Digby," "In the Polluted Cornice of the Day," "Om
Hollow," "Danse Macabre," "Les Combaralles," "The Rancid Moonlight
Hotel," "Dialogue with a Triptych," "Canso," "A Late Evening in July,"
"Study of a Man Staring at a Pillow in the Dark," "Life Then Seems Thicker,"
"This I Call Holding You," "Skeezix Agonistes," "All White Hands On
Deck."

[Note: The Black Sparrow Press promotional catalogue: "New Titles for
Spring Summer 1978, (20.2 × 10.1cm., in cream, blue, green, grey and black
announces the forthcoming publication of What She Means, and nine books by
other authors. It prints (on page 4 of 10 pages) the first fifteen lines and the
last six lines from "Eternity"].

A49   Eternity   1978

35.6 × 21.7cm.; single leaf printed on one side.

[A study of a man playing bocce ball from a collection of the work of
photographer Nicole Gelpi; superimposed on this, in red:] ETERNITY /
[first 19 lines of poem] [below halftone: 13 lines of poem] / clayton eshleman
[on lower left corner of halftone, reading top to bottom parallel to left side:]
nicole gelpi [Paper: Sundance cover stock].

Publication: Printed by George Fuller at the Jazz Press in Los Angeles,
California, in 1978 in an edition of approximately 200 copies; gratis, for a
poetry reading, part of a series of readings given on the occasion of a full
moon. This particular reading celebrated the publication of WHAT SHE
MEANS, [Santa Barbara, Black Sparrow Press, July, 1978]. It was the first
book appearance of the poem "Eternity," [published in *Primer* 3 April 1977];
(see: C250).

Contains: "Eternity"

A50   César Vallejo: The Complete Posthumous Poetry   1978

a. First edition, first printing:

[Thin black rule] / CÉSAR VALLEJO / The Complete Posthumous Poetry / [printer's device] / Translated by / Clayton Eshleman / & / José Rubia Barcia / [printer's device] / UNIVERSITY OF CALIFORNIA PRESS / Berkeley [dot] Los Angeles [dot] London / [thin black rule]

[A bilingual Edition; original Spanish on versos, English on rectos].

26 × 18.5cm.; 192 leaves; [one blank leaf] pp. [i–ix] x–xvii [xviii–xix] xx–xxxvii [xxxviii] [1] 2–339 [340–344]: [one blank leaf]; p. [i] half title; p. [ii] portrait of Vallejo from a photograph taken by Juan Larrea; p. [iii] title page as above; p. [iv] copyright page; p. [v] dedication; p. [vi] blank; p. [vii] acknowledgements; p. [viii–ix] x–xvii indice on versos, contents on rectos; p. [xviii] blank; p. [xix] xx–xxxvii introduction by Clayton Eshleman; p. [xxxviii] blank; p. [1] divisional title; pp. 2–339 text; pp. [340–344] blank. White endpapers.

[Red cloth covered boards; on spine reading top to bottom, in silver:] CÉSAR VALLEJO The Complete Posthumous Poetry [reading side to side:] California [Paper: 50# Boole Natural; all edges trim; false headbands].

Dust jacket: [On spine, on black ground, reading side to side, in white script:] César / Vallejo / [rule] / The / Complete / Posthumous / Poetry / [printer's device] / [printer's device] / California / [rule]. [Front cover, in white script:] César Vallejo / The Complete / Posthumous Poetry / [inside white rule frame, a portrait from a photograph of César Vallejo by Juan Larrea] / Translated by / Clayton Eshleman / & / José Rubia Barcia [Back cover: inside white rule square, in white:] César Vallejo: / The Complete Posthumous Poetry / [a fourteen line excerpt from a poem by César Vallejo] / "BLACK STONE ON A WHITE STONE," / BY CÉSAR VALLEJO / [outside square] UNIVERSITY OF CALIFORNIA PRESS [slash] BERKELEY, CALIFORNIA 94720 / ISBN 0-520-03648-4 [Inside front cover flap, on black ground, in white:] $20.00 / CÉSAR VALLEJO: THE COMPLETE / POSTHUMOUS POETRY / Translated by Clayton Eshleman / and José Rubia Barcia [biographical notes on César Vallejo] [Inside back cover flap: brief biographical note on Clayton Eshleman followed by brief biographical note on José Rubia Barcia] / JACKET DESIGNED BY BOB CATO.

Publication: Published by the University of California Press simultaneously in Berkeley, Los Angeles and London, March 6, 1979. Printed by Malloy Lithographing, Inc. in Ann Arbor, Michigan, December 18, 1978 in an edition of 2000 copies, priced at $20.00 a copy.

b. Second Printing, first paperback edition:
Same as above except: 21.5 × 15.4cm.; [Verso of title page:] First Paperback
Printing 1980 [glued in glossy paper wrappers; spine: on black ground,
reading top to bottom, in white:] César Vallejo [slash] The Complete
Posthumous Poetry [reading side to side:] Cal / 457 [Front cover same as dust
jacket, except upper right corner is triangulated in red, on red band:] [black
rule] / [in white] 1979 / National Book Award / [black rule] [Back cover, on
white ground, in black:] $6.95 / [inside red rule frame, in black:] "César
Vallejo is the greatest catholic poet since Dante / -by catholic I mean universal." -Thomas Merton / [Outside red rule frame: blurbs by translation judges
for National Book Awards: Richard Miller, Alastair Reid, Eliot Weinberger
quoted from the Times Literary Supplement and the San Francisco Review
of Books] / [brief identification of Clayton Eshleman and José Rubia Barcia]
/ University of California Press / Berkeley 94720 / ISBN 0-520-04099-6

Publication: Published simultaneously in Berkeley, Los Angeles, London in
1980. Printed in Ann Arbour, Michigan by Malloy Lithographing, Inc. in an
edition of 3000 copies, priced at $6.95 a copy.

c. Second paperback printing:
Same as b. except: back cover now reads; $10.95. Published in Berkeley, Los
Angeles, London in October, 1984. Printed by Malloy Lithographing, Inc.
in Ann Arbor, Michigan in an edition of 3700, priced at $10.95.

Contains: Introduction by Clayton Eshleman; César Vallejo: from *Payroll of
Bones* (1923–1936): "Payroll of Bones," "Violence of the Hours," "Good Sense,"
"The Gravest Moment in Life," untitled: "The windows shuddered...," "I
Am Going to Speak of Hope," untitled: "We probably already were of a compassionate age...," "Discovery of Life," untitled: "A woman with peaceful
breasts...," untitled: "Longing ceases, ass in the air...," untitled: "-No one
lives in the house anymore...," untitled: "There is a man mutilated...," "I
Am Laughing," untitled: "Behold that today I salute...," "Spine of the Scriptures," "Height and Hair," untitled: "Four consciousnesses are...," untitled:
"Between pain and pleasure...," untitled: "The moment the tennis player
masterfully serves...," "Hat, Overcoat, Gloves," "Angelic Salutation," "Epistle to the Transients," untitled: "And don't say another word to me...,"
"Glebe," "Tuberous Spring," "Black Stone on a White Stone," untitled:
"Sweetness through heartsown sweetness...," untitled: "Until the day I will
return, from this stone...," untitled: "It was Sunday in the clear ears of my
jackass...," untitled: "Life, this life...," untitled: "Today I like life much
less...," untitled: "Today I would like to be happy willingly...," untitled:
"From disturbance to disturbance...," untitled: "Considering coldly, impartially...," untitled: "And if after so many words...," untitled: "Finally,

without that good continuous aroma...," untitled: "Idle on a stone...," untitled: "The miners came out of the mine...," untitled: "But before all this happiness ends...," "Telluric and Magnetic," "Old Asses Thinking," from: *Sermon on Barbaraism* (1936–1938): "Paris, October 1936," "The Hungry Man's Wheel," untitled: "Heat, tired I go with my gold to where...," untitled: "One pillar holding up consolations...," untitled: "Upon reflecting on life...," "Poem to Be Read and Sung," untitled: "The accent dangles from my shoe...," untitled: "The tip of man...," untitled: "Oh bottle without wine...," untitled: "He is running, walking, fleeing...," untitled: "At last, a hill...," untitled: "My chest wants and does not want its color...," untitled: "This / happened between two eyelids...," untitled: "I stayed on to warm up the ink in which I drown...," untitled: "The peace, the whasp, the shoe heel, the slopes...," untitled: "Overcome, solomonic, decent...," untitled: "Well? Does the pallid metalloid heal you?...," untitled: "It is so hot, I feel cold...," untitled: "Confidence in the eyeglass, not in the eye...," untitled: "Speaking of kindling, do I silence fire...," untitled: "Mocked, acclimated to goodness...," untitled: "Alfonso: you keep looking at me, I see...," "Stumble Between Two Stars," "Farewell Remembering a Goodbye," untitled: "Chances are, I am another...," "The Book of Nature," untitled: "I have a terrible fear of being an animal...," "Wedding March," untitled: "The anger that breaks the man into children...," "Intensity and Height," "Guitar," untitled: "Hear your mass, your comet...," untitled: "What's got into me, that I am whipping myself...," "Anniversary," "Pantheon," untitled: "A man is looking at a woman...," "Two Yearning Children," "The Nine Monsters," untitled: "A man walks by with a stick of bread...," untitled: "For several days, I have felt an exuberant, political need...," untitled: "Today a splinter has gotten into her...," "Clapping and Guitar," "The Soul That Suffered from Being Its Body," "Couplings," untitled: "He has just passed by, the one who will come...," untitled: "Let the millionaire go naked, stark naked...," untitled: "That the evil man might come, with a throne...," untitled: "Contrary to the mountain birds...," untitled: "The fact is that the place where...," untitled: "Something identifies you with the one who leaves you...," untitled: "In short, I have nothing with which to express...," untitled: "A little more calm, comrade...," "The Miserable," "Sermon on Death"; from: *Spain, Take This Cup From Me* (1937–1938): "Hymn to the Volunteers for the Republic," "Battles: II–XV as follows: II, untitled: "Man from Estremadura...," III, untitled: "He used to write with his big finger in the air...," IV, untitled: "The beggars fight for Spain...," V, untitled: "There she goes! Call her! It's her side...," VI, "Cortege After the Capture of Bilbao," VII, untitled: "For several days the air, companions...," VIII, untitled: "Back here...," IX: "Short Prayer for a Loyalist Hero," X: "Winter During the Battle for Teruel," XI, untitled: "I looked at the corpse...," XII, "Mass," XIII, "Funereal Drumroll for the

Ruins of Durango," XIV, untitled: "Beware Spain, your own Spain...,"
XV: "Spain, Take this Cup from Me," Facsimilies of Vallejo's worksheets,
Appendix: "Battles in Spain," Notes, including a translation of the Vallejo
poem: "Trilce." (Translated from the Spanish by Clayton Eshleman and José
Rubia Barcia).

A51   Chrysanthemum Lane   1978

14 × 8.9cm.; single leaf printed on both sides.

[On orange, with short side up, in black:] [printer's ornamental device] /
Chrysanthemum Lane / [thick rule / thin rule] / [14 line poem] / [thick rule
/ thin rule] / Clayton Eshleman [on white verso, with long side up, on upper
left in black:] Chrysanthemum Lane © 1978 / by Clayton Eshleman / Printed
by Stuart McCarthy [bisecting the card, top to bottom, in black:] The
Bellevue Press, 60 Schubert St., Binghamton, N.Y. 13905 [on right, reading
length-wise:] [with printer's ornamental rule on left and right sides:] A /
BELLEVUE / PRESS / CARD [Paper: card stock, wove].

Publication: Published by Gil Williams of The Bellevue Press in Binghamton,
New York in 1978. Printed by Stuart McCarty II, at the Geryon Press, Tunnel, New York in 1978, in an issue of 500 copies, 450 of which were for sale,
priced at $.25 a card.

Contains: "Chrysanthemum Lane."

A52   César Vallejo: Paris, October 1936   1978

25.5 × 20.2cm.; single leaf printed on one side.

[On grey, in black:] [printer's ornament] PARIS, OCTOBER 1936 [printer's
ornament] / [16 line poem] / CÉSAR VALLEJO / (Translated by Clayton
Eshleman and José Rubia Barcia.) / 80 copies printed by Stuart McCarty for
the Bellevue Press. / © 1978 by Clayton Eshleman and José Rubia Barcia. /
[printer's ornament]. [Paper: Heavy weight wove, lower edge uncut].

Publication: Published by Gil Williams of The Bellevue Press in Binghamton,
New York in 1978. Printed by Stuart McCarty II at the Geryon Press, Tunnel, New York in 1978, in an issue of 80 copies, 50 of which were for sale,
priced at $5.00 a copy.

Contains: "Paris, October 1936" by César Vallejo (translated from the Spanish
by Clayton Eshleman and José Rubia Barcia).

A53   Dot   1979

33 × 15.1cm.; single leaf printed on one side.

[In black:] DOT [with red "flames" in center of 0] / [9 lines of poem] / [printer's ornament] / [12 lines of poem] / [printer's ornament] / [2 lines of poem] / CLAYTON ESHLEMAN / San Damiano de Stellanello, / 18 [slash] 19 February, 1979 / Printed by Stuart McCarty for The Bellevue Press in a signed / edition of 65 copies of which 15 are reserved for the author. / © 1979 by Clayton Eshleman [Paper: white laid]

Publication: Published by Gil Williams of The Bellevue Press in Binghamton, New York. Printed by Stuart McCarty II at the Geryon Press, Tunnel, New York in 1979 in an issue of 65 copies, 50 of which were for sale, priced at $5.00 a copy.

Contains: "Dot."

A54   A Note on Apprenticeship   1979

CLAYTON / ESHLEMAN / a note / on / apprenticeship / [reproduction of a building] / Two Hands Press / 1979 / Chicago

25.1 × 16.4cm.; 6 leaves: p. [i] title page as above; p. [ii] copyright page; p. [3–9] text; p. [10] blank; p. [11] colophon; p. [12] blank

[Stiff grey wrappers; front cover in black:] Clayton / Eshleman / APPRENTICESHIP SERIES NUMBER 1 [Hand sewn through to the spine in white thread. Paper: white heavyweight; watermark:] RIVES [Top and fore-edge trim, lower edge uncut].

Publication: Published by Two Hands Press at the Two Hands Bookstore in Chicago, Illinois in 1979. Printed in the spring of 1979 by George Ball, Pat Merrill and Douglas Macdonald under the guidance and tutelage of Robi Liscomb, in an edition of 300 copies, 50 copies signed by the author priced at $10.00 a copy; unsigned copies $3.00 a copy. Colophon: [in red:] "...Three hundred copies of this book were hand / printed on Rives heavyweight paper using a / Gordon platen press built around 1880. The / type face is Caslon Old Style. Fifty copies / were signed by the author. This is number / [number and poet's signature written in green ink on signed copies].

Contains: Essay: "A Note on Apprenticeship."

A55   Nights We Put the Rock Together   1980

Nights / We Put / The Rock / Together / Clayton Eshleman / Cadmus Editions 1980 Santa Barbara

21.4 × 14.3cm.; 28 leaves; 1-2⁸, 3-4⁶; pp. [i–viii] [9–46] [47–56]: pp. [i–ii] blank; p. [iii] tipped-in color frontispiece illustration of a woman's head carved in mammoth ivory from Malta, Central Siberia, now in The Hermitage, Leningrad; p. [iv] blank; p. [v] title page as above; p. [vi] copyright page states "First published in 1980. . ."; p. [vii] dedication; p. [viii] blank; pp. [9–46] text; pp. [47–48] blank; p. [49] blank except for the word "Notes" in upper right corner; p. [50] Notes by the author; p. [51] advertisement; p. [52] blank; p. [53] colophon; pp. [54–56] blank. Grey endpapers, with uncut fore-edge.

Three bindings, no priority as follows:
a. [Hand made French marbled paper, red, pink, gold and blue with gilt speckles, folded on top, bottom and fore-edge French style, over unprinted grey wrappers; on spine, cream paper label reading top to bottom in black:] Nights We Put The Rock Together [printer's device] Clayton Eshleman [Front cover, on cream paper label, in black:] Nights / We Put / The Rock / Together / [printer's device] / Clayton Eshleman [Paper: Mohawk Superfine; all edges trim. Hand set in 16 point Van Dyck itallic type and printed letterpress. Hand sewn and bound by Linda Benet of Graham Mackintosh, Inc. p. [49] unprinted but with an original holograph poem and drawing by the author. 33 copies; 26 (hand lettered from A–Z) were for sale, priced at $35.00 a copy, and 7 copies marked "Presentation Copy" were reserved for the author. An additional 7 copies without the holograph poem [1 each marked "Author's Copy," "Printer's Copy," "Binder's Copy," "Publisher's Copy," "File Copy," and 2 "for deposit, library of Congress,") not for sale.

b. Same as a. except: blue, red and gold with gilt speckles. 100 signed copies of which 100 copies (number stamped 1–100) were for sale, priced at $20.00 a copy.

c. Same as above except: 21.6 × 14cm.; glued in white wrappers; [cover fore-edge folds 4.4cm., front and back, over heavy grey-brown paper inner cover, glued at spine; spine reading top to bottom in black:] Clayton Eshleman [in red] Nights We Put The Rock Together [in black] Cadmus [publisher's device] [Front cover, super-imposed over grey-green photograph of unknown subject, in black:] Clayton Eshleman / Nights / We Put / The Rock / Together [On back cover, lower left, in black:] ISBN 0-932274-05-8 [Grey endpapers; all edges trim]. Unprinted glassine dust jacket. 374 copies, priced at $10.00 a copy.

Publication: Published December 1979 By Jeffrey Miller of Cadmus Editions, in Santa Barbara, California. Printed by Alastair Johnston at the Poltroon Press of Berkeley, California. Covers printed by Graham Mackintosh, labels for the signed limited portion of the edition, also printed by Graham Mackintosh. Colophon: [Publisher's device / This first edition of / Nights We Put The Rock Together, / printed letterpress by Poltroon Press of Berkeley, consists / of 374 trade copies and 126 numbered and lettered copies signed by the poet; / each of the lettered copies has a page of holograph in the poet's hand. / Numbered and lettered copies have been sewn and bound by / Linda Benet. Designed and set by Alastair Johnston / in Monotype Van Dijck. / This is copy number [on numbered copies, number stamped in red; on lettered copies, letter inked in by the author in black].

Contains: "Dot," "Adam's Shield," "Airon," "Initial," "Cenote," "Poem Written on a Toothpick," "The Butterpillar," "Meditation on Marwan's Faces," "Hermes Butts In," "The Woman," "Inversion of the Bull's-eye," "Study for 'Silence Raving'," "Master Hanus to His Blindness," Notes by the author.

[Notes: This set of twelve poems was written in February of 1979, while the Eshlemans stayed in Marwan's (Marwan Kassab Bachi) summer cottage in San Damiano de Stellanello, a tiny towm on the Italian Rivera. A promotional pamphlet: *New Titles / Fall 1979,* announces the publication of *Nights We Put The Rock Together.* 20.3 × 12.5cm., cream paper folded to form 2 leaves, prints 13 lines of the poem "Airon" from *Nights We Put The Rock Together:* lists the trade edition at $10.00 a copy. A catalogue of publications dated Spring 1981, includes *Nights We Put The Rock Together.* 23.4 × 9cm., cream paper, 6 leaves stapled through to spine, printed in rust and black, prints 19 lines from the same poem; the cover contains a rust collage of photographs of Cadmus authors with Clayton Eshleman at the upper right corner; lists the trade edition at $9.00 a copy].

A56   The American Sublime   1980

14 × 8.9cm.; single leaf printed on both sides.

[With short side up, in black:] THE AMERICAN SUBLIME / [red rule] / [14 line poem] / [in red:] -Clayton Eshleman [on verso, with long side up, on upper left in black:] TRUMPS / A Periodical of Postcards / Published by Station Hill Press / Produced at Open Studio, Rhinebeck, NY [Bisecting the card, reading from bottom to top, in black:] Copyright © 1980 by Clayton Eshleman [Paper: 10 point cover stock].

Publication: Published by George & Susan Quasha of Station Hill Press, Station Hill, Barrytown, New York in 1980. Printed at Open Studio in Rhinebeck, New York, in 1980 in an issue of approximately 1,000 copies, issued and priced with a set of postcards. (See B31).

Contains: "The American Sublime."

[Note: This title was later changed to "Un Poco Loco" when printed in *The Name Encanyoned River: Selected Poems 1960–1985.* (See A71)].

A57   The Lich Gate   1980

[Within three overlapping pointed arches of thin green, black and grey rule, in green:] THE / LICH GATE / [in black:] Clayton Eshleman / [in green:] station hill [dot] barrytown

22.1 x 14.5cm.; 8 leaves: p. [i] title page as above; p. [ii] copyright page; pp. [3–15] text; p. [16] colophon. Brown free endpapers.

[Stiff green wrappers printed in white:] THE / LICH GATE / [a photograph of a gate, by Richard Gummere] / [in white:] Clayton Eshleman [Back cover in white:] $2.50 [on far right:] POETRY / ISBN 0-93079420-6 / Clayton Eshleman is the author of numerous books in- / cluding INDIANA, ALTARS, THE GULL WALL, and / WHAT SHE MEANS. Formerly the editor of CATER- / PILLAR, he has translated extensively from the Spanish / and French and is co-recipient of the 1979 National Book / Award for translation. / STATION HILL [Stapled twice through to the spine; paper: Warren's Old Style with a 10 point cover 70 lbs.; all edges trim]

Publication: Published by George & Susan Quasha of Station Hill Press, Barrytown, New York, 1980. Printed under the direction of Patricia Nedds at Open Studio in Rinebeck, New York, 1980. Colophon: designed by susan & george quasha / with a photograph by richard gummere / the text was set in times roman / with windsor light & westminster light / & printed on a heidelberg kord / under the direction of patricia nedds / at open studio in rinebeck new york / in an edition of 1000 / of which 43 have been signed by the author [1000 copies, 43 copies hand numbered (1–43) and signed by the author, priced at $2.50 a copy].

Contains: "In Memory of Wallace Berman," "To Myself," "The Lich Gate," "A Muscular Man with Gossamer Ways," "Century Village," "Angry Angel," "For Matthew Rothenberg," "Cato's Altars."

A58   Our Lady of the Three-Pronged Devil   1981

[Light blue ground, in calligraphy (by Alice Koeth), in brown:] OUR / LADY / OF THE / THREE- / PRONGED / DEVIL / [in blue:] THE RED OZIER PRESS / NEW YORK CITY

23.8 × 15.4cm.; 24 leaves; 1^2, 2^4, $3-4^6$, 5^4, 6^2; (a folding painting on linen paper by Paul Wong is bound in center of 4^6): pp. [i–iv] blank; p. [v] author's name; p. [vi] blank; p. [vii] title page as above; p. [viii] copyright page; p. [ix] preface by the poet; p. [x] blank; p. [xi] conclusion of preface; p. [xii] blank; pp. [13–39] text (signed by the author on page 39); p. [40] blank; p. [41] author's holograph poem; p. [42] blank; p. [43] colophon; pp. [44–48] blank. Beige endpapers.

Two bindings, no priority as follows:
a. [Half tan morocco over navy cloth covered boards; on spine, reading from top to bottom, in blind:] Clayton Eshleman OUR LADY OF THE THREE-PRONGED DEVIL [Hand sewn in white thread. Paper: blue Saunders mouldmande; watermark:] T H SAUNDERS. [Uncut, printed in black with titles in blue]. 16 signed copies with linen paper foldout painting by Paul Wong and poet's holograph poem, priced at $150.00 a copy.

b. [Same as above except: 23.2 × 15cm.; p. [41] colophon; pp. [42–48] blank; (signatures 1 and 6 are glued in, not sewn as in a.); hand sewn in tan thread and glued in beige moldmade paper, the same as that used for the endpapers in a., including the watermark; a dust jacket of the same beige moldmade paper reads on spine from top to bottom, in black:] Clayton Eshleman OUR LADY OF THE THREE-PRONGED DEVIL [Front cover printed in calligraphy, in brown:] OUR / LADY / OF THE / THREE- / PRONGED / DEVIL [Uncut]. 199 signed copies lacking linen paper foldout painting by Paul Wong and poet's holograph poem, priced at $50.00 a copy.

Publication: Published and printed Ken Botnick and Steve Miller of the Red Ozier Press, in New York, in 1981. Colophon: This is number [number press printed] of two-hundred & fifteen / copies printed in hand-reset Poliphilus

Monotype / on Saunders mouldmade paper. Wrappers and / endsheets were pulled by the Tidepool Mill / working at Dieu Donne. Alice Koeth did the / title page calligraphy. The first sixteen copies were / hardbound by Wilton Hale Wiggins, and include / a linen paper piece by Paul Wong and a poem / in holograph by the author. Tireless Ozierites / bound the remaining copies at their new shop / in the old Chelsea area of Manhattan Island.

Contains: Preface by Clayton Eshleman, "Silence Raving," "Winding Windows," "Blues," "Clarksville, October, 1979," "Our Lady of the Three-Pronged Devil," "The Countermotion," "The Tears of Perseus," "Cimmeria."

[Note: The endpapers show a watermark of an early sexual sign such as can be found, painted or carved during the Upper Paleolithic period, in the caves of southern of France].

A59   Foetus Graffiti   1981

[On light grey, in black:] Clayton / Eshleman / Foetus / Graffiti / Pharos / 1981

27.9 × 21.6cm.; 4 leaves: p. [i] title page as above; p. [ii] copyright page; pp. [3-6] text; p. [7] colophon; p. [8] blank.

Stiff red unprinted wrappers, stapled twice through to the spine. [Stiff grey linen-finish dust jacket, on front cover, in blind:] Foetus / Graffiti [Paper: grey laid; watermark: Kilmorg; all edges trim].

Publication: Published by Matthew Jennett of Pharos Books in New Haven Connecticut on November 5, 1981. Printed by Branford Printing Company of Branford, Connecticut on November 4, 1981. Designed by Matthew Jennett. Colophon: The first edition of 250 copies of this poem / was printed in conjunction with a reading by / Clayton Eshleman at Calhoun College, Yale University / New Haven, on 5 November, 1981. Of 250 copies, / A to Z are for the poet, / A to Ω are for Pharos / and 1-200 are for sale / No [number press printed] / [publisher's device]. 200 copies, numbered (numbered 1-200) and signed by the author, priced at $20.00 a copy. 26 copies (lettered A-Z) author's copies, not for sale. 24 copies (lettered Alpha to Omega) priced at $35.00 a copy.

Contains: "Foetus Graffiti."

[Note: The original design called for dark drab jacket around blood red wrapper, in an 8vo. format. As Matthew Jennett had only two days to get the book printed for Clayton Eshleman's reading at Yale, the printer was given this description and completed the book via linotype on available paper in the 4to. format, without further supervision].

A60   Hades in Manganese   1981

[In blue:] Clayton Eshleman / [red rule] / [in black:] HADES / [red rule] / [in black:] IN / [red rule] / [in black:] MANGANESE / Santa Barbara / BLACK SPARROW PRESS / 1981

23.5 × 16cm.; 60 leaves; 1^2, 2^8, 3^2, $4-6^{16}$; pp. [i–viii] 9–14 [15–16] 17–114 [115–120]: p. [i] advertisement; p. [ii] three red rules carried over from title page; p. [iii] title page as above; p. [iv] copyright and acknowledgements; p. [v] dedication; p. [vi] blank; p. [vii–viii] table of contents; pp. 9–14 preface by Clayton Eshleman; pp. [15] half title; p. [16] blank; pp. 17–114 text; p. [115] colophon; p. [116] blank; p. [117] portrait of the author from a photograph taken by Al Vandenberg, below this is a brief biography of the poet; pp. [118–120] blank. Black endpapers.

Three bindings, no priority as follows:
a. [Purple cloth spine over grey paper covered boards; light grey paper label reading top to bottom in blue:] Clayton Eshleman [in black:] HADES IN MANGANESE [Front cover, on lavender, purple and silver patterned paper:] [red rule] / [on grey ground, in blue:] Clayton Eshleman / [in black:] HADES IN / MANGANESE / [red rule]. [Back cover: on grey ground, two red rules]. Paper: wove; all edges trim. False headband. Unprinted acetate dust jacket. Numbered and signed; an extra leaf is bound in between pages [iv–v] with an original holograph poem and drawing by the author; hand bound in boards by Earle Gray. 47 copies, of which 35 copies, (numbered 1–35) were for sale, priced at $40.00 a copy; 12 copies (one each marked "Author's Copy," "Publisher's Copy," "Printer's Copy," "Binder's Copy," and a "File Copy"; and 7 copies marked "Author's Presentation Copy") not for sale.

b. Same as a. except: lavender cloth spine; lacks extra leaf. 251 signed copies (numbered 1–250) were for sale, priced at $20.00 a copy. One "File Copy" not for sale.

c. Same as above except: 22.8 × 14.8cm.; glued in grey paper wrappers: [spine, reading top to bottom, in blue:] Clayton Eshleman [red rule which is continued from front and back cover] [in black:] HADES IN MAN-

A60. Hades in Manganese

GANESE [red rule which is continued from front and back cover] [in black:] Black Sparrow Press [Black, free endpapers]. 2081 copies, priced at $5.00 a copy.

Publication: Published by John Martin of the Black Sparrow Press in Santa Barbara, California, February 13, 1981. Printed by Graham Mackintosh and Noel Young in Santa Barbara, California and Edwards Brothers in Ann Arbor, Michigan, January 1981. Colophon: [Publisher's device] / Printed January 1981 in Santa Barbara & Ann Arbor for the / Black Sparrow Press by Mackintosh and Young & Edwards / Brothers, Inc. Design by Barbara Martin. This edition is / published in paper wrappers; there are 250 hardcover copies / numbered & signed by the author; & 35 numbered copies have / been handbound in boards by Earle Gray each with a colored / holograph poem [slash] drawing by Clayton Eshleman.

Contains: Preface by the author; "The Lich Gate," "A Muscular Man with Gossamer Ways," "Cato's Altars," "Frida Kahlo's Release," "Sound Grottos," "Placements." "Turnstiles," "Dot." "Hades in Manganese," "Initial," "The Tourist," "The Butterpillar," "Meditation on Marwan's Faces," "Hermes Butts In," "Etruscan Vase," "The Woman," "The Light," "Silence Raving," "Master Hanus to His Blindness," "From St. -Cirq to Caravaggio," "Self-Portrait," "Nameitsense," "Equal Time," "Winding Windows," "The American Sublime," "Blues," "Tartaros," "Permanent Shadow," "Mother's

Comb," "Voluntary Prayer," "The Aurignacians Have the Floor," "Cuauhx-icalli," "Clarksville, October, 1979," "Narration Hanging from the Cusp of the Eighties," "For Aimé Césaire," "Our Lady of the Three-Pronged Devil," "Ramapithecus," "The Decanting," "The Countermotion," "The Tears of Perseus," "Cimmeria," "The Shaft."

[Note: The Black Sparrow Press promotional catalogue: "New Titles for Fall Winter 1980, (21.6 × 14.5cm., in light blue, green, lavender and black) announces the forthcoming publication of *Hades in Manganese,* and five books by other authors. It prints (on page 4 of 6 pages) the last 20 lines of the poem "From St.-Cirq to Caravaggio"].

A61   Aime Cesaire: Some African Poems in English   1981

[In Gothic Outline:] Munger [in black:] Africana / Library Notes / ISSUE 62, November 1981 / Three Dollars / AIME [sic] CÉSAIRE: / Some African Poems / in English / Translated by / Clayton Eshleman / and / Annette Smith / US ISSN 0047-8350 / © California Institute of Technology

[A bilingual edition; original French on versos, English on rectos].

21.7 × 14cm.; 10 leaves; stapled twice through to spine; pp. [i–ii] 3–19; p. [20]: p. [i] title page as above; p. [ii] blank; pp. 3–4 a note on the translators; p. 5 Introduction by the authors; pp. 6–15 text; pp. 16–19 text and advertisements; p. [20] Announcement].

[On orange-tan stiff paper wrappers, in Gothic outline:] Munger [in black:] Africana / Library Notes / [inside rectangle of black rule:] AIME CESAIRE: / [a photograph of Clayton Eshleman / a photograph of Annette Smith [on right of photographs:] Some African / Poems in / English / Translated by / Clayton Eshleman / and / Annette Smith / [outside black rule rectangle:] November 1981 / 62 [Paper: glossy white wove; all edges trim].

Publication: Published by Ned Munger of the Munger Africana Library, California Institute of Technology in Pasadena, November 1981, as Issue 62 of Munger Africana Library Series. Printed by Castle Press, Pasadena, 1981. 400 copies, priced at $3.00 a copy.

Contains: A Note On The Translators by Ned Munger; Introduction by Clayton Eshleman and Annette Smith; Aimé Césaire; "Hail to Guinea," "The Time of Freedom," "Africa," "A Salute to the Third World." (Translated from the French by Clayton Eshleman and Annette Smith).

A62   Aimé Césaire: The Woman and the Knife   1981

73.3 × 35.5cm.; single leaf printed on both sides.

[On grey, in brown:] THE WOMAN AND THE KNIFE / [in black: a 23 line poem] / [in brown] Aimé Césaire 1946 [on right of poem: a photograph (grey on grey) of an untitled collage by John Digby]. [On verso, in black:] THE WOMAN AND THE KNIFE / by Aimé Césaire, as translated and copyright held by / by (sic.) Clayton Eshleman & Annette Smith with / collage by John Digby. Struck in 1981 at / Red Ozier Press, New York City. [Paper: Laid, Barcham Green handmade (purple)].

Publication: Published and printed by Ken Botnick and Steve Miller of the Red Ozier Press in New York City, New York in 1981, in an edition of 75 copies, priced at $25.00 a copy. Colophon: THE WOMAN AND THE KNIFE / by Aimé Césaire, as translated and copyright held by / by (sic.) Clayton Eshleman & Annette Smith with / collage by John Digby. Struck in 1981 at / Red Ozier Press, New York City.

Contains: Aimé Césaire: "The Woman and the Knife." (Translated from the French by Clayton Eshleman and Annette Smith).

[Note: Although originally designed to fold into 3 panels, after completion it seemed a poor choice to fold the collage. So according to the printer-publishers, they chose to lay it flat, thus explaining the colophon printed on the back. A postcard announced this publication].

A63   Antonin Artaud: Four Texts   1982

a. First edition, first printing:
Antonin Artaud: / Four Texts / Translated by / Clayton Eshleman and / Norman Glass / Panjandrum Books, Inc. [dot] Los Angeles [dot] 1982 [a drawing by Nancy Spero is on the right half of the page].

22.4 × 14.7cm.; 52 leaves; 1–2^{16}, 3^4, 4^{16}; pp. [i–iv] 1–99 [100]: p. [i] half title; p. [ii] blank; p. [iii] title page as above; p. [iv] copyright and acknowledgements; pp. 1–3 Introduction; p. [4] blank; p. [5] divisional title; p. [6] blank; pp. 7–99 text; p. [100] blank. Drawings by Nancy Spero between texts on divisional pages [5], [19], [59], [81]. White endpapers.

Two bindings, no priority as follows:
[Brown leatherette covered boards; on spine reading top to bottom, in gilt:]

A63. Antonin Artaud: Four Texts

Artaud Four Texts [Front cover: a glossy tan label, reads, in brown:] AN-
TONIN / ARTAUD: 4 TEXTS / Translated by / Clayton Eshleman / and
Norman Glass [drawing by Nancy Spero of a brown head with long red
"tongue" is on the right half of the label]. [Back cover: a glossy white label
prints, in black, a blurb for the book and biographical note on authors].
Paper: white wove; all edges trim. Unprinted acetate dust jacket. 150 copies,
priced at $14.95 a copy, 25 of which were numbered (1–25) and signed by
Clayton Eshleman on the title page, priced at $19.95 a copy.

b. Same as above except: 21.6 × 13.6cm.; glued in glossy paper wrappers;
[printed on the spine reading top to bottom, in black:] Artaud Four Texts
[reading side to side: publisher's device]. [Front cover reproduces the same

graphics and picture as on the hardcover label; back cover reproduces that of the hardcover edition with the addition:] Panjandrum, Inc. $6.95 ISBN 0-915572-56-7 [1,342 copies, priced at $6.95 a copy].

Publication: Published by Dennis Koran of the Panjandrum Press in West Los Angeles, California on November 3, 1982. Printed by Publisher's Press, Salt Lake City, Utah, September, 1982.

c. Second printing: Same as above except: [Title page now reads:] Antonin Artaud: / Four Texts / Translated by / Clayton Eshleman and / Norman Glass / Cover and Artwork by Nancy Spero / Panjandrum Books, Inc. [dot] Los Angeles [dot] 1986 [Copyright page prints "Second Printing"]. [Back cover, below blurb, now reads:] From 1969 to 1972, the artist Nancy Spero integrated a wide / range of texts from Artaud into works on paper ranging in size / from 20 inches to 25 feet in length. Spero continues to use Araud / texts intermittently in her work. / Cover and artwork by Nancy Spero. / Panjandrum, Inc. $6.95 ISBN 0-915572-56-7 / Distributed by the Talman Company (NYC) [1045 copies, priced at $6.95 a copy].

Publication: Published by Dennis Koran of Panjandrum Press, March, 1986. Printed by Bookcrafters, Chelsea, Michigan, January, 1986.

Contains: Introduction by Clayton Eshleman; Antonin Artaud: "To Georges Le Breton," (Draft Of A Letter); from: *Artaud The Mômo:* "The Return of Artaud the Mômo," "Center-Mother and Boss-Puss," "Insult to the Unconditioned," "The Execration of the Father-Mother," "Madness and Black Magic"; from: *To Have Done With The Judgment Of God:* "Kré Everything puc te . . .," "Tutuguri: The Rite of the Black Sun," "The Search for Fecality," "To Raise the Question of. . .," "Conclusion"; from: *The Theater Of Cruelty:* and "An Open Letter to the Reverend Father Laval": "The Theater of Cruelty," "Post-Scriptum [I]," "Post-Scriptum [II]," "Open Letter to the Reverend Father Laval." (Translated from the French by Clayton Eshleman and Norman Glass with notes by Clayton Eshleman and Norman Glass).

A64   Visions of the Fathers of Lascaux   1983

[Within a black rectangle of thick rule, in black:] VISIONS / of the / FATHERS / of / LASCAUX / followed by THE STAKED WOMAN / [halftone of a black and white drawing] / Kashkaniraqmi, by Atlementheneira (Lascaux, at the / base of the South Wall of the Apse). / Clayton Eshleman / PANJANDRUM PRESS, INC. [printer's device] LOS ANGELES [printer's device] 1983.

21.5 × 14cm.; 18 leaves; pp. [1–viii] 1–27 [28]: p. [i] half title; p. [ii] blank; p. [iii] title page as above; p. [iv] copyright page, states "First published in 1983 by . . . ," p. [v] foreword by Clayton Eshleman; p. [vi] blank; p. [vii] half-title; p. [viii] blank; pp. 1–27 text; p. [28] blank.

[Stiff glossy grey wrappers; on spine, in black:] VISIONS of the FATHERS of LASCAUX [small red square] Eshleman [Front cover, inside square of thin black rule / thick red rule / thin black rule, on white ground, in black:] VISIONS of the ["of" above "the"] / [thin black rule] / FATHERS / [thin black rule] / of LASCAUX / [below the square, in black:] Clayton Eshleman [Glued in paper wrappers; all edges trim; paper: white wove].

Publication: Published by Dennis Koran of the Panjandram Press, in Los Angeles, California August 26, 1983. Printed by Gemini Graphics in Venice, California, (typeset at New Comp Graphics Center, a part of Beyond Baroque Foundation, Venice, California) July, 1983. Designed by Robin Palanker. 500 wrappered copies; 490 copies priced at $4.50 a copy, and 10 hand numbered 1–10 and signed by the poet on the title page, priced at $15.00 a copy.

Contains: Foreword by Clayton Eshleman, "Visions of the Fathers of Lascaux," "The Staked Woman," Notes by Clayton Eshleman.

A65   Fracture   1983

[Short blue rule] / [in red:] CLAYTON ESHLEMAN / [blue rule] / [in black:] FRACTURE / [blue rule] / [in black:] BLACK SPARROW PRESS / SANTA BARBARA 1983

23.6 × 16cm.; 76 leaves; 1², 2–3¹⁶, 4², 5⁸, 6–7¹⁶; pp. [i–viii] 9–145 [146–152]: p. [i] advertisement; p. [ii] one blue rule carried over from title page; p. [iii] title page as above; p. [iv] copyright and acknowledgements; p. [v] dedication; p. [vi] blank; pp. [vii–viii] table of contents; pp. 9–18 Introduction; p. [19] half title; p. [20] blank; p. [21] divisional title; p. [22] blank; pp. 23–45 text and notes; p. [146] blank; p. [147] colophon; p. [148] blank; p. [149] portrait of the author from a photograph taken by Nina Subin, below this is a brief biography of the poet; pp. [150–152] blank. Black endpapers.

Four bindings, no priority as follows;
a. Red, green, gold and blue striped and dotted tan silk cloth spine over gold and white paper covered boards. [On white paper spine label: gold rectangle, blue verticle rule, reading top to bottom, in black:] CLAYTON ESHLEMAN [in red:] FRACTURE [Front cover, on gold ground in red:] CLAYTON

A65. Fracture

ESHLEMAN / [in black:] FRACTURE / [broken blue rule with gold "fracture" running from blue rule to lower edge of cover; on white ground, to the
left but intersected by, gold "fracture," a red and white photograph reproducing a scene on a wall in the "shaft" of the Lascaux cave (reproduced from
Leroi-Gourhan: *Treasures Of Prehistoric Art,* Abrams, c.1967) p. 414] / [blue
rule]. Back cover: gold and white intersected by a blue rule. Paper: wove; all
edges trim. False headband. Unprinted acetate dust jacket. Numbered and
signed; an extra leaf is bound in between pages [iv-v] with an original
holograph poem and drawing by the author; hand bound in boards by Earle
Gray. 60 copies, of which 49 copies (numbered from 1–49) were for sale, priced at $40.00 a copy. 11 copies (one each marked "Publisher's Copy," "Binder's
Copy," "File Copy," and eight marked "Author's Presentation Copy") not for
sale. [Note: only 49 copies were for sale.]

b. Same as a. except: spine bound in red cloth lacks extra leaf. 203 signed
copies, of which 200 copies (numbered 1–200) were for sale, priced at $25.00,
2 copies (marked "Author's Copy," and "Printer's Copy,") and one "File Copy"
not for sale.

c. Same as above except: blue cloth spine; 219 copies of which 218 copies were
for sale, priced at $14.00 a copy, one "File Copy" not for sale. [Note: 81 less
than the announced limitation.]

d. Same as above except: 22.8 × 14.9cm.; glued in gold and white paper wrappers. [On spine:] [gold ground] [blue rule continued from front and back

cover] [on white ground, reading from top to bottom, in black:] CLAYTON ESHLEMAN [in red] FRACTURE [in black:] BLACK SPARROW PRESS [Gold, front and back, free endpaper]. 1905 copies, priced at $7.50 a copy.

Publication: Published by John Martin of the Black Sparrow Press in Santa Barbara, California, May 12, 1983. Printed by Graham Mackintosh in Santa Barbara, California, and Edwards Brothers in Ann Arbor, Michigan, April 1983. Colophon: [Publisher's device] / Printed April 1983 in Santa Barbara & Ann Arbor / for the Black Sparrow Press by Graham Mackintosh / & Edwards Brothers Inc. Design by Barbara Martin. / This edition is published in paper wrappers; / there are 300 hardcover trade copies; 200 copies / have been numbered & signed by the author; & / 50 numbered copies have been handbound in boards / by Earle Gray each with a colored holograph poem [slash] / drawing by Clayton Eshleman.

Contains: Introduction by the author, "The Kill," "Saturos," "The Soul of Intercourse," "Diamonion Taxi Driver," "A Small Cave," "Inseminator Vortex," "The Terrace at Hotel Du Centenaire," "The Death of Bill Evans," "The Loaded Sleeve of Hades," "Fracture," "Rhapsody," "Magdalenian," Notes, "Tiresias Drinking," "Notes on a Visit to Le Tuc D'Audoubert," "Coproativism," "Cuitlacoche," "The Seeds of Narrative," Introduction to "Visions of the Fathers of Lascaux," "The Fathers of Lascaux," "The Staked Woman," "A Kind of Moisture on the Wall," "Through Breuil's Eyes," Notes, "Apparition of the Duck," "Toddler Under Glass," "The Severing," "Stud Farms of Cooked Shadows," Notes. "Certification," "Millennium," "The Spiritual Hunt," "Tantrik X-Ray," "Nothing Follows," "Inn of the Empty Egg," "The Language Orphan," "The Arcade's Discourse on Method," "Maithuna," "Elegy," "Tangerine Dawn," "The Aurignacian Summation," "The Tears of Christ Pulled Inside Out," "Foetus Graffiti," "Forty-Seven Years," "Terrestrial," "The Bowery of Dreams," "The Color Rake of Time," "Manticore Vortex," Notes.

[Note: The Black Sparrow Press promotional catalogue: "New Titles Spring Summer 1983" (21.3 × 14cm., in creme, red, blue, black grey and yellow) written by Tom Clark, announces the publication of *Fracture* and five books by other authors. It prints (on page 3 of 6 pages) a quote from Doren Robbins' essay on *What She Means,* published in *Third Rail* 5, 1982; along with other new Black Sparrow Press titles].

A66   Aimé Césaire: The Collected Poetry   1983

a. First edition, first printing:
The / Collected / Poetry / [printer's ornament] AIMÉ / CÉSAIRE /

Translated, with an Introduction and Notes by / CLAYTON ESHLEMAN / and / ANNETTE SMITH / UNIVERSITY OF CALIFORNIA PRESS [dot] BERKELEY [Slash] LOS ANGELES [slash] LONDON

[A bilingual edition; original French on versos, English on rectos].

26 × 18.4cm.; 216 leaves; 1–12¹⁶, 13⁸, 14¹⁶; [i–vii] viii–xv [xvi] [1] 2–408 [409–416]: p. [i] half title; p. [ii] frontispiece portrait of Aimé Césaire taken by an unidentified photographer; p. [iii] title page as above; p. [iv] copyright page [states first edition code: 1 2 3 4 5 6 7 8 9]; p. [v] Acknowledgments; pp. [vi]–[vii] viii–xv Table of Contents, (French titles on versos, English translations on rectos); p. [xvi] blank; pp. [1] 2–28 Introduction; pp. [29] 30–31 Notes; p. [32] divisional title; p. [33] photograph of an untitled water-color by Wifredo Lam; pp. 34–399 text; p. [400] blank; pp. [401] 402–408 Notes; p. [409] Credits; pp. [410–416] blank. Green endpapers.

Note: The text is illustrated with reproductions of paintings by Wifredo Lam on the following pages: [33]; [87]; [161]; [227]; [261]; [359].

Two bindings, no priority as follows:
a. [Light brown cloth over boards; spine reading side to side, in green-gilt:] CÉSAIRE / [reading top to bottom:] AIMÉ / [reading side to side:] THE / COLLECTED / POETRY / [Reading top to bottom:] CÉSAIRE / [reading side to side:] CALIFORNIA [On front cover, in blind: a wild plantin: "Balisier" found in the forrests of Martinique] / A C [Paper: offset smooth; all edges trim].

Dust jacket: [Spine, reading side to side:] CÉSAIRE / [reading top to bottom:] Aimé / [reading side to side:] THE / COLLECTED / POETRY / [reading top to bottom:] CÉSAIRE / [reading side to side:] CALIFORNIA [Front cover:] C [centered inside "C," in small capital letters:] AIMÉ [continuing in the same large capital letters as the "C":] ÉSAIRE / THE COLLECTED POETRY / [color reproduction of "Le vent chaud" (1948) by Wilfredo Lam] / TRANSLATED, WITH INTRODUCTION AND NOTES BY / Clayton Eshleman and Annette Smith [Back cover, to the right of reproduction of a painting by Wilfredo Lam:] ". . . that unmistakably major tone that / distinguishes great from lesser poets." / -ANDRÉ BRÉTON / [below painting:] [14 line poem] / -from Aimé Césaire's *Notebook of a Return to the Native Land* / UNIVERSITY OF CALIFORNIA PRESS, BERKELEY 94720 ISBN 0-520-04347-2 [On inside front cover flap:] $25.00 / AIMÉ / CÉSAIRE / Translated, with Introduction and Notes by / CLAYTON ESHLEMAN and / ANNETTE SMITH / In Aimé Césaire the great surrealist tradition draws to / a close, achieves its definitive meaning and is /

destroyed: surrealism, a European movement in / poetry, is snatched from the Europeans by a black man / who turns it against them and assigns a rigorously / defined function to it ... a Césaire poem explodes and / whirls about itself like a rocket, suns burst forth whirling / and exploding like new suns -it perpetually surpasses / itself. / —Jean-Paul Sartre / [biographical note on Aimé Césaire] [Back jacket cover flap:] [Biographical note continued] / [brief biographical note on Clayton Eshleman followed by brief biographical note on Annette Smith] / Jacket art: *Le vent chaud* (1948), by [dot] Wifredo Lam. / Reproduced courtesy of Pierre Matisse / Gallery, New York City. / Jacket design: Bob Cato [2000 copies, priced at $25.00 a copy].

b. Same as above except: 25.4 x 17.4cm.; [the covers reproduce that of the dust jacket described above except spine deletes:] CALIFORNIA [and adds:] CAL / 667 [back cover ISBN number is changed to read:] ISBN 0-520-05320-6 [3690 copies, priced at $11.95 a copy].

Publication: Published by the University of California Press simultaneously in Berkeley, Los Angeles, London October 14, 1983. Printed by Malloy Lithographing, Inc. in Ann Arbor, Michigan, June 8, 1983.

c. Second printing: published in cloth, October 3, 1983, priced at $30.00 a copy. (Edition code: 23456789). Reprinted August, 1984.

Contains: Introduction, by Annette Smith and Clayton Eshleman; Aimé Césaire: *Notebook of a Return to the Native Land,* from: *Miraculous Weapons:* "Gunnery Warning," "The Thoroughbreds," "Have No Mercy," "Serpent Sun," "Sentence," "Poem for the Dawn," "Visitation," "Mythology," "Perdition," "Survival," "Beyond," "The Miraculous Weapons," "Prophecy," "Night Tom-Tom," "Nostalgic," "The Automatic Crystal," "Conquest of a Dawn," "Debris," "Investiture," "The Virgin Forest," ::Another Season," "Day and Night," "Annunciation," "Tom-Tom I," "Tom-Tom II," "High Noon," "Batouque," "The Oubliettes of the Sea and the Deluge," "The Woman and the Knife," "Postface: Myth," from: *Solar Throat Slashed:* "Magic," "The Oricous Have the Floor," "The Law Is Naked," "Velocity," "Tangible Disaster," "Among Other Massacres," "The Griffin," "Redemption," "Mississippi," "Blues of the Rain," "The Scapegoat," "Son of Thunder," "Ex-Voto for a Shipwreck," "Millibars of the Storm," "Your Hair," "The Tornado," "Totem," "Samba," "Interlude," "The Wheel," "Calm," "New Year," "All the Way from Akkad, From Elam, From Sumer," "To Africa," "Demons," "Night Swamp," "Noon Knives," "At the Locks of the Void," "Trite," "Ode to Guinea," "Horse," "Sun and Water," "March of Perturbations," "Barbarity," "Antipode," "Crusades of Silence," "Rains," "Nonvicious Circle," "Different Horizon," "Death at Dawn," "Lynch," "Howling," "The Light's Judgment," from: *Lost Body:* "Word," "Who Then, Who Then," "Elegy," "Presence," "Forloining," "Lost Body," "Your Portrait," "Summons," "Births," "Lay of Errantry," from: *Ferraments:* "Ferraments," "Nursery Rhyme," "Seism," "Spirals," "Hail to Guinea," "Kingdom," "Monsoon-Mansion," "For Ina," "Birds," "Nocturne of a Nostalgia," "To Know Ourselves," "Merciless Great Blood," "Beat it Night Dog," "But There is This Hurt," "Viscera of the Poem," "It is Myself, Terror, It is Myself," "Fangs," "Liminal Vampire," "My Profound Day's Clear Passage," "Corpse of a Frenzy," "Patience of Signs," "Phantoms," "Mobile Beam of Peculiar Dreams," "Bitter Season," "Statue of Lafcadio Hearn," "Beautiful Spurted Blood," "It is the Courage of Men Which is Dislocated," "From My Stud Farms," "Marine Intimacy," "Bucolic," "Ferment," "I Perseus Centuplicating Myself," "Precept," "Feeling the Sand with the Bamboo of My Dreams," "On the Islands of All Winds," "The Time of Freedom," "Gift of Tree Saps," "Tomb of Paul Eluard," "Memorial for Louis Delgrès," "In Memory of a Black Union Leader," "On the State of the Union," "Africa," "Out of Alien Days," "A Salute to the Third World," "Indivisible," "A Blank to Fill on the Travel Pass of the Pollen," "A Little Song to Cross a Big Stream," "In Truth," from: *Noria:* "Letter from Bahia-of-All-the-Saints," "Ethiopia," "The Verb 'Marronner'," "Wifredo Lam," "Voodoo Ceremonial for St. -John Perse," "When Miguel Angel Asturias Disappeared," "In Order to Speak," "I Guided the Long Transhumance of the Herd," "Lagoonal Calendar," "Banal," "Ibis-Anubis," "This Appeal Prohibited Blood," "To Be Deducted," "Annonciades," "Zaffer Sun," "Internuncio," "A Freedom in Passage." (Translated from the French with notes by Clayton Eshleman and Annette Smith).

[Note: Three quarters of the introduction was written by Annette Smith, with Eshleman contributing material for the biographical sketch of Césaire and descriptions of certain books].

A67   Antonin Artaud: (from:) Suppots Et Supplications. 1984

32.4 × 20.3cm.; single leaf printed on one side.

[Superimposed over orange drawing, in black:] Antonin Artaud / [17 line untitled poem] / [thin black rule] / [10 line untitled poem] / [thick black rule] / [thin black rule] / These poems are from the 1978 Gallimard edition of / SUPPOTS ET SUPPLICATIONS / Translated by A. James Arnold & Clayton Eshleman. / Printed at the Red Ozier Press in April of 1984. / The drawing is by Nancy Spero. [Paper: many different types were used, including: Frankfort creme and white, India Office, and Gampi Torinoko according to the printers, although I have seen only the Frankfort white].

Publication: Printed and published by Ken Botnick and Steve Miller of the Red Ozier Press in the fall of 1984 in New York City in an edition of 75 copies, gratis to friends of the Red Ozier Press.

Contains: Two untitled poems by Antonin Artaud: "It is thought from below...," and "The tremendous incurable hiccup sounds so many bodily epidermises...," (translated from the French by A. James Arnold and Clayton Eshleman).

A68   Michel Deguy: Given Giving: Selected Poems   1984

GIVEN GIVING / Selected Poems of Michel Deguy / [thin black rule] / Translated by Clayton Eshleman / With an Introduction by Kenneth Koch / UNIVERSITY OF CALIFORNIA PRESS / Berkeley Los Angeles London

[A bilingual edition; original French on versos, English on rectos]

21.6 × 14.3cm.; 108 leaves; $1-4^{16}$, 5^4, 6^8, $7-8^{16}$; pp. [i-v] vi-xi [xii] xiii-xxiii [xxiv] [1] 2-189 [190-192]: [i] half title; p. [ii] blank; p. [iii] title page as above; p. [iv] copyright page [states first edition code: 1 2 3 4 5 6 7 8 9] p. [v] Acknowledgements; pp. vi-xi Table of Contents, French titles on verso English titles on rectos; p. [xii] blank; pp. xiii-xxiii Introduction by Kenneth Koch; p. [xxiv] blank; p. [1] divisional title; pp. 2-189 text; pp. [190-192] blank. [White endpapers].

[Grey cloth over boards; spine reading top to bottom, in black:] GIVEN GIVING CALIFORNIA / Selected Poems of Michel Deguy [Paper: offset wove, all edges trim. False headbands].

Dust jacket: [On spine reading top to bottom, in grey:] GIVEN GIVING [in black:] CALIFORNIA / Selected Poems of Michel Deguy [On front cover, in grey:] GIVEN / [in black:] Selected Poems of Michel Deguy / [in grey:] GIVING / [thick black rule] / [within a thin black rule frame, a color reproduction of a painting by Jorgé Perez-Roman entitled "Far Away & Long Ago"] / [thick black rule] / [in grey:] Translated by Clayton Eshleman / With an Introduction by Kenneth Koch [On back cover, within a thin black rule frame, a portrait of Michel Deguy by an unknown photographer] / [in black] Michel Deguy / [in grey:] UNIVERSITY OF CALIFORNIA PRESS / Berkeley 94720 / [in black:] ISBN 0-520-04728-1 [On inside front cover flap, in black:] $19.95 / [in grey:] GIVEN / [in black:] Selected Poems of Michel Deguy / [in grey:] GIVING / [thick black rule] / [in black:] Translated by

A68. Michel Deguy: Given Giving

Clayton Eshleman / With an Introduction by Kenneth Koch / [an essay on
the poetry of Michel Deguy, continued on back flap] / [brief biographical
identification of Michel Deguy / [brief biographical identification of Clayton
Eshleman] / [brief biographical identification of Kenneth Koch] / Jacket
painting: Jorgé Perez-Roman / Jacket Design: Linda M. Robertson

Publication: Published by the University of California Press simultaneously in
Berkeley, Los Angeles, London on December 1, 1984. Printed by Braun-
Brumfield in Ann Arbor, Michigan on October 9, 1984, in an edition of 2,000
copies, priced at $19.95 a copy.

Contains: Introduction by Kenneth Koch, Michel Deguy: from: *Fragments Of
The Cadastre:* "The Gulf," "The Cemetery," "The Laundry," "She," from: *Poems*

On The Peninsula: "Threshold," untitled: "O great apposition of the world . . .,"
"The Traitor," "The Apple Tree," "Sun King," "The Mirror," "The Eyes,"
"Effacement," from: *Millraces:* untitled: "Each time that he fixes . . .," untitled:
"Lots of wind . . .," untitled: "This rather peaceful ball . . .," untitled: "A cup
on a telegram . . .," from *By Ear:* untitled: "the poet in profile . . .," untitled:
"A man tired of the genitive . . .," untitled: "When the wind sacks the
village . . .," untitled: "It's between us . . .," untitled: "The days are not
numbered . . .," untitled: "Alluvium of cries . . .," untitled: "Grey pier from
where the snow bait falls . . .," untitled: "You will be astonished . . .," untitled:
"Blue moraine . . .," untitled: "The sky like a child . . .," untitled: "Phases
events demivolts . . .," untitled: "Entanglement of centers in the hall . . .," untitled: "This lady and her beautiful window . . .," untitled: "The air takes her
by the waist . . .," untitled: "Hold this moment . . .," untitled: "No sooner does
she . . .," untitled: "She helps him on with his gown . . .," untitled: "There is
a need . . .," untitled: "To know why you are so dear to me . . .," "(The Ages),"
from: *Acts:* "Vista," untitled: "I call muse . . .," untitled: "At night on the far
shore . . .," from: *Figurations:* "Beautiful Emphases," "Etc.," "Summer Winter
the Night the Night," "Prose," "Quadratures," "Histories of Relapses," from:
At The Tomb of Du Bellay: "Who What," "World Movement," "Blow of Silence,"
untitled: "The wall is massive . . .," "Passim," from: *Couplings* followed by
Made In The USA: "Table of Contents," untitled: "When the world confines . . .," "Voice of the Paleontologist," "Make-up," "To Forget the Image,"
from: *Given Giving:* "The Ballad," "Advanced Study," "Sleeping Under the
Star 'N'," "Iaculatio Tardiva," "Poetic Air 166."

[Note: The "working title" for *Given Giving* was *Quadratures: Selected Poetry of
Michel Deguy].*

A69   Antonin Artaud: Chanson   1985

[In black:] Antonin Artaud [in red:] Chanson / [in black:] translated by A.
James Arnold & Clayton Eshleman / drawings by Nancy Spero / [in red:]
Red Ozier Press [in black:] 1985

21.1 × 13.6cm.; 10 leaves; [i–vi] [7–20]: p. [i] title page as above; p. [ii] blank;
pp. [iii–iv] A Note on Chanson by A. James Arnold & Clayton Eshleman;
p. [v] divisional title, in red; p. [vi] blank; p. [7–17] text; p. [18] colophon;
pp. [19–20] blank. Note: there is a drawing by Nancy Spero in light brown
on pp. [10–11]. Black free endpapers; [a frontispiece drawing by Nancy Spero
in green and gilt is letterpressed on the verso of front endpaper].

[Tan colored wrappers (of INGRES-FABRIANO folded over at fore-edge);
in red:] Chanson by Antonin Artaud / [a drawing by Nancy Spero, printed

in brown]. Sewn in white thread through to spine. Paper: Astrolite (text); and Cansen (endpapers).

Publication: Printed and published by Ken Botnick and Steve Miller of the Red Ozier Press in winter of 1985 in New York City in an edition of 145 copies, priced at $25.00 a copy. Colophon: Futura types are printed on Astrolite text. / Translation Copyright 1985 by A. James Arnold / & Clayton Eshleman. / 145 copies made during the winter months / by Botnick & Miller in New York City.

Contains: Antonin Artaud: "Chanson," from Interjections, the third and final section of *Suppots Et Supplications;* (translated from the French by A. James Arnold and Clayton Eshleman).

[Note: A postcard, 14 × 8.9cm., advertising *Chanson* and a publication of Robert Bly was printed in brown and grey, on the same tan Ingres-Fabriano paper as the book's cover].

A70   Reagan at Bitberg   1985

33.5 × 23.9cm.; single leaf printed on one side.

[In red:] REAGAN AT BITBERG / [thick black rule] / [thin red rule] / [in black:] [30 line poem] / Clayton Eshleman [poet's signature] May 5, 1985 / [thin red rule] / Designed & printed by J. Mudfoot for Table-Talk Press, Santa Barbara, California, in an edition of 100 signed copies. / Copyright 1985 by Clayton Eshleman. / This is number [hand numbered in red ink] [Paper: Rives heavyweight; lower edge uncut].

Publication: Published by Michael J. Sherick of Table-Talk Press in Santa Barbara, California September 15, 1985. Printed and designed by J. Mudfoot in Santa Barbara, August 31, 1985 in an edition of 120 copies, 100 of which were hand numbered in red. Signed by the poet, priced at $15.00 a copy. 20 copies were "overs."

Contains: "Reagan at Bitberg."

[Notes: 3 special copies, 38.1 × 26cm.; on 25% Cattail 75% cotton handmade by Coco Gordon, NYC (which lacks "this is number"), were printed for "Author's Copy," "Publisher's Copy," "Printer's Copy." There were 4 proof copies on newsprint. Also see B45, *Table-Talk Press: Five Broadsides].*

A71   The Name Encanyoned River: 1986
         Selected Poems 1960–1985

[In grey:] CLAYTON [three rose colored rules] / [in grey:] ESHLEMAN / [three rose colored rules] [in black:] THE / NAME / ENCANYONED / RIVER / [in grey:] SELECTED POEMS 1960–1985 / [rose colored rule] / [in grey:] Introduction by Eliot Weinberger / BLack (sic.) Sparrow Press [printer's device] Santa Barbara [printer's device] 1986

23.6 × 16cm.; 126 leaves; 1^2, 2–3^{16}, 4^4, 5^8, 6–10^{16}; pp. [i–viii] 9–245 p. [246–252]: p. [i] advertisement; p. [ii] rose colored rules continued from title page; p. [iii] title page as above; p. [iv] copyright and acknowledgements; p. [v] quotation from Hart Crane; p. [vi–viii] table of contents; pp. 9–15 Introduction by Eliot Weinberger; p. 16 blank; p. 17 divisional title; p. 18 blank; pp. 19–245 text; p. [246] blank; p. [247] colophon; p. [248] portrait of the author from a photograph taken by Nina Subin; p. [249] brief biography of the poet; pp. [250–252] blank. Rose endpapers.

Four bindings no priority as follows:
a. [Purple, grey-green, rose, grey and black patterned silk cloth over cream paper covered boards printed in rose, grey, black and blue. [Cream paper spine label, reading top to bottom, in grey:] Clayton Eshleman [blue vertical rule] [on grey rectangle, in cream:] THE NAME ENCANYONED RIVER [Front cover, on cream ground, a rose rectangle, to the left of lower ¼ of rectangle, in grey:] CLAYTON / [on grey rectangular ground, in black:] ESHLEMAN / [in cream:] THE / NAME / ENCANYONED / RIVER / [below the grey rectangle on cream ground, in grey:] SELECTED POEMS 1960–1985 / [short black rule] / [three short blue rules] / [black rule]. [Back cover:] [rose square] / [three blue rules] / [grey rectangle intersected by a black rule]. Paper: wove; all edges trim. False headband. Unprinted acetate dust jacket. Lettered and signed, an extra leaf is bound in between pages [iv–v] with an original holograph poem and drawing by the author; hand bound in boards by Earle Gray. 41 copies, of which 26 copies (lettered A–Z) were for sale, priced at $40.00, 15 copies, (one each marked "Publisher's Copy," "Printer's Copy," "Binder's Copy," "Editor's Copy," and "File Copy," and 10 marked "Author's Presentation Copy") not for sale.

b. Same as a. except: spine bound in rose cloth; lack extra leaf. 151 signed copies of which 150 copies (numbered 1–150) were for sale, priced at $30.00 a copy, one "File Copy" not for sale.

c. Same as above except: grey corduroy cloth spine. 301 copies of which 300 copies were for sale, priced at $20.00 a copy, one "File Copy" not for sale.

A71d. The Name Encanyoned River: Selected Poems 1960–1985

d. Same as above except: 22.8 × 14.8cm.; glued in cream paper wrappers. [On spine, reading top to bottom, in grey:] Clayton Eshleman [blue vertical rule] [on grey rectangle, in cream:] THE NAME ENCANYONED RIVER [outside grey rectangle, on cream ground, intersecting three blue rules which are continued from front and back cover, in grey:] Black Sparrow Press [black rule which is continued from front and back cover]. Rose, front and back, free endpapers. 2556 copies, priced at $12.50 a copy.

Publication: Published by John Martin of the Black Sparrow Press in Santa Barbara, California, January 27, 1986. Printed by Graham Macintosh and Edwards Brothers in Santa Barbara and Ann Arbor January 1986. Colophon: Printed January 1986 in Santa Barbara & Ann / Arbor for the Black Sparrow Press by Graham / Mackintosh & Edwards Brothers Inc. Design / by Barbara Martin. This edition is published / in paper wrappers; there are 300 hard-cover / trade copies; 150 copies have been numbered / & signed by the author;

& 26 lettered copies / have been handbound in boards by Earle Gray / each with a holograph poem [slash] drawing / by Clayton Eshleman. / [publisher's device]

Contains: Introduction by Eliot Weinberger, "Evocation I," "The Crocus Bud," "The Book of Yorunomado," "Niemonjima II," "Walk VI," "Matthew's Birth," "The 1802 Blake Butts Letter Variation," "The Yellow Garment," "Diagonal," "Soutine," "The Overcoats of Eden," "Ode to Reich," "The Baptism of Desire," "The Bridge at the Mayan Pass," "The Physical Traveler," "Study for a Self-Portrait at 12 Years Old," "Creation," "Sugar," from "Adhesive Love," "Portrait of Vincent Van Gogh," "Frida Kahlo's Release," "Portrait of Francis Bacon," "A Visit from Paul Blackburn," "The Sandstone Gate," "Ira," "The Dragon Rat Tail," "Still-Life with Fraternity," "The Cogolo," "Scorpion Hopscotch," "The American Sublime," "Still-Life, with African Violets," "The Name Encanyoned River," "The Lich Gate," "Placements I," "Hades in Manganese," "Silence Raving," "Master Hanus to His Blindness," "Equal Time," "Un Poco Loco," "The Aurignacians Have the Floor," "Permanent Shadow," "Our Lady of the Three-Pronged Devil," "The Death of Bill Evans," "The Loaded Sleeve of Hades," "Fracture," "Magdalenian," "Tiresias Drinking," "Notes on a Visit to Le Tuc D'Audoubert," "Coproatavism," "Visions of the Fathers of Lascaux," "A Kind of Moisture on the Wall," "Tomb of Donald Duck," "The Language Orphan," "Maithuna," "The Color Rake of Time," "Auto —," "Junk Mail," "An Emergence," "The Natal Daemon," "Lemons," "Nora Jafee," "Tuxedoed Groom on Canvas Bride," "The Excavation of Artaud," "Man and Bottle," "Scarlet Experiment," "Placements II," "The Crone," "Ariadne's Reunion," "I Blended Rose," "Deeds Done and Suffered by Light," "The Man with a Beard of Roses," "Dedication," Notes.

[Note: The Black Sparrow Press promotional catalogue: "New Titles of Fall Winter 1985, (21.3 × 14cm., in red, blue, black and white) written by Tom Clark, announces the forthcoming publication of *The Name Encanyoned River: Selected Poems 1960–1984,* and five books by other authors. It prints (on page 1 of 6 pages) the first three and the last four lines from "The Color Rake of Time"].

A72   Bernard Bador: Sea Urchin Harakiri   1986

BERNARD BADOR / Translation and Introduction / by Clayton Eshleman / Postface by Robert Kelly / SEA URCHIN / HARAKIRI / Panjandrum Books, Inc. / Los Angeles 1986

[A bilingual edition; original French on versos, English on rectos]

23.6 × 15.9cm.; 68 leaves; 1-2^{16}, 3^4, 5-6^{16}; pp. [i-x] 11-15 [16-17] 18-128 [129] 130 [131-136]: p. [i] half title; p. [ii] blank; p. [iii] title page as above; p. [iv] copyright page; p. [v] dedication; pp. [vi-ix] table of contents, French titles on versos, English titles on rectos; p. [x] blank; p. 11-15 Introduction; p. [16] blank; p. [17] divisional title; pp. 18-128 text; p. [129] blank; p. 130 colophon; pp. [131-136] blank. [Rose endpapers].

First issue, five bindings, no priority as follows:

a. [Maroon cloth over boards; on spine reading top to bottom, in gilt:] SEA URCHIN HARAKIRI BERNARD BADOR Panjandrum, Inc. [On front cover, on left top to bottom:] [a label of glossy card stock with a color reproduction of a collage created by Bernard Bador]. [Acid free paper; all edges trim]. 117 copies, priced at $15.95 a copy, of which 25 copies were numbered [1-25] and signed by Bernard Bador, Clayton Eshleman, and Robert Kelly, priced at $30.00 a copy.

b. Same as above except: on right side of cover, hand stenciled in white is a number from 1 to 25; issued loose, with the book, is a collage in color by Bernard Bador, each an original]. [25 copies, priced at $50.00 a copy].

c. Same as above except: 22.9 × 15.2cm.; glued in glossy white paper wrappers. [On spine, on lavender ground, reading from top to bottom, in white:] SEA URCHIN HARAKIRI BERNARD BADOR Panjandrum, Inc. [On front left cover, frop top to bottom, a color reproduction of a collage done by Bernard Bador; on right of picture, in lavender:] BERNARD BADOR / [in black:] Translation and Introduction / by Clayton Eshleman / Postface by Robert Kelly / SEA URCHIN / HARAKIRI [On back cover:] SEA UR-CHIN HARAKIRI / BERNARD BADOR / Translated by Clayton Eshleman / [a 30 line excerpt from Clayton Eshleman's Introduction] / Clayton Eshleman / (from his Introduction) / Panjandrum, Inc. $6.95 ISBN 0-915572-76-1 / (Cloth edition: $15.95 ISBN 0-915572-77-X) / Distributed by The Talman Company [1,024 copies, priced at $6.95 a copy].

d. Same as a. except: on front cover, on right of collage, stamped in gilt: SEA URCHIN HARAKIRI / BERNARD BADOR [Approximately 25 copies, priced at $15.95 a copy].

e. Same as a. except: bound in white silk cloth. [On front cover, on right of collage, stamped in gilt:] SEA URCHIN HARAKIRI / BERNARD BADOR [Unprinted acetate dust jacket]. 26 copies (lettered A-Z) signed by Bernard Bador, Clayton Eshleman, and Robert Kelly are Hors Commerce.

Publication: Published by Dennis Koran of Panjandrum Press in Los Angeles, California February 5, 1986. Printed by Bookcrafters in Chelsea, Michigan in December, 1985 and January, 1986. Designed by Laurie Haycock. Binding of cloth copies done by Earle Gray. Photograph of collage for front cover taken by Daniel Catherine. Colophon: The first edition of this book consists of one thousand copies. / Twenty-five clothbound copies are signed and numbered by / the author, translator, and author of the postface. Each of / these twenty-five has an original tipped-in collage by the / author. An additional twenty-five clothbound copies are signed / and numbered by author, translator, and author of the post- / face. Twenty-six clothbound copies, in an edition *Hors Com- / merce,* are lettered A–Z. / The text was typeset in Goudy Oldstyle, and printed on acid-free paper.

Contains: Introduction by Clayton Eshleman; "Outlaw," "Death of a World," "Essence," "The Sea," "The Transparent Man," "The Green Queen," "Checked," "S-leen," "Suicide," "Evil Port," "Struggles," "Cancer Dreams," "Sabotage," "Journey to the End of Night," "The Judgment," "The Hand," "Momentary Truths," "Archeology," "Surf," "Destiny," "The Fisherman," "Odyssey," "Apocalypse," "Birth," "Progress," "Anabasis," "Cadaver Cracks in the Lotus Pond," "Biography," "Destiny," "Andean Hopes," "Daily Routine," "The Four Seasons of the Night," "The Discovery," "Call of the Caverns," "Impotence," "Secret Entablature," "Royal Hunt," "Diptych," "To the Cannibals," (translated from the French by Clayton Eshleman; the following four poems were written by Bernard Bador in English alone:) "The Coal Orchid," "The Absent from the Night," "A Cape of Wild Flies," "Curdled Skulls," "End of the Walk." Postface: "Prose pour un Lendemain," by Robert Kelly.

A73   Aimé Césaire: Lost Body (Corps Perdu)   1986

LOST BODY / (CORPS PERDU) / BY AIMÉ CÉSAIRE / ILLUSTRATIONS BY / PABLO PICASSO / Introduction and Translation by / CLAYTON ESHLEMAN and ANNETTE SMITH / GEORGE BRAZILLER, INC. NEW YORK

[A bilingual edition; original French printed at the end of the English text].

26.1 x 19cm.; 80 leaves; 1–10⁸; pp. [i–iii] iv–xxvii [xxviii] [1–6] 7–131 [132]: p. [i] half title; p. [ii] from an etching: "corps perdu" inscribed in a vegetable-shaped heart; p. [iii] title page as above; p. iv copyright page [states: "First Printing"]; p. [v] Contents; p. [vi] blank; pp. vii–xxvii Introduction and Notes by Annette Smith and Clayton Eshleman and Publisher's note; p. [xxviii] blank; p. [1] divisional title; p. [2] blank; p. [3] from an etching entitled: "Poeta Laureatus"; p. [4] blank; p. [5] poem title with aquatint; p. [6] blank; pp. 7–131 text; p. [132] colophon. [White endpapers].

Note: The title page illustrations of individual poems are from aquatints and are on the following: pp. [5], [15], [25], [35], [41], [53], [65], [73], [83], [95]; each poem is illustrated by two engravings found on the following: pp. [9], [13], [19], [23], [29], [33], [39], [45], [49], [57], [61], [69], [77], [81], [87], [91], [99], [103], [107]

A66. (page 77). Aimé Césaire: The Collected Poetry; *A73.* Aimé Cesaire: Lost Body

Two bindings, no priority as follows:
a. [Orange cloth over boards; spine reading from top to bottom, in white:]
CÉSAIRE [printer's device] PICASSO LOST BODY GEORGE
BRAZILLER [Front cover, stamped in black:] [from an etching: "Corps
perdu," inscribed in a vegetable-shaped heart] [Paper: Mohawk Vellum
cream; top edge trim, fore-edge and bottom edge uncut].

Dust jacket: [On spine, on orange grund, in black:] CÉSAIRE [printer's
device] PICASSO LOST BODY BRAZILLER [On front cover:] LOST
BODY / POEMS BY AIMÉ CÉSAIRE / [reproduction of an etching of
"poeta laureatus" by Pablo Picasso] / ILLUSTRATIONS BY PABLO
PICASSO [On inside front cover flap, on white ground, in black:] $25.00 /
Lost Body / by Aimé Césaire / Illustrated by Pablo Picasso / Introduction and
Translation / by Clayton Eshleman and Annette / Smith / [a note on the
limited edition of 200 copies of the first printing of the Césaire-Picasso edition
of these poems in French, now translated into English] / [biographical note
on Aimé Césaire continued onto the back flap] / [brief biographical note on
Clayton Eshleman and Annette Smith] / George Braziller, Inc. / One Park
Avenue / New York, New York 10016 / ISBN 0-8076-1147-6 / Designed by
Cynthia Hollandsworth [2006 copies, priced at $25.00 a copy].

b. Same as above except: 25 × 18.7cm.; [cover same as dust jacket except, on
back cover:] $14.95 / [inside white rectangular ground, in black:] Lost

Body / by Aimé Césaire / Illustrated by Pablo Picasso / Introduction and Translation / by Clayton Eshleman and Annette Smith / [reproduces dust jacket front and back flap information; ISBN now reads: ISBN 0-8076-1148-4 [parallel to spine, reading bottom to top, in black:] Designed by Cynthia Hollandsworth [The fore-edge of the front and back cover folds over 7.6cm.; top and bottom edges trim, fore-edge uncut]. 5171 copies, priced at $14.94 a copy.

Publication: Published by George Braziller, Inc. in New York on June 20, 1986. Printing and binding by Murray Printing Company of Westford, Massachusetts, April 21, 1986. Colophon: LOST BODY / [printer's device] / The design of Lost Body is based on Corps Perdu designed by Pablo / Picasso and published by Editions Fragrance (Paris, 1950) in a limited / edition of 219 copies. Picasso chose to set Aimé Césaire's poems in / Erasmus, designed by S.H. de Roos, a medeival-style type dating / from 1923 with light serifs, tall ascenders, short descenders, and an / unusual lower-case g. A new typeface, Vermeer, has been designed / by AlphaOmega especially for this edition of Lost Body, with digital / composition by ASD Typesetting Service of Poughkeepsie, New York, / using High Technology Solutions, Multi-language Publishing System. / Vermeer is based on Erasmus' proportions and feel, but has a / more contemporary appearance. / Lost Body has been designed by Cynthia Hollandsworth / and printed on Mohawk Vellum cream. Printing and / binding by Murray Printing Company / of Westford, Massachusetts.

Contains: Introduction and notes by Annette Smith and Clayton Eshleman, Aimé Césaire: *Lost Body:* "Word," "Who Then, Who Then," "Elegy," "Presence," "Forloining," "Lost Body," "Your Portrait," "Summons," "Births," "Lay of Errantry," (translated from the French by Clayton Eshleman and Annette Smith), *Corps Perdu* (French text).

[Note: This translation was done while, for the most part Smith was in France and Eshleman was in the United States. Therefore, they worked on their own for the sections of the Introduction that each undertook to do. Eshleman's section is from p. xii ("The ten poems...") to the middle of p. xvi, other than this, Smith wrote the introduction. On the translation, they collaborated more closely, Smith giving or dictating to Eshleman a very rough draft, he elaborating and revising these drafts, and later revising the work together until they were both satisfied. She was, generally speaking, responsible for the accuracy of the translation, he for turning it into a polished poem in English].

A74   Brown Thrasher   1986

43.1 × 27.9cm.; single leaf, printed on one side.

[On tan, in black:] BROWN THRASHER / [rule] / [46 line poem] / (3 May 1986) / Clayton Eshleman / [signature of poet; hand numbered] / [colophon] / [lower right corner, printed in rust: a drawing of a traditional tantric yoga design (India)]. Paper: 65 pound cover stock, classic laid, Monterey Sand.

Publication: Published by Karl Pohrt of the Shaman Drum Bookshop in Ann Arbor, Michigan on October 24, 1986. Printed by Kolossos Printing, Inc. in Ann Arbor, Michigan on October 23, 1986 in an edition of 150 copies, priced at $6.00 a copy. Colophon: This Broadside was printed in an edition of 150 copies on the occasion of a reception / for Clayton Eshleman on Friday, October 24, 1986 at Shaman Drum Bookshop, 313 / South State Street, Ann Arbor, Michigan.

Contains: "Brown Thrasher."

A75   César Vallejo: Pain and Circumstances   1987

[In brown:] DOLOR / & / CIRCUNSTANCIAS / TIRAMISU PRESS [printer's device] MADISON WISCONSIN

26.2 × 17cm.; three leaves glued to make one long leaf which is accordion folded into 12 sections with the preceding measurement; 2 tipped-in illustrations by Michael Thomas: pp. [i–iv] [5–11] [12]: pp. [i] title page as above; p. [ii] acknowledgements; pp. [iii–iv] blank; p. [5] (poem:) QUE ME DA QUE ME AZOTO...?; p. [6] tipped-in illustration; p. [7] (poem:) WHAT'S GOT INTO ME, THAT I'M WHIPPING MYSELF?; p. [8] (poem:) INTENSIDAD Y ALTURA; pp. [9–10] double spread tipped-in illustration; p. [11] (poem:) INTENSITY & HEIGHT; p. [12] blank; [on inside back cover: colophon].

Two bindings, no priority as follows:
a. [grey paper wrappers; text accordion folded and stitched at last inner fold into 3 panel grey wrappers; stamped in brown on front cover:] PAIN / & / CIRCUMSTANCES [Paper: Mohawk fine; cover: hand-made 100% cotton "Tairona"; tipped-in illustrations on Japanese Kozo]. 20 copies priced at $85.00 a copy.

b. Same as above except: dark grey paper wrappers; (cover and text) hand-made 100% cotton "Tairona" paper. 5 copies priced at $100.00 a copy.

Publication: Published and printed by Marta Gómez at the Tiramisu Press at the University of Wisconsin in the summer of 1987. Handmade paper by Marta Gómez. [Colophon on inside back cover of a.:] PAIN & CIR-CUMSTANCES brings together two poems / by the Peruvian writer, Cesar Vallejo, in the original Spanish / and in the English translation by Clayton Eshleman. The text / is hand-set in Garamond and Kennerly (sic) Roman. The cover stock / is paper made by the printer, Marta Gómez. The illustrations / are by Michael Thomas and are printed on Japanese Kozo paper. / twenty five (sic) copies were produced towards the end of the Sum- / mer of 1987 by the Tiramisu Press, Madison, Wisconsin. [Colophon on inside back cover b.:] PAIN & CIRCUMSTANCES brings together two poems / by the Peruvian writer, Cesar Vallejo, in the original Spanish / and in the English translation by Clayton Eshleman. The text / is hand-set in Garamond and Kennerly (sic) and printed on Tairona / paper made by the printer, Marta Gómez. The illustrations are / by Michael Thomas and are printed on Japanese Kozo paper, / 25 copies were produced towards the end of the steamy Sum- / mer of 1987 by the Tiramisu Press, Madison, Wisconsin.

Contains: César Vallejo: untitled: "What's got into me, that I'm whipping myself...," "Intensity & Height." (Translated from the Spanish by Clayton Eshleman and José Rubia Barcia).

Note: Both this title and the following title were completely unauthorized printings.

Note: Marta Gómez has printed and published in Spring 1988, a small book (16 mo.:) *After So Many Words: Fragments From Four Poems By Cesar Vallejo* in 2 issues: on hand made and on machine made paper, both with hand made paper covers; text illustrated with graphic devices; using translations by Clayton Eshleman and José Rubia Barcia, in an edition of 55 copies, 15 copies on hand made paper, 40 copies on machine made paper; both issues priced at $85.00 a copy. Colophon: Designed, printed and published / by Marta Gómez in Madison WI / during the Spring of 1988. From an edition of 55 you are holding / number / [number printed in].

A76   Antonin Artaud: Indian Culture   1987

61.2 × 40.7cm.; single leaf, printed on one side.

[On orange, in black:] ANTONIN ARTAUD / INDIAN CULTURE / Translated from the French by Clayton Eshleman and / Bernard Bador, with art work by Nancy Spero / [rule] / [poem in two columns of 47 and 51 lines each, with small figures in black to the right of column one, large figures in red below column two:] 1946 / [colophon]. Paper: 80 lb. Strathmore Gold.

Publication: Printed and published by Pat Smith and Keith Taylor at Other-Wind Press in Ann Arbor , Michigan in November 1987. 150 copies priced at $15.00 a copy. Colophon: Of the 150 copies printed by OtherWind Press, / signed by Clayton Eshleman and Nancy Spero, / this is number [number inked in].

Contains: Antonin Artaud: "Indian Culture." [Translated from the French by Clayton Eshleman and Bernard Bador].

B. Contributions to Anthologies

B1   **Erotic Poetry**   1963

[Double spread title page, in black:] Erotic Poetry / [in blue:] DECORA-
TIONS BY WARREN CHAPPELL [on recto, in blue and black: a drawing
of "Pan" and a female figure] / [in black:] The Lyrics, Ballads, Idyls / and
Epics of Love — / Classical to Contemporary / Edited by WILLIAM COLE
/ Foreword by Stephen Spender / [in blue: publisher's device] / [blue rule]
/ [in black:] RANDOM HOUSE / [in blue:] 1963

24.5 × 16.5cm.; 280 leaves; [one blank leaf] [i-vi] vii-Liv [1-4] 5-501
[502-504]: blank leaf; p. [i] blank; p. [ii] advertisements; p. [iii] half-title; p.
[iv-v] title pages as above; p. [vi] copyright page (states "FIRST PRINT-
ING"); pp. vii-xxi acknowledgments; p. [xxii] personal acknowledgments;
pp. [xxiii] xxiv-xxvii Foreword by Stephen Spender; p. [xxviii] blank; pp.
[xxix] xxx-xLvii contents; p. [xLviii] blank; pp. xLix-Liv Introduction; pp.
[1-4] 5-501 text; p. [502] blank; p. [503] a note on the editor; p. [504] blank.
Light brown endpapers.

Green cloth stamped in gilt and red-brown on spine; cover: title stamped in
gilt with two figures stamped in red-brown. Top edge stained red, top
and lower edges trimmed, fore-edge untrimmed; false headbands. Paper:
wove.

Dust jacket: red, orange and yellow, printed in red and black with figures in
Greek costume on front and spine. A portrait of the editor, William Cole from
a photograph by Elliott Erwitt, is on the inside back flap.

Publication: Published by Random House in New York in 1963 in an edition
of an unknown number of copies priced at $8.95 a copy.

Contains: two poems by Pablo Neruda: "Lone Gentleman" pp. 100-101,
"Materia Nupical" pp. 212-213, (translated from the Spanish by Clayton
Eshleman).

B2 Poetas Norteamericanos 1966

POETAS NOR [dash] / TEAMERICA [dash] / NOS / BLACKBURN [dash] CORMAN / ESHLEMAN [dash] ENSLIN / EDICIONES SUNDA

16.1 × 10.5cm.; 26 leaves; [1–6] 7–49 [50–52]: pp. [1–2] blank; p. [3] title page as above; p. [4] Editado en el Cuzco [dash] Perú / derechos reservados / Ediciones Sunda [;] pp. [5–6] 7–49 text p. [50] blank; p. [51] Indice; p. [52] colophon

Glued in stiff glossy white pictorial wrappers; printed in black and orange; all edges trim. Paper: wove.

Publication: Published in Lima, Perú, Julio, 1966 in a small edition of around 50 copies. Price unknown. Colophon: ESTE LIBRO HA SIDO IMPRESO EN LA / "EDITORIAL GARCILASO" EN LA CIU [dash] / DAD DEL CUSCO / EN EL MES DE JULIO DE 1966. / CON LA AYUDA DE LA CASA DE LA CULTURA / DEL CUSCO

Contains: brief biographical note; "Despues Del Amor," "El Reconocimento," "Barbara Enferma," "Mano," "Las Piedras De Sanjusangendo," "puerta Del Sol," translated into Spanish by Carlos German Belli, excepto el último poema cuya versíon es de César Levano. pp. 27–38.

B3 Artists and Writers Protest 1967
Against the War in Viet Nam Poems

[On beige in black:] ARTISTS AND WRITERS PROTEST / AGAINST THE WAR IN VIET NAM / [red rule] / POEMS / [red rule] 45.8 × 30.8cm.; 14 leaves: p. [1] title page as above; p. [2] copyright; p. [3] introduction by Max Kozloff; p. [4] acknowledgments; p. [5] contents; p. [6]–[26] text; p. [27] blank; p. [28] colophon.

Beige paper, sewn through to the spine. [A rust paper dust jacket folds over front and back fore-edge of the book; on front dust jacket cover in black:] POEMS [Paper: Niddegen, a mold-made German paper].

Publication: Published by Artists & Writers Protest in New York in 1967. Printed by the Profile Press in New York in an edition of 500 copies, price unknown. 100 copies numbered and signed by the poets, price unknown. Colophon: This volume of poetry was designed / and produced for Artists & Writers Protest / by Rudi Bass with the assistance of S.S. Five hundred copies /

have been printed at the Profile Press in New York, N.Y. / on Niddegen, a mold-made German paper. The text / was set in Monotype Perpetua by the Press of A. Colish / in Mount Vernon, N.Y. One hundred copies, / signed by the various poets, are / numbered 1 to 100. / This is copy number / [red parenthesis].

[Note: I have not seen a signed, numbered copy].

Contains: "Lachrymae Mateo"

B4   The Genre of Silence   1967

THE GENRE OF SILENCE / A One-Shot Review / June, 1967 / Editor, Joel Oppenheimer / Associate Editor, Joel Sloman / Production Editor, Anne Waldman / Cover photography by Joe Dankowski

22.8 × 15.3cm.; 48 leaves; [1–6] 7–72 [96]: p. [1] title page as above; p. [2] copyright page; p. [3] contents; p. [4] blank; p. [5] introduction [by Joel Oppenheimer]; p. [6] blank; pp. 7–72 [73–96] text and eight photographs by Joe Dankowski.

Glued in black and white wrappers; front cover a photograph of a figure with umbrella, title in white, $1.00 on lower right corner; white title on spine; back cover white. Paper wove. All edges trim with cover.

Publication: Published by the Poetry Project at St. Mark's Church In-The-Bowery, in New York, June 1967. Financed by a government grant. "This then will be the first and last issue of THE GENRE OF SILENCE" (from introduction). Printed in an unknown number of copies priced at $1.00 a copy.

Contains: Selections from "The Book of Eternal Death," pp. 50–52.

B5   Poets for Peace   1967

POETS FOR PEACE / Poems from the Fast / The present committee includes Esther Aronson, Lynne / Banker, David Henderson, K K, Bill Little and Gary Youree. / Henri Percikow, Carol Rubenstein and Leo Young were on the / Fast Committee, and Carol assisted in the compilation of this / anthology. Poets for Peace was originally organized by Henri / Percikow and the idea of the January Fast was his. / Members of Poets for Peace are available for readings in / colleges, churches, high schools, Elks Clubs, etc.

For in- / formation, and for additional copies of the anthology, contact / Bill Little, 146–11 Hillside Ave., Jamaica, N.Y. 11435, tel: / 523–8234; or Gary Youree, 102 E. 4th St., New York, N.Y. / 10003, tel: 674-7612. / Maggie Dominic's "This Man That Weeps" copyright 1966 by / *The Worksheet Directory,* Maine; Barbara Holland's "To / Rachel" if from *Imprints Quarterly:* Denise Levertov's / "Advent 1966" was first printed in *The Nation,* February 13, / 1967; Lenore Marshall's "Gogglehead" first published in *The / Saturday Review* and later in her *Other Knowledge;* "The / War Comes into My Room" will be in Muriel Rukeyser's next / book of poems, *The Speed of Darkness.* / Copyright 1967 by Lynne Banker. / All rights reserved by the authors. / Cover designed by Cliff Joseph.

21.6 × 17.8cm.; 48 leaves; [i–iv] v–vi 1–90: p. [i] (mis-numbered "1") title page as above; p. [ii] reproduction of a black and white drawing of St. Mark's Church by P.T. Eley; p. [iii] dedication; p. [iv] Foreword; pp. v–vi poem by Ed Blair pp. 1–90 text; (inside back cover: poem by Sotere Torregian).

Black and white printed wrappers, stapled twice through to the spine. Paper: wove. All edges trim with cover.

Publication: Publisher not indicated. Probably published by the Poetry Project at St. Mark's Church-In-The-Bowery, in New York, 1967. Price unknown, probably gratis.

Contains: "Stele" pp. 20–21.

B6   Mad Windows   1969

MAD / WINDOWS / Selected by Phil Perry / LIT PRESS 1969

22.3 × 14.3cm.; 55 leaves; one blank leaf [i–iv] [5] 6–106 [107–110]: pp. [i] title page as above; p. [ii] copyright page; p. [iii] contents; p. [iv] blank; pp. [5] 6–106 text; pp. [107–110] blank. White endpapers.

Two bindings, no priority as follows;
a. Light Blue stamped front and spine in black; all edges trimmed. Paper: wove.

White unprinted pictorial dust jacket (a drawing of a man's head by Gino).

b. Same as above except: 21.5 × 13.9cm.; glued in wrappers; front cover reproduces dust jacket black and white art by Gino.

Publication: Published by The Lit Press, Notre Dame, Indiana 1969 by Phil Perry. Printed in an unknown number of copies, prices unknown.

Contains: "Theseus Ariadne," pp. 32–36. First published in *The Lit*, 7 May 1968; (see C98).

B7   The Triquarterly Anthology of Contemporary   1969
Latin American Literature

The TriQuarterly / Anthology / of Contemporary / Latin American / Literature / edited by / JOSE DONOSO and WILLIAM A. HENKIN / with the staff of *TriQuarterly* / [publisher's device] / NEW YORK: E.P. DUTTON & CO., INC.

21 × 15.1cm.; 256 leaves; [one blank leaf] [i–vi] vii–xi [xii] [1–2] 3–496 [497–498]: blank leaf; p. [i] half title; p. [ii] About the Editors; p. [iii] title page as above; p. [iv] copyright page [states "FIRST EDITION"]; p. [v] acknowledgments; p. [vi] blank; pp. vii–xi contents; p. [xii] blank; p. [1] half title; p. [2] title and illustrations for first selection; pp. 3–496 text; pp. [497–498] blank. 29 black and white illustrations. White endpapers.

Light green cloth stamped on spine in gilt; all edges trimmed. False head-bands. Paper: wove.

White pictorial dust jacket printed in black on spine, front, and back: a white, red, green, blue, pink, yellow, and brown figure is pictured on a tan ground on front dust jacket. Dust jacket designed by Seymour Chwast.

Publication: Published by E.P. Dutton in New York in 1969, in an edition of 2,000 copies, priced at $8.95 a copy. "Published simultaneously in Canada by Clarke, Irwin & Company Limited, Toronto and Vancouver."

Contains: "Translating César Vallejo: an Evolution" [divided into three sections as follows:] A. "The Encounter" (from "The Book of Yorunomado"), B. "Letter to César Calvo concerning the inauguration of a monument to César Vallejo," C. "The Black Cross: a preface to *Human Poems*"; author's note pp. 29–56. Six poems by César Vallejo: untitled: "It was Sunday in the fair ears of my burro...," untitled: "The point of the man...," untitled: "But before all this lady runs out...," untitled: "Today I like life much less...," untitled:

"The windows . . . ," untitled: "The one who will come . . . ," (translated from the Spanish by Clayton Eshleman). pp. 58–65.

[Notes: According to archival records, the *TriQuarterly* editors planned a simultaneous edition in wrappers of 8,000 copies, priced at $3.95 a copy. I have been unable to locate any copies. Note: This edition reproduces the contents of *TriQuarterly* Thirteen [slash] Fourteen. Fall [slash] Winter 1968 [slash] 69 Contemporary Latin American literature; (see C119)].

B8   The Voice That Is Great Within Us: 1970
American Poetry of the Twentieth Century

THE VOICE / THAT IS GREAT / WITHIN US / AMERICAN POETRY OF THE / TWENTIETH CENTURY / Edited by / HAYDEN CARRUTH / [publisher's device] / BANTAM BOOKS / [rule] / TORONTO [slash] NEW YORK [slash] LONDON / [rule] / A NATIONAL GENERAL COMPANY

17.7 × 10.6cm.; 384 leaves; [i–iv] v–xlv [xlvi] [1–2] 3–722: pp. [i] half title and blurbs for book; [ii] blurbs for book continued; p. [iii] title page as above; p. [iv] copyright page; pp. v–xvi acknowledgments; [xvii] dedication; p. [viii] blank; pp. xix–xxiii foreword; p. [xxiv] blank; pp. xxv–xlv contents; p. [xlvi] blank; p. [1] half-title; p. [2] blank; pp. 3–722 text.

Glued in white pictorial wrappers printed on spine, front and back in black, red, orange, and tan. All edges trimmed. Paper: wove.

Publication: Published by Bantam Books in New York, November 1970, in a first edition of 50,000 copies, priced at $1.95 a copy. There have been many later printings.

Contains: "The Black Hat" pp. 695–699.

B9   A Caterpillar Anthology   1971

[Double spread title page:] A CATERPILLAR ANTHOLOGY / A Selection of Poetry and Prose from CATERPILLAR Magazine / Edited by CLAYTON ESHLEMAN / Anchor Books / Doubleday & Company, Inc. / Garden City, New York / 1971

18 × 10.7cm.; 260 leaves; [i–v] v–xvi [1–2] 3–503 [504]: p. [i] half-title; pp. [ii–iii] title pages as above; p. [iv] copyright page [states: "First Edition"]; pp.

[v–ix] contents; p. [x] blank; pp. [xi–xvi] Introduction; p. [1] divisional title; p. [2] blank; pp. 3–503 text; p. [504] blank.

Glued in turquoise wrappers; with a yellow, red, blue, green and purple deisgn; printed in white on spine and white and yellow on front. All edges trimmed. Paper: wove.

Publication: Published by Anchor Books, Garden City, New York in 1971, in an edition of 10,000 copies, priced at $2.50 a copy.

Contains: Introduction by Clayton Eshleman pp. xi–xvi; [*Caterpillar* 2:] "The Test of Translation IV: Basho," pp. 74–79. [*Caterpillar* 6:] "The Lay of Phi Delta Theta: section 5," pp. 174–177. [*Caterpillar* 8–9:] "An Ode to Autumn," pp. 299–302. [Caterpillar 11:] "The Gates of Capricorn," pp. 405–411. [See: C92, C124, C131, C146; D5, D10, D12.

B10   The Box   1971

[Cover title; on a tan wraparound band, in black:] California Institute of the Arts Vol. 1, No. 1, MARCH, 1971 / BOX $ 2½ / (A QUARTERLY)

40 × 40 × 2.7cm.; one roll of music, 5 loose leaves, a record cover containing 15 loose leaves.

A square black box, the shape of a record album container, with a tan wraparound band which reads on front as above; on back there is a long poem quote from Plato's *Republic* with the names of the participants in *The Box* as follows: JULES ENGEL CLAYTON ESHLEMAN / LEO HAMALIAN DICK HIGGINS / ALAN KAPROW / ALISON KNOWLES RICHARD KOSTELANETZ / BEN LIFSON NAM JUNE PAIK VICTOR PAPANEK / ARAM SAROYAN PETEN VAN RIPER / THE CENTER FOR THE STUDY OF TECHNOLOGICAL EXPERIENCE. [Three more lines from the Plato quote].

Publication: Published by Peace Press, [students of California Institute of the Arts in Vallencia, California] in 1971 in an unknown number of copies (possibly 300 copies) priced at $2.50 a copy. Printed by Western Screen Printers of Sun Valley, California in 1971.

Contains: The broadside poem: "The Bridge at the Mayan Press;" (see A19).

[Note: This was the first issue of what was intended as a quarterly magazine to be published four times a year by the students of California Institute of the Arts with issues in March, May, October and January. However, there was only one issue produced].

B11   Art Poetry Melodrama   1972

[On grey clasp envelope in red:] WINTER 1972 [in upper left corner in black:] [publisher's device] / The Alternative Press / 4339 Avery Detroit, Michigan 48208

31.8 × 24.1cm.; 11 loose leaves of varying sizes, colors and papers which include, 6 postcards (including the Eshleman contribution), one bookmark, and 4 broadsides; all work by various poets, artists, photographers, etc., mailed in the grey clasp envelope described above.

Publication: Published by Ken Mikolowski of The Alternative Press in Detroit, Michigan in early 1972, in an edition of 400 copies priced at $10.00 a subscription (four issues). Printed by Ken Mikolowski in Detroit, Michigan, November 1971, on an old 1904 Chandler letter press. This was then a quarterly issue and is presently a yearly publication of two issues.

Contains: untitled 6 line poem beginning: "One of the oldest dreams...," (See A22).

B12   Doors and Mirrors   1972

[In black, on left:] Doors / and / Mirrors [on right:] Fiction and Poetry / from Spanish America / 1920 [dash] 1970 / Selected and Edited by / Hortense Carpentier / and Janet Brof / Grossman Publishers / New York 1972 [below: printer's device]

[A bilingual edition; original Spanish on versos, English on rectos].

23.4 × 16cm.; 239 leaves; [one blank leaf] [i–iv] v–xvi [1–3] 4–13 [14–15] 16–454 [455–460]: p. [i] half title; p. [ii] blank; p. [iii] title page as above; p. [iv] copyright page [states: First published in 1971; copyright 1972 by Hortense Carpentier and Janet Brof] and acknowledgments; p. v–vi continuation of acknowledgments; p. [vii] dedication; p. [viii] blank; pp. [ix] x preface; pp. [xi] xii–xvi contents; p. [1] half title; p. [2] blank pp. [3] 4–13 introduction; pp. [14–15] 16–454 text; pp. [455–456] blank; p. [457] colophon; pp. [458–460] blank; orange endpapers.

Two bindings, no priority as follows:

a. Tan cloth stamped in gilt and bronze on spine; top edge stained red; all edges trimmed; false headbands. Paper: wove. Dust jacket not seen.

Publication: Published by Grossman Publishers in New York in 1972 in an edition of an unknown number of copies, priced at $15.00 a copy. Published simultaneously in Canada by Fitzhenry and Whiteside, Ltd.

b. Published in wrappers by Viking Press in 1972 in an edition of an unknown number of copies at $3.50 a copy. I have not seen a copy.

Contains: César Vallejo: "I am Going to Speak of Hope," "Stumble Between Two Stars," "Palms and Guitar," "The Wretched of the Earth," (translated from the Spanish by Clayton Eshleman) pp. 49–59.

**B13   Open Poetry: Four Anthologies of   1973
        Expanded Poems**

OPEN POETRY / Four Anthologies of Expanded Poems / EDITED BY / Ronald Gross and George Quasha / WITH / Emmett Williams, / John Robert Colombo / and Walter Lowenfels / SIMON AND SCHUSTER New York

24.5 x 17.5cm.; 320 leaves; [one blank leaf] [i–iv] v–xix [xx] [1–2] 3–614 [615–618]: [one blank leaf]; p. [i] publisher's device; p. [ii] blank; p. [iii] title page as above; p. [iv] copyright page [states "First printing"]; pp. v–xii acknowledgments; pp. xiii–xiv preface; pp. xv–xix contents; p. [xx] blank; p. [1] divisional title; p. [2] blank; pp. 3–614 text; pp. [615–618] blank. White endpapers.

Light orange cloth stamped on spine in brown; all edges trimmed. False headbands. Paper: wove.

White dust jacket printed on spine, front, and back in black, brown, and purple.

Publication: Published by Simon and Schuster in New York in 1973, in an edition of an unknown number of copies, priced at $14.95 a copy. Printed by The Murray Printing Company, Forge Village, Massachusetts. Designed by Irving Perkins.

Contains: "Lachrymae Mateo," "Soutine," "The Meadow," pages 79–90; César Vallejo: "Telluric and Magnetic," (translated from the Spanish by Clayton Eshleman); pp. 274–275.

**B14   America A Prophecy: A New Reading of   1973
American Poetry from Pre-Columbian Times
to the Present.**

[In block letters:] AMERICA / A PROPHECY / [in black:] A New Reading
of American Poetry / from Pre-Columbian Times to the Present / Edited by
GEORGE QUASHA / and JEROME ROTHENBERG / Random House
[publisher's device] New York

21.4 × 14.4cm.; 320 leaves; pp. [iii–vi] vii–xv [xvi] xvii–xxxviii [1–2] 3–603
[604]: p. [iii] half title; p. [iv] blank; p. [v] title page as above; p. [vi]
copyright page; pp. vii–xv acknowledgments; p. [xvi] blank; pp. xvii–xxvi
contents; pp. [xxvii–xxviii] xxix–xxxviii introduction; p. [1] divisional title;
p. [2] blank; pp. 3–603 text; p. [604] about the editors. White endpapers.
[Note: there are only two preliminary leaves, although the publisher begins
the numbering of the preliminary pages with p. vii].

Two bindings, no priority as follows:
a. Black cloth stamped in gilt and black. All edges trimmed, false headband.
Paper: wove.

Blue dust jacket printed in red, white, black and yellow.

Publication: Published by Random House in New York in 1973, in an edition
of an unknown number of copies, priced at $12.95 a copy.

b. Same as above except: 20.2 × 13.1cm.; [title page deletes:] Random House
[publisher's device] New York [but adds:] [publisher's device] Vintage Books
/ A Division of Random House / New York [Glued in wrappers; cover same
as dust jacket except on spine on white ground, reading top to bottom, in
red:] America a Prophecy [in black:] EDITED BY / JEROME
ROTHENBERG AND / GEORGE QUASHA [reading side to side, in
black:] [publisher's device] / V-976 / VINTAGE [Front cover, upper
right corner, adds:] $3.95/V-976 [left top corner, reading bottom to top,
adds:] 394-71976-X [back cover reproduces that of the dust jacket except that it is printed in black and adds to the upper left corner:]
POETRY

Publication: Published by Vintage Books, a division of Random House in New
York in January, 1974, in an edition of an unknown number of copies, priced
at $3.95 a copy.

Contains: "Ode to Reich" pp. 502–506.

B15   Sparrow 1-12   1973

[No separate title page, white label on front cover within an orange single rule frame, in orange:] SPARROW / 1-12 / Autographed edition / limited to 50 copies / Black Sparrow Press / Los Angeles — 1973

23.7 × 15.7cm.; 96 leaves; text consists of separate issues of *Sparrow 1-12* bound together. Grey endpapers.

Light blue boards with white label as described above. All edges trimmed. False headbands. Unprinted acetate dust jacket.

Publication: Published by John Martin of the Black Sparrow Press in Los Angeles, California, September 25, 1973, in an edition of 59 copies, priced at $40.00 a copy. This "autographed" edition of *Sparrow 1-12* consists of all first printings each signed by the individual author on the cover of their work. A trade edition of 65 copies containing various printings of the 12 pamphlets was published simultaneously and priced at $15.00 a copy. Additional copies containing mixed printings were issued in varying bindings as deemed necessary.

Contains: Sparrow 2: The Sanjo Bridge; (see A23).

B16   Messages: A Thematic Anthology of Poetry   1973

Messages / A Thematic Anthology of Poetry / Edited by X.J. Kennedy Tufts University / Little, Brown and Company / Boston

21.8 × 16.1cm.; 208 leaves; [i-v] vi-xiii [xiv] xv-xvii [xviii] xix [xx] [1-4] 5-386 [387-396]: pp. [i-ii] blank; p. [iii] half title; p. [iv] blank; p. [v] title page as above; pp. vi-xiii copyright [states "First Printing"] and acknowledgments; p. [xiv] blank; pp. xv-xvii preface; p. [xviii] blank; p. xix contents; p. [xx] blank; p. [1] half title; p. [2] black and white photograph; p. [3] divisional title; p. [4] blank; pp. 5-386 text; pp. [387-396] blank. Black and white photographs on pages [2], [22], [50], [84], [114], [138], [162], [194], [216], [252], [276], [304].

Glued in stiff glossy black wrappers printed in red, blue, green, yellow, orange and white. All edges trimmed. Paper: wove.

Publication: Published by Little, Brown & Company in Boston, Massachusetts in 1973. Published simultaneously in Canada by Little, Brown & Company (Canada) Limited, in an edition of an unknown number of copies, priced at $5.50 a copy. There is a second printing.

Contains: "A Very Old Woman" pp. 310–311.

B17   Active Anthology   1974

AN /ACTIVE ANTHOLOGY / edited by / GEORGE QUASHA / contributing editor / SUSAN QUASHA / THE SUMAC PRESS / Fremont, Michigan [publisher's device on right].

25.4 × 17.8cm.; 128 leaves; [1–8] 9–256: p. [1] black and white photograph; p. [2] advertisements p. [3] title page as above; p. [4] copyright [states "First Edition"] and acknowledgments; p. [5] black and white photograph; p. [6–7] contents; p. [8] black and white photograph; pp. 9–11 preface by George Quasha; pp. 12–256 text [illustrated with black and white photographs and drawings].

Glued in white wrappers printed in red and black with a black and white photograph on cover. All edges trimmed. Paper: wove.

Publication: Published by Dan Gerber of the Sumac Press in Fremont, Michigan in 1974, in an edition of 3,000 copies, priced at $4.95 a copy.

Contains: "Study for a Self-Portrait at 12 Years Old," "Creation," "Portrait of Antonin Artaud" pp. 185–187.

B18   Sparrow 13–24   1974

[No separate title page, white label on front cover, within a blue single rule frame, in blue:] SPARROW / 13–24 / Autographed edition / limited to 50 copies / Black Sparrow Press / Los Angeles—1974

23.7 × 15.7cm.; 96 leaves; text consists of separate issues of *Sparrow 13–34* bound together. White endpapers.

Blue cloth with white label as described above. All edges trimmed. False headbands. Unprinted acetate dust jacket.

Publication: Published by John Martin of the Black Sparrow Press in Los Angeles, California, September 21, 1974, in an edition of 60 copies, priced at $40.00 a copy. This "autographed" edition of *Sparrow 13–24* consists of all first printings each signed by the individual author on the cover of their work. A trade edition of 100 copies containing various printings of the 12 pamphlets was published simultaneously and priced at $15.00 a copy. Additional copies containing mixed printings were issued in varying bindings as deemed necessary.

Contains: Sparrow 18: Aux Morts; (see A27); *Sparrow 23: Antonin Artaud: Letter to André Breton:* (translated by Clayton Eshleman); (see A29).

B19   Giant Talk: **1975**
An Anthology of Third World Writings

[In block letters:] GIANT / TALK / [in black:] An Anthology of Third World Writings / Compiled and Edited by / Quincy Troupe and Rainer Schulte / Random House [publisher's device] New York

24 × 15.8cm.; 296 leaves; [i–xv] xvi–xxi [xxii–xxiii] xxiv–xLiv [1–3] 4–546 [547–548]: p. [i] half-title; p. [ii] blank; p. [iii] title page as above; pp. [iv–xiii] copyright [states "First Edition"] and acknowledgments; p. [xiv] blank; pp. [xv] xvi–xxi contents; p. [xxii] blank; pp. [xxiii] xxiv–xLiv introduction; p. [1] divisional title; p. [2] blank; p. [3] 4–546 text; p. [547] about the authors; p. [548] blank. White endpapers.

Two bindings, no priority as follows:
a. White cloth stamped in green on spine. All edges trimmed. False headbands. Paper: wove.

Dust jacket, (I have not seen a jacketed copy).

Publication: Published by Random House in New York 1975 and simultaneously in Canada by Random House of Canada Limited, Toronto in an edition of an unknown number of copies, priced at $20.00 a copy.

b. Same as above except: 23.4 × 15cm.; [title page ads:] [publisher's device] Vintage Books / A Division of Random House, New York [deletes:] Random House [publisher's device] New York. [Copyright page states "First Vintage Books, September 1975"]. Glued in white pictorial wrappers printed in blue, black and green on spine and blue, green, yellow and black on front and back covers.

Publication: Published by Random House in New York in 1975 and simultaneously in Canada by Random House of Canada Limited, Toronto; and by Vintage, A Division of Random House, September 1975, in an edition of an unknown number of copies, priced at $6.95 a copy.

Contains: César Vallejo: untitled: "The anger that breaks the man into children...," p. 3; "I Am Going to Speak of Hope," pp. 63–64; untitled: From pure heat I am freezing..." pp. 329–330 (translated from the Spanish by Clayton Eshleman).

B20   **The Negritude Poets**   1975
        An Anthology of Translations from the French

[Double spread title page:] [printer's device] / An Anthology of Translations
from the French / [printer's device] / Edited and with an Introduction by
Ellen Conroy Kennedy / [printer's device] / A Richard Seaver Book [on recto:] The Negritude Poets / The Viking Press New York

23.9 × 16.4cm.; 160 leaves; [i–iv] v–xxxiii [xxxiv] [1–2] 3–284 [285–286]: p.
[i] half title; pp. [ii–iii] title page as above; p. [iv] copyright page (states "First
published in 1975 by Viking Press, Inc."); pp. v–vii acknowledgments; p.
[viii] blank; p. [ix] dedication; p. [x] blank; p. xi personal acknowledgments;
p. [xii] blank; pp. xiii–xviii contents; pp. xix–xxix introduction; p. [xxx]
blank; pp. xxi–xxxiii chronology; p. [xxxiv] printer's device; p. [1] divisional
title; p. [2] blank; pp. 3–284 text; pp. [285–286] blank. White endpapers.

Black cloth stamped in orange and fushia gilt on spine; over pale orange and
black patterned paper covered boards. All edges trimmed. False headband.
Paper: wove.

Black pictorial dust jacket printed in white, orange, and grey.

Publication: Published by Viking Press in New York in 1975 (a Richard Seaver
Book), in an edition of an unknown number of copies priced at $15.00 a copy.
Published simultaneously in Canada by The Macmillan Company of Canada
Limited.

Contains: Aimé Césaire: "Notes on a Return to the Native Land" (abridg-
ment), "First Problem," "The Wheel," "Magic," "Mississippi," "Beat it Night
Dog," (translated from the French by Clayton Eshleman and Denis Kelly)
also "State of the Union," (translated from the French by Denis Kelly). pp.
66–85.

B21   **The Gist of Origin 1951–1971**   1975
        An Anthology

The Gist of Origin / 1951–1971 [slash] an anthology / edited by Cid Corman
/ [thin rule rectangle] / Grossman Publishers / A Division of The Viking Press
[slash] New York [slash] 1975

23.4 × 14.5cm.; 282 leaves; [i–iii] iv–xxxvii [xxxviii] [1–2] 3–525 [526]: p. [i]
half title; p. [ii] blank; p. [iii] title page as above; p. iv copyright page

(states: "First published in 1975 by Grossman Publishers") pp. v–xiv contents; pp. xv–xxxvii introduction; p. [xxxviii] blank; p. [1] divisional title; p. [2] blank; pp. 3–525 text; p. [526] blank. White endpapers.

Blue cloth, stamped in orange on spine, over orange paper covered boards. All edges trimmed. False headbands. Paper: wove.

Blue dust jacket printed in orange and white.

Publication: Published by Grossman a division of Viking Press in New York in 1975, in an edition of an unknown number of copies priced at $17.50 a copy.

Contains: César Vallejo: untitled: "In sum, to express my life I have only my death...," untitled: "exists a man mutilated not from combat...," "I Am Going to Speak of Hope," "Discovery of Life," "Common Sense," "Violence of the Hours," untitled: "The windows have been shaken, elaborating...," (translated from the Spanish by Clayton Eshleman) pp. 290–298. [From: *Origin* 13 (Second Series) April 1964; (see C39)].

B22   Sparrow 25–36   1975

[No separate title page, white label on front cover, within a green single rule frame, in green:] SPARROW / 25–36 / Autographed edition / limited to 50 copies / Black Sparrow Press / Los Angeles — 1975

23.7 × 15.7cm.; 100 leaves; text consists of separate issues of *Sparrow 25–36* bound together. Tan endpapers.

Green cloth with white label as described above. All edges trimmed. False headbands. Unprinted acetate dust jacket.

Publication: Published by John Martin of the Black Sparrow Press in Los Angeles, California, September 29, 1975, in an edition of 62 copies priced at $40.00 a copy. This "autographed" edition of *Sparrow 25–36* consists of all first printings each signed by the individual author on the cover of their work. A trade edition of 110 copies containing all first printings of the 12 pamphlets was published simultaneously priced at $15.00 a copy. Additional copies containing mixed printings were issued in varying bindings as deemed necesary.

Contains: Sparrow 34: To Have Done With The Judgment Of God By Antonin Artaud (translated from the French by Clayton Eshleman and Norman Glass); (see A33).

B23   Sparrow 37–48   1976

[No separate title page, white label on front cover within a brown single rule frame, in brown:] SPARROW / 37–48 / Autographed edition / limited to 50 copies / Black Sparrow Press / Santa Barbara — 1976

23.7 × 15.7cm.; 100 leaves; text consists of separate issues of *Sparrow 37–48* trimmed and bound together. Cream endpapers.

Light brown cloth with white label as described above. All edges trimmed. False headbands. Unprinted acetate dust jacket.

Publication: Published by John Martin of the Black Sparrow Press in Santa Barbara, California, October 14, 1976, in an edition of 60 copies. Priced at $40.00 a copy. This "autographed" edition of *Sparrow 37–48* consists of all first printings each signed by the individual author on the cover of their work (except No. 43 by Charles Olson). A trade edition of 146 copies containing all first editions of the 12 pamphlets was published simultaneously priced at $15.00 a copy. Additional copies containing mixed printings were issued in varying bindings as deemed necessary.

Contains: Sparrow 47: Artaud the Momo by Antonin Artaud (translated from the French by Clayton Eshleman and Norman Glass); (see A36).

B24   New Directions 33   1976

[Superimposed over large grey N D in black:] New Directions in Prose and Poetry 33 / [on white:] Edited by J. Laughlin / with Peter Glassgold and Frederick R. Martin / [publisher's device: a drawing by Heinz Henghes] A New Directions Book.

20.9 × 14.2cm.; 96 leaves; [i–vi] 1–186; p. [i] half-title; p. [ii] dedication; p. [iii] title page as above; p. [iv] copyright page [states: "First published cloth-bound (ISBN: 0-8112-0616-5) and as New Directions Paperbook 419 (ISBN: 0-8112-0617-3) in 1976"]; pp. [v–vi] contents; pp. 1–186 text. White endpapers.

Two bindings, no priority as follows:
a. Brown and tan "tweed-type" paper over boards, printed in black on spine, with the publisher's device stamped in blind on front cover. All edges trimmed. Paper: wove.

White dust jacket printed in blue on spine; front cover, printed in white on blue. 1500 copies priced at $12.00 a copy.

b. Same as above except: 20.2 x 13.1cm.; glued in stiff glossy blue wrappers; [cover same as dust jacket except: back cover reproduces the information on the series printed on the inside flaps. A New Directions Paperbook NDP419. $3.95 is added to the lower back cover. 2500 copies priced at $3.95 a copy.

Publication: Published for James Laughlin by New Directions Publishing Corporation in New York, in 1976. Published simultaneously in Canada by McClelland & Stewart, Ltd.

Contains: "Variations Done for Gary Snyder," pp. 160–163.

**B25   The Borzoi Anthology of Latin American   1977
Literature Volume II**

THE BORZOI / ANTHOLOGY / OF LATIN AMERICAN / LITERATURE / Volume II / The Twentieth Century — from / Borges and Paz to Guimarães Rosa / and Donoso / Edited by / EMIR RODRÍGEZ MONEGAL / With the assistance of / THOMAS COLCHIE / [publisher's device] / Alfred A. Knopf New York 1977

23.2 x 15.5cm.; 255 leaves; [one blank leaf] [i–vi] vii–x [xi] xii [xiii] xiv [495] 982 [983–990]: blank leaf; p. [i] half title; p. [ii] blank; p. [iii] title page as above; p. [iv] copyright page (states "FIRST EDITION"); p. [v] acknowledgments; pp. [vi] vii–x permissions and acknowledgments; pp. [xi] xii contents; pp. [xiii] xiv preface to the second volume; pp. [495] 496–982 text; pp. [983–984] blank; p. [985] a note about the editor; p. [986] blank; p. [987] a note on the type; pp. [988–990] blank.

Glued in blue wrappers printed in orange, yellow and white; back cover: orange ground printed in brown. All edges trimmed. Paper: wove.

Publication: Published by Alfred A. Knopf in New York, and simultaneously in Canada by Random House of Canada Limited, Toronto in 1977, in an edition of an unknown number of copies priced at $7.95 a copy. There was a second and third printing.

Contains: César Vallejo: untitled: "Considering coldly, impartially...," untitled: "Alfonso, I see you watching me...," untitled: "The fact is the place where I put on my...," "The Wretched of the Earth," "Sermon on Death," "Paris, October 1936," "Black Stone on a White Stone," (translated from the Spanish by Clayton Eshleman and José Rubia Barcia), pp. 589–596.

B26   Sparrow 49-60   1977

[No separate title page, white label on front cover within a lavender single rule frame, in lavender:] SPARROW / 49-60 / Autographed edition / limited to 50 copies / Black Sparrow Press / Santa Barbara—1977

23.7 × 15.7cm.; 100 leaves; text consists of separate issues of *Sparrow 49-60* bound together. Cream endpapers.

Light purple corduroy cloth with white label as described above. All edges trimmed. False headbands. Unprinted acetate dust jacket.

Publication: Published by John Martin of the Black Sparrow Press in Santa Barbara, California, October 28, 1977 in an edition of 59 copies, priced at $40.00 a copy. This "autographed" edition of *Sparrow 49-60* consists of all first printings each signed by the individual author on the cover of their work, except No. 52 (by Charles Reznikoff) and No. 58 (by Paul Goodman). A trade edition of 114 copies containing all first printings of the 12 pamphlets was published simultaneously priced at $15.00 a copy. Additional copies containing mixed printings were issued in varying bindings as deemed necessary.

Contains: Sparrow 57: Core Meander; (see A38).

B27   The Little Magazine in America: 1978
A Modern Documentary History

THE LITTLE MAGAZINE / IN AMERICA: / A MODERN / DOCUMENTARY HISTORY / edited by Elliott Anderson and Mary Kinzie / [publisher's device]

24 × 16.8cm.; 392 leaves; [i–xiv] [1–2] 3–770: pp. [i–ii] blank; p. [iii] publisher's device; p. [iv] blank; p. [v] half-title p. [vi] blank; p. [vii] title page as above; p. [viii] copyright page (states "First printing, November, 1978); p. [ix] dedication; p. [x] publisher's note; p. [xi] half-title; p. [xii] blank; pp. [xiii–xiv] [1] contents; p. [2] blank; pp. 3–5 prefatory note; pp. 6–770 text. Color and gilt patterned endpapers.

Two bindings, no priority as follows:
a. Black cloth stamped in gilt and red on spine. All edges trimmed. False headbands. Paper: wove.

Black dust jacket printed in gold, white, and black. 2,000 copies priced at $25.00 a copy.

b. Same as above except: 23.5 × 15.3cm.; glued in paper wrappers; [cover same as dust jacket except:] $14.95 / ISBN 0-916366-13-8 (s.c.) [has been added to the spine; front cover now includes, below the title:] –42 lively, anecdotal chapters by the / outstanding editors of our time / –Illustrated with over 140 photographs / and documents / –Including an annotated checklist of 85 / magazines and an Index [expanded number of blurbs on back cover]. 500 copies priced at $14.95 a copy.

Publication: Published by Bill Henderson of The Pushcart Press in Yonkers, New York November 1978. Printed by Roy Freiman & Company, Stamford, Connecticut, in 1978.

Contains: "Doing *Caterpillar,*" by Clayton Eshleman pp. 450–471.

[Note: The Little Magazine In America was published simultaneously with *Tri-Quarterly* 43 Fall 1978, from the sheets of the latter publication. See: *Tri-Quarterly* 43 Fall 1978, (see C277). [From p. [x]:] PUBLISHER'S NOTE / THE LITTLE MAGAZINE IN AMERICA: *A Modern Documentary History* / is the product of a unique cooperation between two small presses - / *Tri-Quarterly* and *Pushcart.* I would especially like to thank Elliot / Anderson, Mary Kinzie and the *TriQuarterly* staff for their superb job / in editing and collecting this book over a four year period, and Cynthia / Anderson for her art direction. Thanks also to Michael McDonnell for / his Index, created specially for this book edition of *TriQuarterly's* his- / tory, and to Russell Maylone, Special Collections, Northwestern Uni- / versity, for his help in assembling the photographs and documents].

B28   Sparrow 61–72   1978

[No separate title page, tan label on front cover, within a red single rule frame, in red:] SPARROW / 61–72 / Autographed edition / limited to 50 copies / Black Sparrow Press / Santa Barbara—1978

23.7 × 15.7cm.; 98 leaves; text consists of separate issues of *Sparrow 61–72* bound together. Tan endpapers.

Red cloth with tan label as described above. All edges trimmed. False headbands. Unprinted acetate dust jacket.

Publication: Published by John Martin of the Black Sparrow Press in Santa Barbara, California, October 13, 1978 in an edition of 60 copies priced at $40.00 a copy. This "autographed" edition of *Sparrow 61–72* consists of all first

printings each signed by the individual author on the cover of their work. A
trade edition of 120 copies containing first printings of all 12 pamphlets was
published simultaneously, priced at $15.00 a copy. Additional copies contain-
ing mixed printings were issued in varying bindings as deemed necessary.

Contains: Sparrow 65: Battles In Spain: Five Unpublished Poems By César Vallejo,
(translated from the Spanish by Clayton Eshleman & José Rubia Barcia):
"Trilce," untitled: "We probably already were of a compassionate age...,"
untitled: "There she goes! Call her...," "Battles in Spain, I–VIII," "Funereal
Hymn for the Ruins of Durango." (See A47).

B29   Poetry in English Now   1978

[Cover title:] POETRY IN ENGLISH NOW / williambronk cidcorman
robert / creeley claytoneshleman philipga / rrison ronloewinsohn georgeoppe
/ POETRY IN ENGLISH NOW / n carlrakosi brucerichman jimb / urns an-
drewcrozier royfisher le / eharwood johnjames timlongvill / POETRY IN
ENGLISH NOW / e yannlovelock paulmatthews ed / winmorgan johnriley
peterriley / rsthomas charlestomlinson chris / torrance gaelturnbull /
POETRY IN ENGLISH NOW / blackweir press

20.7 × 15cm.; 56 leaves; 1–112: [Inside front cover:] contents; p. 1 foreword by
John Freeman; pp. 2–110 text; p. 111 acknowledgments; p. 112 colophon and
list of subscribers.

[Stiff glossy white wrappers, stapled twice through to the spine, printed on
front cover as above; on back cover:] POETRY IN ENGLISH NOW /
BLACKWEIR PRESS / £ 1.80.

Publication: Published in Cardif, England by John Freeman of the Blackweir
Press in 1978, in an edition of 500 copies. Priced at £ 1.80 a copy. Printed by
University College, Cardiff, Wales. Colophon: *Poetry in English Now* was conceived and compiled in the first place as a / special issue of the international
magazine *Lettera,* in response to an / invitation from its editor, Spartaco
Gamberini. *Lettera* is distributed / to a restricted list of correspondents and
not for sale to the public. It / seemed appropriate to offer the material
gathered to a wider audience, and / so this Blackweir Press edition was arranged. I am grateful to Mr. / Gamberini for permission to reprint the contents of his magazine, as well / as for his help in numerous ways.

Contains: "Satanas" (a prose poem) pp. 26–31.

[Note: Lettera 15, Quaderno 3, Febbraio, 1978, a special issue of *Lettera* magazine was sent and given to a mailing list of recipients, most of them in Italy, by Spartaco Gamberini of the Derpartment of Italian, University College, Cardiff, Wales. *Poetry in English Now* was publsihed by John Freeman of the English Department, University College, Cardiff, Wales in order to bring this selection of poets to a wider reading public in the United Kingdom and the United States. The 500 copies sold out and another printing was planned: however, because copyright permission from one of the English poets was accidentally omitted, the publication was withdrawn; (see: C270)].

B30   Out of the West   1979

[In black:] Out of the [in orange:] WEST / [in black:] Poems by / William Everson, Gary Snyder, Philip Levine / Clayton Eshleman & Jerome Rothenberg / [in orange:] [device] / [in black:] Lord John Press: Northridge, California / 1979

27 × 19.8cm; 32 leaves; [i–xii] 1–47 [48–52]: p. [i–ii] blank; p. [iii] half title; p. [iv] blank; p. [v] title page as above; p. [vi] copyright; p. [vii] contents; p. [viii] blank; p. [ix] half title; pp. 1–47 text; p. [48] blank; p. [49] colophon; pp. [50–52] blank. Light brown map endpapers.

[Brown cloth stamped in gilt on spine, over orange paper covered boards, stamped dark orange with:] [device] / [poet's names]. Top edge trim, fore-edge and lower edge untrimmed; false headbands. Paper: Frankfurt, laid. Issued without dust jacket.

Publication: Published by Herb Yellin of the Lord John Press in Northridge, California November 23 1979. Printed by Vance Gerry. Colophon: This first edition of / OUT OF THE WEST / is limited to 350 numbered copies, / all of which have been signed by each poet. / The type is Caslon & Janson and the paper / is Frankfurt. Designed and printed by / Vance Gerry for the Lord John Press. / Binding by Bela Blau. / This is number [number inked in]. Published in an edition of an unknown number of copies. 350 copies priced at $35.00 a copy, were for sale, however there are an unknown number of copies designated "Presentation Copy" on colophon page, also signed by the four poets which are presently for sale from the publisher.

Contains: "Variations Done for Jerry Rothenberg," "Frida Kahlo's Release," pp. 31–37.

[Note: Each poet has signed, below his printed name, the leaf which appears before his poetry contribution].

B31   Trumps II   1980

[Title card, in black:] BIALY CALLAHAN ENSLIN ESHLEMAN
GRENIER MCCLELLAND MCNAUGHTON / [on red rectangle
ground, in white:] TRUMPS II / [below rectangle, in black:] MALONE
MEYER MILLER NEDDS QUASHA SCHNEEMANN SCHWERNER
STEIN

14 × 8.9cm.; [except the Bruce McClelland postcard, which is 14 × 9.3cm.] 16
postcards, each printed in red and black on recto, [on verso, with long side
up, on upper left in black:] TRUMPS / A Periodical of Postcards / Published
by Station Hill Press / Produced at Open Studio, Rhinebedk, NY [Bisecting
the card, reading from bottom to top, in black:] Copyright © 1980 by [name
of author] plus title card [which lacks postcard printing on verso]

Glossy white cover stock, issued in an acetate pocket.

Publication: Published by George and Susan Quasha at the Station Hill Press,
Station Hill, Barrytown, New York in 1980. Printed at Open Studio in
Rhinebeck, New York in 1980, in an issue of approximately 1,000 sets priced
at $2.50 a set.

Contains: The American Sublime. (See A56)

B32   Vingt Poètes Américains   1980

Vingt poètes / américains / David Antin–John Ashbery–Paul Blackburn / Cid
Corman- / Robert Duncan–Larry Eigner / Clayton Eshleman–Kenneth
Koch–Denise Levertov / Harry Mathews–William Merwin–Charles Olson /
George Oppen–Jerome Rothenberg–James Schuyler / Jack Spicer–Gertrude
Stein–Nathaniel Tarn / Rosmarie Waldrop–Louis Zukofsky / ÉDITION
BILINGUE / Versions française de: / Anne-Marie Albiach, Michel
Couturier, / Michel Deguy, / Alain Delahaye, Michel de Fornel, / Domi-
nique Fourcade, Denise Getzler, Roger Giroux, / Joseph Guglielmi, Janet
Litman, Didier Pemerle, / Georges Perec, Jacques Roubaud, Claude Roy,
/ Claude Royet-Journoud, Roy Skodnick, / Kenneth White. / PRÉSENTA-
TION DE JACQUES ROUBAUD / CHOIX DE MICHEL DEGUY / ET
JACQUES ROUBAUD / CHOIX DE MICHEL DEGUY / ET JACQUES
ROUBAUD / nrf / GALLIMARD

[A bilingual edition; original English on verso, French on recto].

26 × 14.1cm.; 248 leaves; [i–vi] 9–493 [494–498]: p. [i] Du Monde En-
tier; p. [ii] blank; p. [iii] title page as above; p. [iv] copyright page; p. [v]

présentation; p. [vi] blank; pp. 9–493 [494–495] text; p. [496] blank; p. [497] colophon; p. [498] 27531.

Signatures sewn; glued in glossy white wrappers printed in red and black on spine, front, and back covers; all edges trimmed. Paper: wove.

Publication: Published by Editions Gallimard in Paris, France October 27, 1980 in an edition of around 10,000 copies priced at 136 French francs a copy. Colophon: Cet ouvrage / a été composé / et achevé d'imprimer / par l'Imprimerie Floch / à Mayenne le 27 octobre 1980. / Dépôt légal: 4ᵉ trimestre 1980. / Nº d'édition: 27531. / Imprimé en France. / (18208).

Contains: "The Name Encanyoned River" / "Fleuve encaissé d'un nom" (translated into French by Michel Deguy, Michel de Fornel, Janet Litman and Didier Pemerle) pp. 418–[437].

B33   Conjunctions: I   1980

[One thick rule, four thin rules] / CONJUNTIONS: I / [four thin rules, one thick rule] / BI-ANNUAL VOLUMES OF NEW WRITING / IN-AUGURAL DOUBLE-ISSUE / A Festschrift in honor of James Laughlin, / Publisher of New Directions / [device] / Edited by Bradford Morrow / [one thick rule, four thin rules] / consulting Editor: Kenneth Rexroth / contributing Editors: Edouard Roditi (PARIS); Walter Abish, / Guy Davenport, Claude Fredericks, Donald Hall, Nathaniel Tarn (USA)

23.5 × 15.7cm.; 152 leaves (with an inset of four unnumbered leaves of black and white photographs on simi-glossy stock between p. 144 and p. 145); [1–2] 3–295 [296–304]: p. [1] title page as above; p. [2] copyright page; pp. 3–4 editor's note, pp. 5–7 contents, pp. 8–10 letters to the editor; pp. 11–295 text; pp. [296–304] advertisements. White endpapers.

Two bindings, no priority as follows:
a. Grey cloth boards stamped in red gilt on spine, with publisher's device stamped in red gilt on front cover; all edges trimmed. False headbands. Paper: wove.

Cream colored laid paper dust jacket printed in rust, black, and turquoise. 307 copies priced at $22.50 a copy.

b. Same as above except: 22.7 × 14.9cm.; glued in laid paper wrappers [cover reproduces the dust jacket with the addition of the following to the front cover:] $9.00 (USA) £ 5.00 (England). [2,500 copies priced at $9.00 a copy].

Publication: Published by Bradford Morrow in New York City, New York, December 14, 1981 (wrappers) and December 29, 1981 (cloth). Printed and bound by Edwards Brothers, Ann Arbor, Michigan, November 1981.

Contains: "The Joy of Persephone" pp. 225–226.

[Note: See *Conjunctions:* I (C334)].

**B34   The Random House Book of Twentieth-Century   1982
French Poetry**

The Random House Book of / TWENTIETH-CENTURY / FRENCH POETRY / with Translations / by American and British Poets / [double rule] / Edited by Paul Auster / [publisher's device] / Random House New York

[A bilingual edition; original French on versos, English on rectos].

24.2 × 16.8cm.; 344 leaves; [I–VII] VIII–XLIX [L] [1] 2–635 [636–638]: p. [I] blank; p. [II] advertisements; p. [III] half-title; p. [IV] blank; p. [V] title page as above; p. [VI] copyright page (states "First Edition"); p. [VII] VIII–XXV contents; p. [XXVI] blank; p. XXVII–XLIX Introduction; p. [L] blank; p. [1] divisional title; pp. 2–635 text; p. [636] blank; p. [637] brief biography of the editor. p. [638] blank. White endpapers.

Two bindings, no priority as follows:
a. Maroon cloth stamped in pink gilt and gilt on spine over dark pink paper covered boards; all edges trimmed. False headbands. Paper: wove.

Maroon dust jacket printed in grey, on front cover: a photographic reproduction by Robert E. Mates of the painting "Red Eiffel Tower, 1911–1912" by Robert Delaunay. Jacket design by Susan Shapiro. Published by Random House in New York in 1982 in an edition of 4,000 copies priced at $25.00 a copy.

b. Same as above except: 23.3 × 15.5cm.; [title page deletes:] [publisher's device] / Random House New York [but adds:] [publishers device] / Vintage Books a Division of Random House New York [Glued in light blue covers printed in tan, and dark grey ruled in taupe]. Published by Vintage Books, a division of Random House in New York in January 1984 in an edition of 10,000 copies, priced at $11.95 a copy.

[Note: Information as to the number of copies printed in both bindings was not forthcoming from the publisher. These figures are from *Paul Bowles: A Descriptive Bibliography* by Jeffrey Miller. (Santa Barbara, Black Sparrow Press, 1986)].

Contains: Aimé Césaire: "Have No Mercy," "Serpent Sun," "Sentence," "Perdition," "Beyond," "Prophecy," (translated from the French by Clayton Eshleman and Annette Smith). pp. 418–425. Michel Deguy: untitled: "O great apposition...," "The Eyes," untitled: "Alluvium...," untitled: "When the wind...," untitled: "The wall...," (translated from the French by Clayton Eshleman), pp. 507–513.

B35   Sparks of Fire: Blake in a New Age   **1982**

sparks of fire / Blake in a New Age / edited by / James Bogan & Fred Goss / North Atlantic Books / Richmond, California

23.5 × 16cm.; 240 leaves; [i–xviii] [1] 2–458 [459–462]: p. [i] linocut by Paul Piech; p. [ii] LC catalogue data; p. [iii] half-title; p. [iv] blank; p. [v] title page as above; p. [vi] copyright page, and credits; p. [vii] dedication; p. [viii–ix] acknowledgments; p. [x–xiii] introduction; p. [xiv–xvii] contents; p. [xviii] "What to Do with This Book"; p. [1] linocut by Paul Piech; p. 2 black and white illustration; pp. 3–458 text, illustrated throughout with black and white photographs, music, and drawings; p. [459] "Enough, or too much!;" p. [460] "Oddements and 'Spare Parts';" p. [461] about the editors; p. [462] advertisement. Blue endpapers.

Two bindings, no priority as follows:
a. Blue cloth stamped in gilt on spine. All edges trimmed; false headbands. Paper: wove. Issued without dust jacket. Approximately 100 copies priced at $35.00 a copy.

b. Same as above except: 22.7 × 15cm.; glued in yellow pictorial [a reproduction of a linocut by Paul Piech on front cover] wrappers printed in blue on spine, front, and back. Approximately 2,000 copies priced at $12.95 a copy.

Publication: Published by North Atlantic Books in Richmond, California in 1982 under the auspices of the Society for the Study of Native Arts and Sciences; part of a series of anthologies called *Io. Sparks of Fire* is *Io* # 29. Typeset by Open Studio, Rhinebeck, N.Y.

Contains: "Niemonjima," pp. 318–330.

[Note: Io was published in journal format between 1964 and 1979, a span covering the first 23 issues, cloth editions were issued occasionally after issue #28].

B36   Studies in Honor of Jose Rubia Barcia   1982

ROBERTA JOHNSON and / PAUL C. SMITH, Editors / STUDIES IN HONOR OF / JOSE RUBIA BARCIA / [publisher's device] / SOCIETY OF SPANISH AND SPANISH-AMERICAN STUDIES

21.4 × 13.9cm.; 102 leaves; [1–6] 7–204: p. [1] half title; p. [2] frontispiece portrait of Jose Rubia Barcia; p. [3] title page as above; p. [4] copyright page; p. [5] contents; p. [6] blank; pp. 7–204 text.

Glossy white wrappers printed in black and red. All edges trimmed. Paper: wove.

Publication: Published by the Society of Spanish and Spanish-American Studies [a non profit educational organization sponsored by the University of Nebraska-Lincoln] in Lincoln Nebraska in 1982 in an edition of an unknown number of copies priced at approximately $20.00 a copy.

Contains: "Working with José," pp. 13–16.

B37   Symposium of the Whole   1983
A Range of Discourse Toward an Ethnopoetics

SYMPOSIUM / OF THE / WHOLE / [rule] / A Range of Discourse Toward an Ethnopoetics / Edited with Commentaries / by / Jerome Rothenberg / & / Diane Rothenberg / UNIVERSITY OF CALIFORNIA PRESS / Berkeley Los Angeles London

25.9 × 18cm.; 264 leaves; [i–vi] vii–xviii [1–2] 3–503 [504–510]: p. [i] half-title; p. [ii] blank; p. [iii] title page as above; p. [iv] copyright page, [states first edition code: 1 2 3 4 5 6 7 8 9]; p. [v] dedication; p. [vi] blank; pp. vii–ix contents; p. [x] blank; p. xi–xviii preface; p. [1] divisional title; p. [2] blank; pp. 3–503 text; p. [504] credits; pp. [505–510] blank. White endpapers.

Two bindings, no priority as follows:
a. Black cloth stamped in gilt on spine. All edges trimmed. Paper: wove. Issued without dust jacket. 1,000 copies priced at $27.50 a copy. There is a second printing.

b. Same as above except: 25.4 × 17cm.; glued in glossy black pictorial wrappers printed in white and orange on spine, front, and back covers; [a color reproduction of a collage by Wallace Berman on front cover]. 7,200 copies priced at $12.95 a copy.

Publication: Published by the University of California Press simultaneously in Berkeley, Los Angeles, London 1983. Printed by Malloy Lithographing, Inc. in Ann Arbor, Michigan, 1983.

Contains: Aimé Césaire: Notebook [a quote, only], (translated from the French by Clayton Eshleman). p. 52. "The Preface to *Hades In Manganese,*" pp. 446–450.

B38   Conjunctions 4   1983

[One thick rule, four thin rules] / CONJUNCTIONS / [four thin rules, one thick rule] / BI-ANNUAL VOLUMES OF NEW WRITING / Edited by Bradford Morrow / [device] [one thick rule, four thin rules] / Contributing Editors: Edouard Roditi (PARIS); Walter Abish, / Guy Davenport, Kenneth Irby, Ann Lauterbach, Nathaniel Tarn (USA)

23.5 × 15.7cm.; 116 leaves; [1–6] 7–226 [227–232]: p. [1–2] advertisements; p. [3] title page as above; p. [4] copyright page; pp. [5–6] contents; pp. 7–226 text; pp. [227–232] advertisements. White endpapers.

Two bindings, no priority as follows:
a. Green cloth boards stamped in silver on spine with publisher's device stamped in silver on front cover; all edges trimmed. False headbands. Paper: Wove.

Cream colored laid paper dust jacket printed in black and grey with a color reproduction of a painting by T.L. Solien: "Death Waites for Whimsy" on front cover. 400 copies, priced at $22.50 a copy.

b. Same as above except: 22.7 × 14.9cm.; glued in laid paper wrappers [cover reproduces the dust jacket with the addition of the following to the front cover:] $7.50. [2,000 copies priced at $7.50 a copy].

Publication: Published by Robert M. McKinney in New York City, New York, May 30, 1983. Printed and bound by Edwards Brothers in Ann Arbor, Michigan.

Contains: Aimé Césaire: "High Noon." (translated from the French by Clayton Eshleman and Annette Smith), pp. 212–219. [See: *Conjunctions:* 4 (C366)].

B39   Conjunctions: 6   1984

[One thick rule, four thin rules] / CONJUNCTIONS / four thin rules, one thick rule] / BI-ANNUAL VOLUMES OF NEW WRITING / Edited by Bradford Morrow / [device] / [one thick rule, four thin rules] / Contributing Editors: Edouard Roditi (PARIS); Walter Abish, / Guy Davenport, Kenneth Irby, Ann Lauterbach, Nathaniel Tarn (USA)

23.5 × 15.7cm.; 160 leaves; (includes glossy numbered leaves); [1–6] 7–306 [307–320]: pp. [1–2] advertisements; p. [3] title page as above; p. [4] copyright page; pp. [5–6] contents; pp. 7–306 text; pp. [307–320] advertisements. White endpapers.

Two bindings, no priority as follows:
a. Black cloth over boards stamped in silver on spine, with publisher's device stamped in silver on front cover; all edges trimmed. False headbands. Paper: wove.

Cream colored laid paper dust jacket with red and grey trim printed in grey, black and red. 220 copies priced at $22.50 a copy.

b. Same as above except: 22.7 × 14.9cm.; glued in laid paper wrappers [cover reproduces the dust jacket with the addition of the following to the front cover:] $7.50. [1838 copies priced at $7.50 a copy].

Publication: Published by Bradford Morrow in New York City, New York August 1, 1984. Printed and bound by Edwards Brothers, Ann Arbor, Michigan in 1984.

Contains: Bernard Bador: "Checkmate," "Irritations," "Archeology," "Cancer Dreams" (translated from the French by Clayton Eshleman). pp. 221–222. [See: *Conjunctions:* 6 (C399)].

B40   Blast 3   1984

[Within a yellow rectangular frame, in red:] BLAST 3 / [thick yellow rule] / [in black:] EDITED BY SEAMUS COONEY / [thick yellow rule] / CO-EDITED BY / BRADFORD MORROW, BERNARD LAFOURCADE / AND HUGH KENNER / BLACK SPARROW PRESS [dot] 1984

31.3 × 23.9cm.; 182 leaves (with an inset of four unnumbered leaves of color illustrations on simi-glossy stock between p. 236 and p. 237; laid in loose, in a white paper sleeve, is a 7" 33⅓ RPM STEREO record: "The Maker of the Sound" by K.R. Campbell); [1-10] 11-356 [357-364]: p. [i] blank; p. [2] frontispiece illustration; p. [3] title page as above; p. [4] copyright page; p. [5] acknowledgments; p. [6] list of plates; p. [7] contents; p. [8] blank; p. [9] half-title; p. [10] blank; pp. 11-356 text; p. [357] colophon; pp. [358-364] blank. Black endpapers.

Four bindings, no priority as follows:
a. Red cloth over yellow paper covered boards printed in red, black, grey and olive. Spine label of yellow and grey, printed in black. All edges trimmed; false headband. Paper: wove.

Unprinted textured yellow paper dust jacket. 26 lettered copies, priced at $40.00 a copy.

b. Same as above except: black cloth spine. 400 copies priced at $30.00 a copy.

c. Same as above except: 30.4 × 22.9cm.; glued in textured yellow wrappers printed same as above. 3,504 copies priced at $15.00 a copy.

d. Same as a. except: yellow cloth spine. Distributed gratis to the contributors and to the Wyndham Lewis Estate. 40 copies.

Publication: Published by John Martin of the Black Sparrow Press in Santa Barbara, California September 21, 1984. Printed by Graham Mackintosh in Santa Barbara, California and Edwards Brothers Inc. in Ann Arbor Michigan August 1984. Colophon: [two thick black rules] / Printed August 1984 in Santa Barbara & Ann Arbor / for Black Sparrow Press by Graham Mackintosh & / Edwards Brothers Inc. Typesetting by Eildon Graphica / of Toronto. Color reproductions by The Paget Press / of Toronto. Designed by Barbara Martin & Peter / Sibbald Brown. This first edition is published in / paper wrappers & 426 deluxe numbered copies have / been handbound in boards by Earle Gray. / [two thick rules / three inverted triangles].

Contains: "Lemons" pp. 258-260; Aimé Césaire: "Lay of Errantry" (translated by Clayton Eshleman & Annette Smith), pp. 261-263.

B41   Conjunctions 7   1985

[One thick rule, four thin rules] / CONJUNCTIONS / [four thin rules, one thick rule] / BI-ANNUAL VOLUMES OF NEW WRITING / Edited by

Bradford Morrow / [device] / [one thick rule, four thin rules] / Contributing Editors: Edouard Roditi (PARIS); Walter Abish, / Guy Davenport, Kenneth Irby, Ann Lauterbach, Nathaniel Tarn (USA) / Publisher: David R. Godine

23.5 × 15.7cm.; 142 leaves; (with an inset of six leaves of halftone illustrations on semi-glossy stock, included in the pagination); [1–6] 7–275 [276–284]: p. [1] advertisement; p. [2] editor's note; p. [3] title page as above; p. [4] copyright page; pp. [5–6] contents; pp. 7–275 text; pp. [276–284] advertisements. White endpapers.

Two bindings, no priority as follows:
a. Grey cloth stamped in green gilt on spine, with device stamped in green gilt on front cover; all edges trimmed. False headbands. Paper: wove.

Cream colored laid paper dust jacket printed in green, blue grey and black with detail, in black and grey, of "Mirror Piece" by Elizabeth Diller on front cover. 1500 copies priced at $20.00 a copy.

b. Same as above except: 22.7 × 14.9cm.; glued in laid paper wrappers cover reproduces the dust jacket with the substitution of $8.95 for $20.00 on the back cover. 4,000 copies priced at $8.95 a copy.

Publication: Published by David R. Godine in New York City, New York, May 1, 1985 in wrappers and cloth. Printed and bound by Edwards Brothers, Ann Arbor, Michigan in April 1985.

Contains: untitled: "O-shock of a fresh deadman . . . ," untitled: "Turned off . . . ," pp. 209. [See: *Conjunctions:* 7 (C415)].

B42   When Poetry Really Began   1986
**   It Practically Included Everything**

[On cream in brown:] WHEN POETRY REALLY BEGAN IT PRAC-TICALLY INCLUDED EVERYTHING / Transcriptions From Poetry Readings & Talks Presented as / "Poets on Poetry, Art & the Quest for Humanistic Knowledge" / at the Boise Gallery of Art / Edited by Gail Kirgis & Norman Weinstein

22.8 × 15.2cm.; 80 leaves; [one blank leaf] i–iii [iv] v–vii [viii] 1–149 [150]: blank leaf; p. i title page as above; pp. ii–iii copyright and acknowledgments; p. [iv] blank; p. v–vi introduction by Norman Weinstein; p. vii contents; p. [viii] blank; pp. 1–149 text; p. [150] blank.

Glued in pictorial ["Celestial Alphabet Event" by Jacques Gaffarel (17th century)] cream wrappers printed in brown on spine and front cover. Paper laid, printed in brown throughout. All edges trim with cover.

Publication: Published by Norman Weinstein in Boise, Idaho on December 12, 1986. Printed by Boise State University Print Shop in Boise, Idaho on December 5, 1986, in an edition of 500 copies gratis. Given as a gift with purchase through Small Press Distribution Inc.

Contains: "A talk by Clayton Eshleman about his explorations in the paleolithic caves in France." Poems included: "Dot," "Permanent Shadow," "Rhapsody," "Magdalenian," "Silence Raving," pp. 1–7.

B43   Best Minds: A Tribute to Allen Ginsberg   1986

BEST MINDS / A TRIBUTE TO / ALLEN GINSBERG / EDITED BY BILL MORGAN / & BOB ROSENTHAL / LOSPECCHIO PRESS / NEW YORK / 1986

26.3 × 18cm.; 164 leaves; [i–iv] v–xiv [xv–xvi] 1–311 [312]: p. [i] half title; p. [ii] black and white frontispiece portrait of Allen Ginsberg by Naomi Ginsberg, circa. 1948; p. [iii] title page as above; p. [iv] copyright and limitation page [states "First Edition" and:] This is Copy / [number or letter inked in over short black rule, where called for] / of the Limited Edition / [signatures linked in below, where called for]; p. v acknowledgments; p. vi blank; pp. vii–ix contents; p. x blank; p. xi introduction by Bob Rosenthal; p. xii blank; p. xiii–xiv introduction by Bill Morgan; p. [xv] excerpts from "Allen's Public School #6 Autograph Book"; p. [xvi] blank; pp. 1–311 text; p. [312] colophon. Red endpapers.

Three issues, no priority:
a. Lettered and signed with a black and white self-portrait photograph by Allen Ginsberg tipped-in on page [312] signed by the poet. 26 copies priced at $125.00 a copy. Black cloth stamped in gilt on spine and front cover; all edges trimmed. False headbands. Paper: wove. Issued without dust jacket.

b. Same as above except numbered and signed on limitation page by the editors; lacks tipped-in portrait. 200 copies priced at $75.00 a copy.

c. Same as above except unsigned and unnumbered. 500 copies; 250 hors commerce copies for the writers of these tributes, and 250 copies priced at $25.00 a copy.

Publication: Published by Bill Morgan of the Lospecchio Press in New York on June 3, 1986. Colophon: This first printing of *Best Minds* is published on

June 3, 1986 and is limited to an edition of / 226 copies, 200 of which are numbered and signed by the editors and 26 of which are let- / tered A to Z and signed by the editors and Allen Ginsburg and contain an additional self- / portrait photograph by the poet. In addition, 500 contributors' [sic] copies in special binding / have been printed, 250 of which are numbered and 250 of which are hors commerce / copies for the writers of these tributes.

Contains: "A Note on Allen Ginsberg," pp. 103–104.

B44   The Poet Exposed   1986

[Rule] / THE / [rule] / POET / [rule] / EXPOSED / [rule] / Portraits by Christopher Felver / Prologue by Gary Snyder / Foreword by Robert Creeley / Afterword by William E. Parker / [publisher's device] / ALFRED VAN DER MARCK EDITIONS [dot] NEW YORK

31.2 × 23.5cm.; 72 leaves; [i–vi] 7–9 10–144: p. [i] half-title; p. [ii] blank; p. [iii] title page as above; p. [iv] copyright page, (states "First printing June 1986); p. [v] dedication; p. [vi] blank; p. 7 prologue by Gary Snyder; pp. 8–9 foreword by Robert Creeley; pp. 10–144 text and afterword by William E. Parker. White endpapers.

Two bindings, no priority as follows:
a. Dark grey cloth stamped in silver on spine and cover. All edges trimmed. False headbands. Paper: wove.

Dust jacket: glossy black paper printed in white on spine, pictorial front and back printed in white; photograph of Christopher Felver by Jay Daniel on inside back flap. 1500 copies priced at $26.95 a copy.

b. Same as above except: 30.4 × 23.1cm.; glued in stiff glossy black wrappers; [cover same as dust jacket except, in upper left corner of back cover:] $16.95 [inside a white rectangle, printed in black, in lower right corner of back cover:] ISBN 0-912383-23-2. [3500 copies priced at $16.95 a copy].

Publication: Published by Alfred Van Der Marck Editions in New York in June 1986. Printed in Italy by Poligrafiche Bolis, Bergamo. Photographic printing: Professional Photographic Services, Eddie Dyba [slash] Timothy Berman, San Francisco.

Contains: Portrait photograph of Clayton Eshleman by Christopher Felver on p. 84, "Un Poco Loco" (reproduced from Eshleman's holograph, signed and: dated, L.A. 1980), p. 85.

B45   Table-Talk Press: Five Broadsides   1986

[Cover title, white paper label, in blue:] TABLE-TALK PRESS / Five Broadsides / Philip Whalen / Leslie Scalapino / Clayton Eshleman / Diane Wakoski / Michael McClure / Santa Barbara, California / 1985–1986

36.8 × 26.8cm.; five loose leaves, most with lower edge uncut; paper: Rives.

Blue striped cloth over boards, white label as above. Five loose broadside poems by five poets. Designed and printed by three different printers, David Dahl (one broadside), Graham Mackintosh (one broadside), and J. Mudfoot (three broadsides).

Publication: Published by Michael K. Sherick of Table-Talk Press in Santa Barbara, California June 3 1986. Portfolio designed, bound, and printed by Judyl Mudfoot in Santa Barbara, California, 1986.

14 portfolios, (one for publisher, one for printer) and 12 portfolios for sale priced at $100.00 each portfolio.

Contains: "Reagan at Bitberg." [See A 70].

B46   Talking Poetry   1987
Conversations in the Workshop with Contemporary Poets

[One thin rule] / [one thick rule] / Talking Poetry / Conversations in the Workshop / with Contemporary Poets / Lee Bartlett / UNIVERSITY OF NEW MEXICO PRESS / ALBUQUERQUE / [one thick rule] / [one thin rule]

24.1 × 16.3cm.; 156 leaves; [i–vi] vii–x 1–295 [296–302]: p. [i] half-title; p. [ii] blank; p. [iii] title page as above; p. [iv] copyright page [states "First edition"]; p. [v] contents; p. [vi] quote from Charles Olson; p. vii–x preface; p. 1–295 text; pp. [296–302] blank. White endpapers.

Two bindings, no priority as follows:
a. Grey cloth stamped in red gilt on spine. All edges trimmed; false headbands. Paper wove.

Red dust jacket printed in black and white on spine and front; white ground printed in black on back cover. 522 copies priced at $29.95 a copy.

b. Same as above except: 23.4 × 15.2cm.; glued in wrappers reproducing the dust jacket described above, with back cover reproducing the front and back flaps of dust jacket but lacking photograph of Lee Bartlett. 1,491 copies priced at $15.95 a copy.

Publication: Published by the University of New Mexico Press April 12, 1987. Printed by Thompson Shore in February, 1987. Designed by Joanna V. Hill

Contains: An interview with Clayton Eshleman; a brief biography; portrait of Clayton Eshleman from a photography by Nina Subin; "The Lich Gate," "Equal Time," "For Aimé Césaire," "Fracture," "Manticore Vortex," pp. 40–63.

B47   Michigan Broadsides   1987

[Title leaf, laid in loose, of stiff blue paper, in white:] [printer's device] / [on a black rectangle in white:] MICHIGAN / [on a thick white rule, in black:] Broadsides / [in two columns in white:] [in left column:] Charles Baxter / Ann Arbor / Andrew Carrigan / Saline / Nicholas Delbanco / Ann Arbor / Michael Delp / Interlochen / Jack Driscoll / Interlochen / Stephen Dunning / Ann Arbor / Clayton Eshleman / Ypsilanti / Linda Nemec Foster / Grand Rapids / Dan Gerber / Fremont / Conrad Hilberry / Kalamazoo / Janet Kauffman / Hudson [in right column:] Josie Kearns / Flint / Elizabeth Kerlikowske / Kalamazoo / Ken Mikolowski / Grindstone City / Kofi Natambu / Detroit / Danny Rendleman / Flint / Herbert Scott / Kalamazoo / Marc Sheehan / Lansing / John Sinclair / Detroit / Richard Tillinghast / Ann Arbor / Eric Torgersen / Mt. Pleasant / Diane Wakoski / East Lansing [a white half-hand print on upper left and a complete hand print on lower left, each partially on the black rectangle].

30.4 × 22.8cm.; 23 loose leaves of varying sizes, colors and papers [Gainsburough, Teton, and Filare all 80% cover weight] which include: two 15.2 × 11.4cm. broadsides, tan; nine 22.8 × 15.2cm. broadsides: two blue, three tan, and four grey; eleven 30.4 × 22.8cm. broadsides: three blue, four grey, and four tan; one title leaf as described above with copyright on verso.

Two issues, no priority as follows:
a. Issued in a stiff blue four leaf fold-over case sealed in center with white wax. Each leaf has been signed by its author [some numbered by them]; the copyright page is numbered and signed by Patrick A. Smith, Keith Taylor, Christine A. Golus and Marla H. Smith. 25 numbered sets priced at $30.00 a set.

b. Same as above except: unnumbered, unsigned issued in plastic "zip-lock" bag instead of blue case. 500 sets priced at $10.00 a set.

Publication: Published by Pat Smith and Keith Taylor of the OtherWind Press in Ann Arbor, Michigan on September 18, 1987. Printed at Kolossos Printing of Ann Arbor, Michigan 1987. Designed by Christine A. Golus.

[Note: The Eshleman broadside, which was not issued seperately, is as follows: 30.4 × 22.8cm.; [on blue, printed in black:] BUDDHA HEAD / for Nina Subin / [27 line poem] / Clayton Eshleman / 24 Nov 1986 / [a white print]. Paper: Gainsburough].

Contains: "Buddha Head"

B48   Paul Blackburn: The Parallel Voyages   1987

a. First edition, first printing:

[Double spread title page, on grey, in black:] THE PARALLEL VOYAGES / Paul Blackburn [in blue outline: a drawing of three birds] [on recto:] [in blue outline: a drawing of three birds] / [in black:] Selected and introduced by Clayton Eshleman / Edited and annotated by Edith Jarolim / Drawings by Ellen McMahon / Sun Lizard Book Number Three / [in outline, a drawing of a lizard] / SUN-gemini Press / Tuscon, Arizona, 1987

26 × 21cm.; 68 leaves; [i-viii] 1-123 [124-128]: p. [i] blank; pp. [ii-iii] title pages as above; p. [iv] copyright and acknowledgments; pp. [v-vi] contents; p. [vii] Paul Blackburn quote; p. [viii] blank; pp. 1-12 Introduction and Notes by Clayton Eshleman; p. [13] illustration by Ellen McMahon; p. [14] blank; pp. 15-123 text; p. [124] brief biography of Paul Blackburn; p. [125] illustration by Ellen McMahon; p. [126] blank; p. [127] colophon; p. [128] blank. (errata leaf laid in loose); blue endpapers.

Two bindings, no priority as follows:
a. Tan morocco over navy blue cloth, gilt stamped navy blue morocco spine label. 24 copies, 4 are hors commerce, 20 copies (numbered I-XX) were for sale priced at $200.00 a copy.

b. Same as above except: yellow, blind stamped on front and back covers, grey spine label printed in blue and black; paper: Ingres Antique silver-grey; uncut; false headbands. 53 copies, 10 are hors commerce, 43 copies (numbered 1-43) were for sale priced at $100.00 a copy.

Publication: Published by Clint Colby of Sun-gemini in Tucson, Arizona in 1987. Printed by Charles Alexander at Chax Press, Tucson, Arizona in 1987. Designed by Clint Colby and Charles Alexander. Colophon: Printed in an edition of 77 copies of which- / 14 copies (10 in cloth, 4 in quarter leather) are *hors commerce,* / 43 copies, numbered 1–43, are bound in full cloth, / 20 copies, numbered I–XX, are bound in quarter leather and are / signed by Clayton Eshleman and Edith Jarolim. Number inked in.

c. Second printing:

Same as a. except: 21.6 × 15.1cm.; glossy yellow wrappers, printed on spine, front and back cover in black; offset. A corrected copy without the errata. Colophon: This offset edition of 1000 copies was printed by Fabe Litho, Tucson, / and was Smythe sewn by Roswell Bookbinding, Phoenix. [1,000 copies priced at $8.95 a copy.]

Contains: Introduction and Notes by Clayton Eshleman.

B49   New Directions 51   1987

[Superimposed over large grey N D in black:] New Directions in Prose and Poetry 51 / [on white:] Edited by J. Laughlin / with Peter Glassgold and Grieselda Ohannessian / [publisher's device: a drawing by Heinz Henghes] A New Directions Book

20.9 × 14.2cm.; 96 leaves; [i–vi] 1–186: p. [i] half-title p. [ii] dedication; p. [iii] title page as above; p. [iv] copyright page [states: "First published clothbound (ISBN: 0-8112-1033-2) and New Directions Paperbook 644 (ISBN: 0-8112-1034-0) in 1987"]; pp. [v–vi] contents; pp. 1–186 text. White endpapers.

Two bindings, no priority as follows:
a. Black cloth stamped in silver on spine and stamped in blind on front cover. All edges trimmed. Paper: wove.

Red dust jacket printed in black and white on spine, front, and back cover. 750 copies priced at $23.95 a copy.

b. Same as above except: 20.2 × 13.2cm.; glued in stiff glossy red wrappers; [cover same as dust jacket except: back cover, which gives information from inside dust jacket flaps, deletes:] NEW DIRECTIONS 80 EIGHTH AVENUE NEW YORK 10011 [and adds:] A NEW DIRECTIONS PAPERBOOK

NDP644 / [inside white rectangle:] FPT ISBN 0-8112-1034-0 $11.95 [2500 copies priced at $11.95 a copy].

Publication: Published for James Laughlin by New Directions Publishing Corporation in New York, in 1987. Published simultaneously in Canada by Penguin Books Canada Limited.

Contains: "Children of the Monosyllable," pp. 54–57. (See C457.)

**B50   Contemporary Authors: Autobiography Series   1988
        Volume 6.**

ISSN 0748-0636 / Contemporary / Authors / Autobiography Series / Adele Sarkissian / Editor / volume 6 / GALE RESEARCH COMPANY [dot] BOOK TOWER [dot] DETROIT, MICHIGAN 48226

28.6 × 22cm.; 228 leaves; [1–4] 5 [6] 7–11 [12–14] 15–329 [330–338] 339–453 [454–456]: p. [1] half-title; p. [2] blank; p. [3] title page as above; p. [4] copyright page; p. 5 contents; p. [6] blank; pp. 7–10 preface; p. 11 Authors Forthcoming in CAAS; p. [12] blank; p. [13] half-title; p. [14] blank; pp. 15–329 text; pp. [330–336] blank; p. [337] divisional title; p. [338] blank; pp. 339–453 cumulative index; p. [454–456] blank. White endpapers.

Blue, pink, purple and black cloth printed in white on spine and front cover. All edges trimmed; false headbands. Paper wove. Issued without dust jacket.

Publication: Published by Gale Research in Detroit, Michigan in November 1987, in an edition of 3000 copies priced at $88.00 a copy.

Contains: Autobiographical essay, illustrated with photographs of the poet and his family; bibliographical list including poetry, translations, and editorship of magazines [through 1986], pp. 123–150.

C. Contributions to Periodicals

1959

C1 "Us." *Folio* Vol. XXIV, #1, Winter 1959. p. 48. This 14 line poem, C.E.'s first appearance in print, is in the Indiana University student literary magazine which was edited by Aubrey Galyon with C.E. listed as associate editor.

C2 "Cat," "We." *Bread* #1, August 1959. np.

C3 "Guernica." *Collage Art Journal* Fall 1959. p. 76.

1960

C4 "You Might Say," "Degas: The Absinthe Drinkers," pp. 31–32. Pablo Neruda: "The Law of Wine," (translated from the Spanish by Walter Compton and C.E.) "Taste," (translated from the Spanish by Walter Compton, C.E. and Cecila Ugarte). "Ode to Frederico Garcia Lorca," (translated from the Spanish by Al Perez and C.E.) pp. 48–61. *Folio* Vol. XXV, #1, Winter 1960. [C.E. is listed as editor of the magazine, with cover design by William Paden who designed the cover of *Caterpillar* 13. (See D14, C151) and who did the woodcut illustrations for *Brother Stones* (See A11)].

C5 "Word for the Magician's Wife." Pablo Neruda: "Walking Around," "Sonata and Destructions," (translated from the Spanish by C.E.). *Hip Pocket Poems* #1, n.d. (ca. Winter 1960). np.

C6 "Lament for October." *Poetry Dial* Vol. #1, Wintertime n.d. (c. 1960–61). p. 46.

C7 César Vallejo: Four Poems: "The Spider," (translated from the Spanish by C.E.); "The Hungry Man's Rack," (translated from the Spanish by C.E. and Maureen Lahey). *Folio* Vol. XXV, #3, Summer 1960. pp. 6–12. [On inside back cover:] PLEASE NOTE: with the Summer issue (Volume XXV–3) the English / Department of Indiana University will discontinue the publication of FOLIO. / A new poetry journal is being planned by the present editor, Clayton / Eshleman, and will be publicized in the fall of 1960. (See D3.)

C8 Pablo Neruda: from *Residence in the Earth:* "Ritual of My Legs," (translated from the Spanish by C.E.). *Beatitude* Number 17, Oct–Nov. 1960. np. [Note: The table of contents has intentionally mis-spelled the authors names, Clayton Eshleman becomes Clayton Echelon (sic)].

C9 From *Mexico & North:* "I (Caletilla Beach)," "II (Caleta Beach)," "III (Envoi: 1960)." *Hip Pocket Poems* #3, December 1960. np.

C10 Pablo Neruda: "Withdrawal," "There's No Forgetting," "Dream Horse," (translated from the Spanish by C.E.) *San Francisco Review* #7, December 1960. pp. 15–18.

C11 Pablo Neruda: "Lone Gentleman," "Death," (translated from the Spanish by C.E.). *Big Table* Vol. II, #5, 1960. pp. 74–77.

C12 "The Roaches." *Trobar* 1960. pp. 6–7.

1961

C13 "Evocation," "Danger." Pablo Neruda: "Serenade," "Barcarola," "Sick in My House," (translated from the Spanish by C.E.). *Coastlines* 17, Vol. 5, #1, 1961. pp. 9–15.

C14 Pablo Neruda: "Alberto Rojas Jimenes Comes Flying," (translated from the Spanish by C.E.). *Damascus Road* #1, 1961. pp. 37–40.

C15 "The Strong." *Trobar* 3, 1961. p. 27.

C16 Pablo Neruda: "Melancholy in the Families," (translated from the Spanish by C.E.). *The Nation* Vol. 192, #7, February 18, 1961. p. 149.

C17 "The End," "A Come On," "A Very Old Woman." *San Francisco Review* #8, March 1961. pp. 11–13.

C18 "The Hitch-Hiker." *The Nation* April 29, 1961. p. 380.

C19   "Amadeo's Women." *Poetry Dial* Vol. 1, #2, Spring 1961. p. 32.

C20   "Red Shoes." *The Outsider* 1, Fall, 1961. p. 86.

C21   Pablo Neruda: from *Residence in the Earth:* "Autumn Returns," (translated from the Spanish by C.E.). *Chelsea* 10, September 1961. pp. 97–98.

C22   Pablo Neruda: from *Residencia En La Tierra:* "Next to Each Other," "Unity," (translated from the Spanish by C.E.). *Mica* 4, Fall 1961. pp. 27–28.

C23   Aimé Césaire: "Among Other Massacres," "The First Problem," "Son of Lightning," (translated from the French by C.E.). *San Francisco Review* #10, December 1961. pp. 49–50.

C24   "Son of Lightning," "Little Song for a Departure." *Choice* 2, 1962. pp. 16–17.

C25   "Dark Blood." *Chelsea* 11, March 1962. pp. 51–52.

C26   "Prothalamion." *San Francisco Review* 11, March 1962. pp. 16–21.

C27   "Inheritance," "Las Brujas." *El Corno Emplumado* 2, April 1962. pp. 16–17.

C28   "The Kingdom," "Taiwan." *Orient-West* Vol. 7, #5, May 1962. pp. 71–72.

C29   "Fire!" *Mica* 6, June 1962. pp. 28–29.

1963

C30   Pablo Neruda: from *Residencia En La Tierra:* "Unidad," "Sabor," "Tango Del Viudo," (translated from the Spanish by C. E.) *El Cornodo Emplumado* #5, January 1963 pp. 36–38. Also a letter to the editor dated Kyoto-October 22, 1962 re: poetry criticism, p. 153.

C31   "The Translation," "The Crocus Bud," pp. 21–25. Letter to the editor from C.E. dated 17 May 1963, titled: "Tsuhyginomiya," re: *El Corno Emplumado* issue #6. *El Corno Emplumado* #7, July 1963. pp. 177–78. There is also an unsigned letter to the editor re: Eshleman's translation of Neruda's *Residence In (sic) The Earth* dated 2–15–63.

C32 "The U.S. Army," from *Mexico & North:* "Water Song." *Burning Water* Fall 1963. pp. 55–56.

C33 Comments by Eshleman on the composition of Mr. Motohiro Takiuchi. *So 'E Sez* Vol. II, #3, November 1963. [a Matsushita English Newsletter of Matsushita Electric Industrial Company, Ltd. Kodoma, Osaka, Japan, Educational & Training Dept.]. p. 7.

1964

C34 "Barbara Sick," "The Leg." *Coyote's Journal* No. 1, 1964. pp. 8–9.

C35 "One Morning," untitled: "I am taking a walk...," *Origin* 12 (Second Series) January 1964. p. 37.

C36 from "The Book of Coatlicue." *Matter* #2, July 1964. np.

C37 César Vallejo: from *Poemas Humanoes — Human Poems:* untitled: "At last, without that good repetitive smell...," untitled: "He goes running, wandering, fleeing...," untitled: "Heated up, tired, I'm off with my gold...," untitled: "O bottle without wine...," (translated from the Spanish by C.E.). *Burning Water* Winter 1964 pp. 15–18.

C38 "Seppuku," "The Koreans," "The Second," "February 25," "The Ascent." *Poetry* Vol. 103, No. 6, March 1964. pp. 359–363.

C39 César Vallejo: untitled: "Desire ceases, tail to the air...," untitled: "Something identifies you...," untitled: "No one now lives in the house...," untitled: "A woman with peaceful breasts...," untitled: "In sum, I've got it in me...," untitled: "Exists a man mutilated...," "I Am Going to Speak of Hope," "Discovery of Life," "Common Sense," "Violence of the Hours," untitled: "The windows have been shaken...," (translated from the Spanish by C.E.). *Origin* 13 (Second Series) April 1964. pp. 48–61.

C40 César Vallejo: from *Poemas Humanos:* untitled: "It's here today I salute...," untitled: "Confidence in the eyeglass...," untitled: "Caviling at life...," untitled: "A column supporting solace...," "The Hungty Man's Rack," untitled: "It was Sunday in the pale ears of my burro...," untitled: "Today I love life much less...," untitled: "Alfonso you're looking at me...," untitled: "Considering coldly, impartially...," "Stumble Between Two Stars," "Black Stone on a White Stone," "Two Gssping Children," untitled: "Sweetness by sweetness crowned...," untitled: "Contrary to the birds of the hill...," untitled: "There're days there comes to me...," "Anniversary," untitled: "What gets into me that I'm whipped with the line...," untitled: "And if after so many words...," "Hat, Coat, Gloves," untitled: "And get off my back about...," (translated from the Spanish by C.E.). pp. 29–47. [An introduction to these peices is supplied by William Paden]. (Review:) *Twenty Poems of Cesar Vallejo*. (translated by John Knoepfle, James Wright, Robert Bly), pp. 88–93. (Review:) *Alain Bosquet: Selected Poems*. (translated by Samuel Becket, Charles Guenther, Edward Roditi and Ruth Whitman), p. 102. *Kulchur* Vol. 4, No. 14, Summer 1964.

C41   "Tomorrow's Lunch," "The Life," "Working Vallejo (III)," "First Morning in a New Back Yard," *Burning Water* Fall 1964. pp. 19–20.

1965

C42   "The Water-Closet," "After Love." *Burning Deck* 4, Spring 1965. pp. 171–72.

C43   César Vallejo: from *Poemas Humanos:* untitled: "Hot, tired, I'm off with my gold...," "Letter to the Transient," untitled: "My chest wants and doesn't want...," untitled: "Until the day in which it turns...," "Paris, October 1936," "Death Sermon," untitled: "Of pure heat I'm freezing...," untitled: "Walk stript, naked the millionaire...," "The Soul that Suffered Being It's Body," untitled: "Who will come has just passed...," "Palms and Guitar," "The Fallen," "Height and Hair," "Guitar," untitled: "Starved with pain...," untitled: "The anger that breaks man into children...," "Bone List," untitled: "Between pain and pleasure...," untitled: "Four consciences...," "The Gravest Moment in Life," (translated from the Spanish, with a note by C.E.). *Kulchur* Vol. 5, No. 17, Spring 1965. pp. 39–56.

C44   "The Book of Coatlicue," "The Stones of Sanjusangendo," "Poem, Note & Statement," (poem and essay:) "Notes on Nightmare." *El Corno Emplumado,* 14 April 1965. pp. 7–18.

C45   "Tsuruginomiya (I)," "Sungate." *From A Window* Number Two, June 1965. np. [Note: the table of contents states that these three poems "...will appear in *Gatetime;* however this book was never published]..

C46   "The Book of Yurunomado." *Poetry* Vol. 106, No. 4, July 1965. pp. 257–269.

C47   "The Creation," "Death and Transfiguration." *Work* 1, Summer 1965. pp. 5–8.

C48   (Review) Raquel Jodorosky: *Ajy Tojen* [which appeared in *El Corno Emplumado* No. 12, 1964]. *Kulchur* Vol. 5, No. 19, Autumn 1965. pp. 96–97.

C49   "Vallejo en Engles: Escribe: César Lavano." [includes a photograph of C.E.; biography; quotes C.E.]; "Puerta del Sol," ("Sun Gate," done into Spanish by César Levano). *Caretas*, November 10–22, 1965. p. 62.

C50   "The Flyer" *Some/thing* 2, Winter 1965. pp. 52–54.

C51   "Book of Niemonjima: Third Movement." *Imago* (four), n.d. (c. 1965–66). pp. 3–8.

1966

C52   César Vallejo: from *Poemas Humanos:* "Tuberous Spring," untitled: "He is running, walking, fleeing...," "Epistle to the Pedestrians," untitled: "My chest wants and doesn't want...," untitled: "Finally, a mountain...," untitled: "It was Sunday in the fair ears of my burro...," untitled: "Until the day I return...," untitled: "From disturbance to disturbance...," "Tulluric and Magnetic," (translated from the Spanish by C.E.). *Origin* 2 (Third Series) 1966. pp. 43–52.

C53   "Hand." *El Corno Emplumado* No. 17, January 1966. p. 33.

C54   "Las Piedras De Sanjusangendo," ("The Stones of Sanjusangendo"). Translated into Spanish by Carlos Germán Belli. *Ciempies* No. 2, April 1966. np.

C55   César Vallejo: 5 poems from *Poemas Humanos:* (all untitled:) "Mocked on a stone...," "This happened between two eyelids...," "Mocked, acclimatized to good...," "Contrary to those mountain birds...," "Life, this life...," (translated from the Spanish by C.E.). *Tish* 36, May 18, 1966. pp. 2–6.

C56   "The Rehab Contrary." *Work* 4, Summer-Fall-Winter 1966. pp. 3–4.

C57   "Explorations in the A-Political," (essay). *The Nation* Vol. 203, #9, September 26 1966. pp. 285–287. [The story of C.E.'s assignment in Lima, Peru, to publish "Quena" and his troubles with censorship].

C58   "Near Cieneguilla," "Stele," "The Hill." *Haravec* #1, November 1966. pp. 21–23.

C59   César Vallejo: untitled: "There comes over my days...," (translated from the Spanish by C.E.) *East Village Other* Vol. 1, #23, November 1–15, 1966.

C60   "Poem to Accompany Mary." *Poetry* Vol. 109, No. 2, November 1966. pp. 75–76.

C61   "Rehab," "Tsuruginomiya (I)." *Camels Coming* 6, December 1966. np.

C62   "Hand," "Violent Sunset," "Hibernaculum (II)." César Vallejo: from *Poemas Humanos:* untitled: "I have a terrible fear of being an animal...," (translated from the Spanish by C.E.). *Maps* 1, n.d. (c. 1966–67). np.

C63   "October 9: Cycle." *Island* 7–8, n.d. (c. 1966). pp. 62–64.

C64   "Walk I," "Walk III." *Grist* 12, n.d. (c. 1966–67). pp. 22–23.

C65   "The Recognition," "The Parent-Power." "Tsuruginomiya (III)." *From a Window* n.d. (This issue states: "The Swan Song" c. 1966–67). np.

C66   "Bud Powell." (essay). *For Now* 6, n.d. (c. 1966). pp. 18–19. [A tribute to the jazz pianist, Bud Powell].

C67   "The Dreyer St. Joan." *For Now* 7, n.d. (c. 1966). pp. 12–13.

1967

C68   "A Note for the World." *The World* 6, 1967. np.

C69   From "The Book of Eternal Death." *The Genre of Silence 1967. (see B4).*

C70   César Vallejo: "Old Asses Thinking," (translated from the Spanish by C.E.). *Camels Coming* #7, 1967. p. 3.

C71   "Washington Square Park," untitled: "Writing you, to...," untitled: "You'll never...," [three peices from "Adrienne Messenger."] *City Two*, 1967. pp. 4–5.

C72   "Burn, Baby Burn." (essay). *The International Times* #9, February 27–March 12, 1967. pp. 6, 12. [Sub-title: A Proposal to the North American People.].

C73 "Walk (I)," "Walk (V)," "Walk (VIII)." *Haravec* #2, March 1967. pp. 52–55.

C74 "The Book of Niemonjima," (first movement). *Tish* #40, March 6, 1967. pp. 7–12.

C75 "The Caterpillar." *Kauri* #19, March–April 1967. p. 11.

C76 (Untitled) "You'll never...," *Hika* Spring 1967. p. 7.

C77 "Sense of Beauty in New Ireland." César Vallejo: (untitled) "Starved with pain, solomonic, proper...," "Wedding March," (translated from the Spanish by C.E.). *Potpourri* IX, Spring 1967. np.

C78 Translating Vallejo. (essay) including César Vallejo: "Intensity and Height," (translated by C.E., English and Spanish given). *The Nation* April 24, 1967. p. 540.

C79 "Burn, Baby Burn: A Proposal to the North American People." (essay) *Open City* Vol. 2, #1, May 5-11, 1967. p. 2. [Re-printed from *The International Times* #9, February 27–March 12, 1967.] (See C72).

C80 "After Han-san," "July 15." *The Aligraph* May 1967. np.

C81 "O Apollonian." *Maps* 2, May 1967. p. 30.

C82 "A Marriage Song for Denis and Kathy." *Kauri* 20, May–June 1967. p. 35.

C83 "The Sylvia Likens Poem." *Kauri* 21, July–August 1967. p. 5.

C84 "The Goddess (II)," "The Quarter," "For Cid Corman," "The Sense of Beauty in New Ireland," "The Heavens Over Tsuruginomiya." *New Measure* 6, Summer 1967. pp. 34–39.

C85 "Meditation Out of Hart Crane." *Hanging Loose* 3, Summer 1967. [loose unnumbered pages, rectos only].

C86 "The Book at War." *El Corno Emplumado* 24, October 1967. pp. 50–57.

C87 "Test of Translation II." [an essay which includes: César Vallejo: untitled: "A man is watching a woman...," (translated from the Spanish by

C.E.)]. *Caterpillar* 1, October 1967. pp. 99–102. [This essay (part of a series of essays on translation to appear in future *Caterpillar* magazines) also includes the translation of the above poem by Lillian Lowenfels and Nan Braymer (from: *Modern Poetry From Spain And Latin America.* Corinth, 1964), with comment by C.E.]. (See: D4).

C88   "Nonomiya," "Sensing Duncan," "To Crane," "Little Moon Worm," "Poem." *Poetry* Vol. III, #2, November 1967. pp. 76–81.

C89   "Lines for the Bread and Puppet Theatre Dramatic Production of Bach's Cantata 140." *The World* 8, 1967. np.

C90   "The Mill." *the* 2, n.d. (c. 1967). np.

C91   "Stele." *Poets For Peace* 1967. pp. 20–21. ("Poets who were at the 3 hour poetry reading at St. Mark's Church in the Bowerie (sic) climaxing The Poets Fast For Peace, January 13–14, 1967, some of whom did not get to read their poems" [from: *Poets For Peace]*). (See B5).

1968

C92   César Vallejo: 9 poems from *Poemas Humanos:* untitled: "The point of the man . . . ," untitled: "This happened between two eyelids . . . ," "Farewell Remembering a Goodbye," untitled: "Chances are, I'm another . . . ," "The Book of Nature," "Pantheon," "Two Anxious Children," untitled: "A man is watching a woman . . . ," "The Nine Monsters." pp. 5–17. (essay:) "A Note on 'Fuses'" [a film by Carolee Schneemann with stills in *Caterpillar* 2]. pp. 18–19. "The Bank," "The Origin," pp. 35–40. "A Test of Translation IV: Basho," comment by C.E. pp. 62–65. *Caterpillar* 2, January 1968. (See: B9, D5).

C93   "The Woman From Tasilli," "The Orange Gate." *Kauri* 24, January–February 1968. p. 5.

C94   "Bear Field." *The Lit* 5, February 22, 1968. pp. 11–13.

C95   "The Matisse 1914 Colligure," "The Caterpillar." *The Lit* 6, March 18, 1968. pp. 9–10.

C96   "The Moistinsplendour," pp. 238–270. Aimé Césaire: from *Les Armes Miraculeuse:* "The Miraculous Arms," (translated from the French by C.E. & Denis Kelly). pp. 144–146. *Caterpillar* 3–4, April–July 1968. (See D6).

C97   César Vallejo: from *Poemas Humanos:* untitled: "The fact is the place where I put on my . . . ," (translated from the Spanish by Clayton Eshleman). *East Village Other* Vol. 3, #23, May 10, 1968. p. 11.

C98   "Theseus Ariadne," *The Lit,* 7, May 1968. np.

C99   César Vallejo: from *Human Poems:* "The Soul that Suffered from Being Its Body," "Height and Hair," "Black Stone on a White Stone," untitled: "There comes over me days a feeling. . .," "The Starving Man's Rack," (translated from the Spanish, with an introductory essay by C.E.) *Evergreen Review* #55, June 1968. pp. 23–25.

C100   (untitled:) "Ibuki Masuko tonight again walking. . .," *Io* #5, Summer 1968. p. 91.

C101   "The Bedford Vision," pp. 26–30. Note on content of magazine, note on Wright review of Pablo Neruda, p. 139; (reviews of:) D. Alexander: *Mules Balk,* pp. 141–142; Lynne Banker: *Rain,* p. 141; *Basho: Back Roads To Far Towns* (translated by Cid Corman and Kamaike Susumu), p. 142; Carol Berge: *Poems Made Of Skin,* p. 144–5; note on Philip Corner's Commentary on the Midrash, p. 146; (reviews of:) Wilhelm Reich: *Reich Speaks Of Freud,* pp. 148–51; Diane Wakoski: *Greed,* pp. 152–3; Robert Kelly: *Finding The Measure,* p. 154. *Caterpillar* 5, October 1968. (See D7).

C102   "Visionary Note on César Vallejo," pp. 75–81; César Vallejo: from *Poemas Humanos:* untitled: "And if after so many words. . .," "Let the Millionaire Walk Naked," "Farewell Remembering a Goodbye," "The Nine Monsters," "A Bone Catalogue," untitled: "There comes over me days a feeling so abundant. . .," pp. 75–81. *Caw* #1, February 1968.

C103   "Two Struggling Blacks," pp. 63–64. *Chelsea* 24–25, October 1968.

C104   César Vallejo: "Loin of the Scriptures," untitled: "The accent hangs from my shoe. . .," untitled: "Today a splinter has entered her. . .," "Gleb," (translated from the Spanish by C.E.) *Contemporary Literature In Translation* #1, n.d. (c. 1968). pp. 15–18.

C105   "The House of Okumura XIV," "Hymn 2." *El Corno Emplumado* 28, October 1968. pp. 79–82.

C106   "Public Bath," *Gnosis* Fall 1968. p. 5.

C107   "The Sepik River Ode," *Helicon* Vol. 6, #2, 1968. pp. 53–54.

C108   "Belsen." *The Lit* 9–10, n.d. (c. 1968). pp. 17–18.

C109   "X Glyph on the 9th Maximus." *The Literary Magazine of Tufts University* Vol. 3, #2, Spring 1968. pp. 13–16.

C110   "Poetry," "The Black Hat," "Cantaloups and Splendour," *Odda-Tala* 1, 1968. np.

C111   "Enter August Night Raga." *Odda Tala* 2, 1968. np.

C112   "The Book of Barbara." *Poetry* May 1968. pp. 109–115.

C113   "Marie Valentine." *Origin* 10 (third series) July 1968. pp. 45–46.

C114   "On Mules Sent from Chavin." *Some/thing* 4–5, Summer 1968. pp. 42–71.

C115   "The 1802 Butts Letter Variation." *The South Florida Poetry Journal* Fall 1968. pp. 11–13.

C116   "The Yellow Garment." *Sou'wester* Vol. 11, #2, Fall 1968. pp. 62–63.

C117   "Eshleman Raps," [an interview with Clayton Eshleman, visiting poet, after his poetry reading at the University of Indiana]. *The Spectator* November 12, 1968. [University of Indiana student paper]. pp. 8–9.

C118   "The Book of Niemonjima." *Stony Brook* 1–2, Fall 1968. pp. 65–69.

C119   "Translating César Vallejo: An Evolution," pp. 55–82. César Vallejo: (all untitled:) "It was Sunday in the fair ears of my burro...," "The point of the man...," "But before all this lady runs out...," "Today I like life much less...," "The Windows have been shaken...," "The one who will come...," (translated from the Spanish by C.E.). *TriQuarterly* 13–14, Fall–Winter 1968. pp. 84–91. (See B7).

C120   "V Night ii." *Vincent The Mad Brother of Theo* #2, 1968. np.

C121   "Sogipo," untitled: "Tonight the window's open...," [mis-titled in this magazine as "The Matisse 1914 Colligure"] "My anus...," [an untitled poem also mis-titled as "Human Universe" in this magazine] *Work* 5, 1968. pp. 2–4.

C122   "Hymn 27." *the 4* n.d. (c. 1968). np.

1969

C123   "Hand." *Evergreen* #62, January 1969. p. 29.

C124   from: "The Lay of Phi Delta Theta," sections 1–5, pp. 58–65. (Reviews:) *Concrete Poetry: A World View.* edited by Mary Ellen Solt, p. 136. Cid Corman: *In Good Time.* pp. 155–157. *Caterpillar* 6, January 1969. (See: B9, D8).

C125   "Watchtowers," "The Taylor Shop," "The Red Mantle," "The Shelf," untitled: "Why get angry...," untitled: "Two tiny cockroaches...," "Fang of Eden," "Sensing Duncan V," pp. 100–111. (Reviews:) Allen Ginsberg: *Planet News.* p. 239: Carlos Castaneda: *The Teachings of Don Juan,* pp. 240–241; Gilbert Sorrentino: *The Perfect Fiction,* pp. 246–247; Cid Corman: *Words for Each Other,* pp. 247–248; Robert Kelly: *Axon Dendron Tree,* pp. 249–252; *Black Elk Speaks,* as told through John G. Neihardt, pp. 231–232. *Caterpillar* 7, April 1969. (See D9).

C126   "The Book of the Formation of Mercy." *Gnosis* Spring 1969. p. 12.

C127   "Neruda: An Elemental Response," (essay), pp. 228–237. Ricardo Paseyro: "The Dead World of Pablo Neruda" (essay, translated from the Spanish by Clayton Eshleman) pp. 202–227. *TriQuarterly* 15, Spring 1969.

C128   "Blood." *Lampeter Muse* Vol. III, #IV, Spring 1969. pp. 22–25.

C129   "Sunday Afternoon." *Sumac* Vol. I, #3, Spring 1969. pp. 45–48.

C130   "Dinosaurs." *Lampeter Muse* 1969. pp. 8–9.

C131   "Ode to Autumn." pp. 49–55, "An Open Letter to George Stanley, Concerning the State of Our Nation, The American Spiritual Body, Which I First Glimpsed in Peru. pp. 145–149. *Caterpillar* 8–9, July–October 1969. (See: B9, D10).

C132   "Diagonal," "Hymn 3," "Hymn 5." *The Park* 4–5, Summer, 1969 [also known as *The Wivenhoe Park Review].* pp. 82–88.

C133   "Datura." *The World* 16, 1969. np.

C134   "Night Entering Vala August Intensity Raga." *Bricoleur* September, 1969. np.

C135   "The King I." *Roots Forming* 2, Fall 1969. pp. 7–9.

C136   "The House of Okumura: VI: A Tale," "The House of Okumura: VII: Commentary." *Ant's Forefoot* #3, Winter 1969. pp. 7–10.

C137   "Diagonal." *Sumac* Vol. II, #1, Fall 1969. pp. 110–113.

C138   "Soutine." pp. 95–98. (Review) Robert Kelly: *Songs* I–XXX, p. 389. *Stony Brook* 3–4, 1969.

C139   "Chords." *Big Venus* 1969. p. 1.

C140   "The Post-Office," untitled: "You are surprised to see me...," "The Shoe-Shop," untitled: "Jeanetta, you came in...," "Ochre." *Big Big Venus* 1969. pp. 1–5.

C141   "Cyclings." pp. 18–29. Short letter by Clayton Eshleman to editor (Kirby Congdon) regarding Robert Kelly's poetry. p. 85. *Mag* 4, 1969.

C142   "The Moat." *the* 6, n.d. (c. 1969–1970). np.

1970

C143   (Untitled:) "A Caldron on the Blackburn table...," "The Mountain," "The Plum." pp. 105–117. A letter from C.E. to Peter Quartermain, pp. 236–240. (Review) Gary Snyder: *Earth House Hold.* pp. 216–220. *Caterpillar* 10, January 1970. (See D11).

C144   "Altars," "Racepoint." *Sumac* Vol. 2, #II & III, Winter–Spring 1970. pp. 54–58.

C145   "Segments." *Corpus* Vol. I, #4, February 1970. np.

C146   "The Gates of Capricorn," "The Rapture," "The Scolopender." *Caterpillar* 11, April 1970. pp. 26–49. (See: B9, D12).

C147   from: "The Lay of the Phi Delta Theta." *Writing* 4, May 6–13, 1970 (also known as *Georgia Strait Writing Supplement*). p. 12.

C148   "Marie Valentine," (translated into Japanese by Obata Mitsumasa) *Ho Sen* [a translation of the Japanese characters on the front cover, which mean *"The Sailing Boat"*] June 3, 1970. [A Japanese literary magazine, the work it contains is taken from *Origin* 10 (third series) July 1968 and is given in the original English with a Japanese translation]. pp. 13–15.

C149   (untitled:) "I pressed the red...," *Origin* 18 (third series) July 1970. p. 59.

C150 (Essay) "Who is the Real Enemy of Poetry?: An Open Letter to George Stanley Concerning the State of Our Nation, the American Spiritual Body, Which I First Glimpsed in Peru." *L.A. Free Press* Part II, September 11, 1970. pp. 49, 56.

C151 "October Notations." *Caterpillar* 13, October 1970. pp. 42–45. (See D14).

C152 "The Cusp." *Vigilante* 2, Fall 1970. pp. 4–7.

C153 "Visions of the Sons of Cancer." *Sumac* Vol. 2, #IV, Fall 1970. pp. 16–19.

C154 "Soliloquy For Tom Meyer." *Lampeter Muse* Vol. V, #1, Fall 1970 pp. 36–39.

C155 "The Meadow." *Tree* 1, Winter 1970. pp. 96–100.

C156 "Heaven Bands 1–42." *Io* Winter 1970. pp. 128–136.

C157 "V Night." *Maguey* 3–4, Winter 1970. pp. 8–11.

C158 "Ode to Reich." *Big Venus* #4, *(Queen Camel)* 1970. np.

C159 "Kansas-Illinois." *Arts In Society* 1970. pp. 261–263.

C160 "Heaven Bands 43–72." pp. 51–62. (Review) John Berryman: *His Toy, His Dreams, His Rest.* pp. 79–80. *The Minnesota Review* Vol. X, #1, 1970.

C161 "Draft for the Moat," "The Moat." *Opus* VIII, 1970. p. 34.

C162 "Feet," "Mint," "Children's Games," "Merton," *The South Florida Poetry Journal* 4–5, 1970. pp. 18–22.

C163 "Hymn 3," "Comment." *Choice* 6, 1970. p. 6.

C164 "Ode to Reich," "Lustral Waters from the Spring of Aires." *Tansy* 2, n.d. (c. 1970). pp. 13–22.

C165 "Female Will." *the* 9, n.d. (c. 1970–71). np.

1971

C166 "The Overcoats of Eden," pp. 9–13. "The Golden String," pp. 140–141. *Caterpillar* 14, January 1971. (See D15).

C167   "The Golden String." *Earth Ship* 3, February–April 1971. p. 4.

C168   "The Stan Brakhage Altarpiece." *Athanor* Vol. I, #1, Winter–Spring 1971. pp. 61–65.

C169   "In Memoriam, Paul Celan." *Sumac* Vol. 3, #III, 1971. p. 79.

C170   "The Baptism of Desire," pp. 83–87. "Notation on Fielding Dawson's *The Black Mountain Book*" (in poem form), pp. 286–287. *Caterpillar* 15–16, April–July 1971. (See D16).

C171   "The Bridge at the Mayan Pass." *Madrona* Summer 1971. pp. 15–17.

C172   "The Tourbillions." *Crazy Horse* 8, September 1971. pp. 24–25.

C173   "Trenches." *Caterpillar* 17, October 1971. pp. 113–117. (See D17).

C174   "In Memorian, Paul Blackburn." *The Nation* October 25, 1971. p. 410.

C175   "The Snake's Lover," (A new working of a South American Indian poem by Clayton Eshleman and Halma Cristina Perry). *Alcheringa* 3, Winter 1971. pp. 51–57.

C176   "Notation on the Amber Necklaces Poured into the Stomach's Cave." *Sumac* Vol. 3, #II, Winter 1971. pp. 144–150.

C177   "Commentary." *Rain* 1–2, 1971. pp. 80–82.

C178   "To the Angel." *Toothpick, Lisbon & The Orcas Islands* 1971. np.

C179   "Passion." *Io* 8, 1971. pp. 220–226.

C180   "The Diamond." *Second Aeon* 15, n.d. (c. 1971–72).

1972

C181   (Review) "In Defense of Poetry: *Neruda and Vallejo: Selected Poems.*" Edited by Robert Bly. Translated by Robert Bly, John Knoepfle & James Wright. *Review* 72, Winter–Spring 1971–1972. pp. 39–47.

C182   "Brief Hymn to the Body Electric." *Aux Arcs* 2, Spring 1972. p. 83.

C183   "Laocoon." *Open Reading* 1, March 1972. pp. 22–24.

C184   "Credo." *The Nation* March 6, 1972. p. 317.

C185   "Poet-Teachers on the Teaching of Poetry: A Symposium." (Clayton Eshleman, with other poetry teachers: Phillip Darce, Greg Juzma, Morton Marcus, Dabney Stuart, Stephen Dunn, Peter Cooley, Van K. Brock, Michael Dennis Browne, and Anselmo Hollo). *Journal of English Teaching Techniques* Vol. 5, #5, Spring 1972. pp. 1–13. [C.E. pp. 8–9].

C186   Artaud, Antonin: *Artaud Le Momo:* "The Return of Artaud the Mômo," "Mother Center and Kitty Owner," "Insult to the Unconditioned," "The Execration of the Father-Mother," "Madness and Black Magic." (French and English versions given with translations from the French by Clayton Eshleman. "A Note on The Mômo" by Clayton Eshleman). *Caterpillar* 18, April 1972. pp. 32–77. (See D18).

C187   (Review) Bern Porter: *Found Poems. Library Journal* Vol. 97, #14, August 1972. p. 2611.

C188   (Review) *Finding The Center: Narrative Poetry Of The Zuni Indians.* Translated by Dennis Tedlock. *Library Journal* September 1, 1972. p. 2737.

C189   (Review) Wole Soyinka: *A Shuttle In The Crypt. Library Journal* September 1, 1972. pp. 2737.

C190   (Review) Nicolás Guillén: *Man-Making Words: Selected Poems.* Translated, annotated & introduction by Robert Marquez & David Arthur McMurray. *Library Journal* September 15, 1972. pp. 2845, 2847.

C191   (Review) Al Levine: *Prophecy In Bridgeport And Other Poems. Library Journal* October 15, 1972. p. 3318.

C192   "Coils." pp. 135–148. César Vallejo: "Hymn to the Volunteers for the Republic," pp. 121–126, (translated from the Spanish, with a translator's note, by Clayton Eshleman). *Caterpillar* 19, October 1972. (See D19).

C193   "Octopus Delivery." *Poetry Review* Vol. 63, #4, Winter 1972–73. p. 353–357.

C194   "Origin." *Sesheta* 4, Winter 1972–73. pp. 70–77.

C195   "The Emerald." *Tree* #3, Winter 1972. pp. 82–84.

C196   "The Cusp." *The World* 24, Winter 1972. np.

C197   "Hearing Bruckner." *Hellcoal Annual* Two, 1972. p. 14.

C198   "Left Hand of Gericault." *Salamander* 1972. pp. 56–59.

C199   "Prayer at the Trunk." *Equal Time* 1972. p. 14.

C200   "Her Eyes Are Stables Filled with Bleeding Cattle," untitled: "It seems to me a god she is...," *Circular Causation* #11, 1972. np.

C201   "Coils." pp. 165–175. Letter from C.E. to Peter Finch. pp. 203–204. *Second Aeon* 16–17, n.d. (c. 1972).

1973

C202   "Origin," with an Introduction to "Origin." *Los* Vol. I, #1, April 1973. pp. 4–9.

C203   "Adhesive Love." pp. 85–95. César Vallejo: "Spanish Image of Death," (translated from the Spanish by C.E. and José Rubia Barcia). pp. 8–9. *Caterpillar* 20, June 1973. (See D20).

C204   César Vallejo: "Cortege After the Capture of Bilbao," (translated from the Spanish by C.E. and José Rubia Barcia). *The World* #27 April 4 1973. p. 72.

C205   (Essay) "César Against Vallejo." *Parnassus* Vol. I, #2, Spring–Summer 1973. pp. 38–41.

C206   César Vallejo: from: *Spain Take This Cup From Me:* (untitled:) "Malaga without father nor mother...," "Winter During the Battle for Tervel," (translated from the Spanish by C.E. and José Rubia Barcia). *Sesheta* 5, Summer 1973. pp. 25–28.

C207   "Soutine," (fragment, translated into French by J. Guglielmi). pp. 34–48. "Sept Poètes de *Caterpillar*" (mentions *Caterpillar* magazine and presents translation of the work of seven poets published in the magazine). pp. 28–60. *Action Poetique* 56, December 1973.

C208   "To the Creative Spirit." *Sixpack* 6, Winter 1973–74. pp. 14–19.

C209 "Mokpo." *Hellcoal Annual Three* 1973. p. 35.

C210 "Hart Crane," "California." *Stooge* 9, n.d. (c. 1973–74). np.

C211 "Van Gogh," "Hart Crane," "For Hans Bellmer, Paralized." pp. 106–109. César Vallejo: "A Short Prayer for a Dead Loyalist Hero," (translated from the Spanish by C.E. & José Rubia Barcia). p. 175. *Second Aeon* 19–21, n.d. (c. 1973–74).

C212 "Sugar." *Poetry Review* Vol. 64, #4, 1973–74. pp. 341–344.

1974

C213 "Charlie Parker," "Hart Crane," "Van Gogh." pp. 557–561. "A Mint Quality," a review of Paul Blackburn: *Early Selected Y Mas,* (with introduction by Robert Kelly); and Paul Blackburn: *Peire Vidal:* (with introduction by George Economou). pp. 640–648. *Boundary* 2, Spring 1974.

C214 Letter by C.E. in response to Diane Wakoski's column in *American Poetry Review* Vol. 2, #5, September–October 1973. *American Poetry Review* Vol. 3, #2, 1974. pp. 53–54.

C215 "T.R." César Vallejo: from: *Poemas Humanos:* untitled: "Standing on a stone...," untitled: "And if after so many words...," (translated from the Spanish by C.E. and José Rubia Barcia). *The Yale Lit.* 143, April 1974. pp. 60–62.

C216 "En le tumba de Vallejo," (translated into Spanish by José Rubia Barcia). *Mester* (Numero 2), Abril de 1974. pp. 125–126.

C217 "The Gull Wall." pp. 128–141. "Tequila," (written with Paul Blackburn). pp. 32–36. *Sixpack* 7–8, Spring–Summer 1974.

C218 (Review) *America A Prophecy.* Edited by George Quasha & Jerome Rothenberg. (See B14). *Poetry Information* 11, Autumn 1974. pp. 27–34.

C219 "Gargoyles." *Fiction International* 2–3, 1974. pp. 111–112.

1975

C220 (Essay: autobiographical article). *Journal L.A.: Institute of Contemporary Art* Number 4, February 1975. pp. 22–23.

C221   "Narration Occurring in the Life of Caryl Eshleman," February 1975." *The Back Door* 7–8, Spring 1975. pp. 46–57.

C222   "The Gull Wall." *Boundary* 2, Vol. III, #3, Spring 1975. pp. 761–773.

C223   "Portrait of Frances Bacon." Arthur Rimbaud: "Le Bateau Ivre," (translated from the French by C.E.) *Stooge* #13, Spring 1975. np.

C224   "A Vist from Paul." *Truck* #15, Spring 1975. pp. 170–171.

C225   (Reviews) *Cesar Vallejo: Spain, Let This Cup Pass From Me.* Translated by Alvaro Cardona-Hine. pp. 61–63. Jeremy Reed: *Posthumous But Still Living.* pp. 39–40. Paul Vangelisti: *Air.* pp. 40–41. *Poetry Information* 12–13, Spring 1975.

C226   "Portrait of Francis Bacon," (untitled:) "Leon Golub working on a painting. . .," *Journal L.A. Institute of Contemporary Art* #6, June–July 1975. pp. 26–29.

C227   "The Female Gate." *Margins* #23-25-26, September–October–November 1975. pp. 49–50.

C228   "Portrait of Charlie Parker." p. 60. Interview with C.E. by Pierre Joris. pp. 49–59. *Sixpack* #9, Fall 1975.

C229   "Bud Powell." *Gravida* Vol. 2, #1, Winter 1975. pp. 40–41.

C230   Letter (in poetic form) from C.E. to Ronald E. Wray, editor of *Primer.* Letter to C.E. from Ronald E. Wray. *Primer* 1, December 1975. p. 1.

C231   (Review) *America A Porphecy.* Edited by George Quasha & Jerome Rothenberg. (See B14). *The Shore Review* #14, 1975. pp. 112–120.

C232   "Robert Duncan," "Rotunda." *Poetry Review* Vol. 66, #1, 1975. p. 42.

C233   "My Gargoyle." *Los* I, 1975. pp. 35–36.

C233a   "A Vision of Robert Peters Metamorphosing Into Ann Lee," p. 27. Antonin Artaud: "Letter on Nerval" translated by Clayton Eshleman, pp. 4–7. *Margins* #27, December 1975.

1976

C234 (Untitled:) "Unexpectedly this morning I grasped...," *Bezoar* Vol. 3, #3, Summer 1976. np.

C235 César Vallejo: from *Payrll Of Bones:* untitled: "Today I would like to be happy...," untitled: "Today I like life much less...," "Epistle to the Transients," from *Sermon On Savagery:* untitled: "Chances are, I am another...," untitled: "One pillar holding up...," untitled: "My chest wants and does not want...," (translated from the Spanish by C.E. and José Rubia Barcia). *Pequod* Vol. 2, #1, Summer 1976. pp. 83–88.

C236 "Drafts of 'For Milena Vodickova'." *La-Bas* #3, October 1976. np.

C237 "Translating Vallejo." (A review of:) *César Vallejo: España, Aparta De Mí Esta Cáliz.* Translated by Alvaro Cardona Hine. Includes: César Vallejo: from *Battles:* untitled: "Malaga without father nor mother...," (translated from the Spanish by C.E. and José Rubia Barcia, and another version translated by Alvaro Cardona Hine). *Invisible City* #18–20, October 1976. pp. 31–32.

C238 "36 Variations on Shiki's 'furukabe no sumi ni ugokazu harami gumo'." *The Spirit That Moves Us* Vol. 2, #1, Fall 1976. pp. 38–39.

C239 César Vallejo: from *Poemas Humanos:* "I Am Going to Speak of Hope," "Discovery of Life," untitled: "A woman with peaceful breasts...," "Height and Hair," "Epistle to the Transients," untitled: "And don't say another word...," "Black Stone on a White Stone," "Until the Day on Which I Return," "Life, This Life," untitled: "Today I would like to be happy willingly...," untitled: "The Miners came out of the mine...," untitled: "But before all this happiness ends...," (translated from the Spanish by C.E. and José Rubia Barcia). *Latin American Literary Review* Vol. IV, #9, Fall–Winter 1976. pp. 144–165.

C240 "A Climacteric," "The Cogollo," untitled: "There is something in him...," untitled: "Making love to you this morning..." *Shell* 1, Fall–Winter 1976. pp. 101–106.

C241 "Some Recent American Poetry." (Reviews of:) Theodore Enslin: *The Median Flow (Poems 1943–73.): Synthesis:* and *Landler.* Louis Zukofsky: *"A" 22 & 23.* Frank Samperi: *The Prefiguration; Quadrifariam; Lumen Gloria.* Robert Kelly; *The Loom. Poetry Information* #16, Winter 1976-7. pp. 30–38.

C242 "Dummies," "Still Life, With Fraternity," "36 Variations on Shiki's 'furukabe no sumi ni ugokazu harami gumo'." pp. 31–37. (Essay) "A Note on the N.E.A. Poetry Fellowships." pp. 79–83. *Text* Winter 1976–77.

C243   "The Dragon Rat Tail," pp. 58–61. "Study for a Portrait of Hans Bellmer," pp. 190–191. Michel Deguy: from *Figurations:* "Histories of Relapses," (translated from the French by C.E.). pp. 181–184. *Curtains* #14–17, 1976.

C244   "The Sandstone Gate." *American Poetry Review* Vol. 5, #4, 1976. pp. 18–19.

C245   "Variations Done for Gary Synder." *New Directions* #33, 1976. pp. 160–163. (See B24.)

C246   "Portrait of Diane Wakoski." *Margins* #28–29–30, 1976. p. 129.

1977

C247   "Archai," "Archai Link." *New Wilderness Letter* Vol. 1, #1, January 1977. np.

C248   "At the Tomb of Abigdor Kara," "After the Second Death." *Pearl* #3, Spring 1977. pp. 12–13.

C249   César Vallejo: from *Payroll of Bones:* untitled: "Upon reflecting on life . . . ," untitled: "Oh bottle without wine . . . ," untitled: "This happened between two eyelids . . . ," untitled: "I stayed on to warm up the ink in which I drown . . . ," untitled: "Alphonso, you keep looking at me . . . ," "Farewell Remembering A Goodbye," untitled: "Chances are, I am another . . . ," (translated from the Spanish by C.E. and José Rubia Barcia). *Boundary* 2, Vol. 5, #3, Spring 1977. pp. 743–751.

C250   "36 Variations on Shiki's 'furukabe no sumi ni ugokazu harami gumo'," "The English Department of the Spirit," "The Wood of Isis." *Montemora* 3, Spring 1977. pp. 41–46.

C251   "Study for a Portrait with Norman," "Study of a Shadow," "Eternity," "School Days Turned Around," "7 Scenes from the Life of Peter Bleguad," "Assassin," "The Cogollo," "Lines Driving South." *Primer* 3, April 1977. pp. 9–22.

C252   (Essay) "A Note on the Malcolm Parr Review of the Dorn Brotherston Vallejo Translation." *Poetry Information* #17, Summer 1977. pp. 84–87.

C253   "The Dragon Rat Tail," untitled: "For your father she said...,"
Pequod Vol. 2, #3, Summer 1977. pp. 26–35.

C254   Horrah Pornoff [pseudonym for Clayton Eshleman] (untitled:)
"When I hear St. Sebastian I hear Frida Kahlo...," *Fag Rag* 20, Summer
1977. p. 10.

C255   "Jalapa." *Impact* Vol. 1, #3, September 1977. pp. 79–80.

C256   Horrah Pornoff [pseudonym for Clayton Eshleman] Drafts from
"Homuncula:" (all untitled:) "Sometimes I look...," "A dice game behind the
office...," "The play I wanted to put on with Adrienne Rich...," "Ass iffy
nation...," "Adrienne, how much you remind me of the poet...," "The
problem in the Mr-Sisterline...," "Second-rate people excite me...," "Frida
Kahlo on my mind...," "Moat where men walk on water...," "To think is
to be sucked back...," "Compressed charwoman- I said to a fire hydrant...,"
"Lorca in Goya-light...," "I was turned in...," "A secretary, leg crossed...,"
"Out on the beach, at Ocean Park...," "I think of my cell with its plateglass
side...," "Feel soft tonight, less wounded...," "Rational, to put myself this
way...," "Aimé Césaire, like Frida Kahlo...." *Momentum* #9–10, Fall 1977.
pp. 3–29.

C257   (Essay by Clayton Eshleman on Jack Spicer:) "The Lorca Working." *Boundary* 2, Vol. 6, #1, Fall 1977. (Jack Spicer issue). pp. 31–49.

C258   César Vallejo: from *Payroll Of Bones:* untitled: "The fact is that the
place where I put on...," (translated from the Spanish by C.E. and José
Rubia Barcia). *California State Poetry Quarterly* Vol. 5, #1, Fall 1977. pp. 6–7.

C259   César Vallejo: from *Poemas Humanos:* untitled: "The windows
shuddered...," "Epistle to the Transients," "Glebe," untitled: "Sweetness for
heart sown sweetness...," untitled: "It was Sunday in the clear ears of my
jackass...," untitled: "And if after so many words...," untitled: "Idle on a
stone...," (translated from the Spanish by C.E. and José Rubia Barcia). *Text*
2, October 1977. np.

C260   "Portrait of Charlie Parker," (selected by Pierre Joris). *Anglo-
French Poetry Translation* October 1977. pp. 88–89.

C261   "Study for a Self-Portrait," "Study of a Shadow." *Boundary* 2, Vol.
5, #2, Winter 1977. pp. 552–555.

C262   "The Woman Who Saw Through Paradise." *Flute* Winter 1977. np.

C263   "Allelula Choruses," "Ixcuina." César Vallejo: untitled: "Considering coldly, impartially . . . ," untitled: "There exists a man mutilated not from combat . . . ," (translated from the Spanish by C.E. and José Rubia Barcia). *River Styx* #2, Winter 1977. np.

C264   "Rancid Moonlight Hotel." *Sarcophagus* IV, December 1977. pp. 54–55.

C265   (Untitled:) "So much feeling about September . . . ," "August Senex." *Text* 3, December 1977. np.

C266   "Tholos." *Jargon* #66, 1977. (A Festschrift for Basil Bunting). np.

C267   Antonin Artaud: "The Theatre of Cruelty with 2 Post-Scriptums and Open Letter to the Reverend Father Laval." (Translated from the French, with a note by C.E. and Norman Glass). *The Bitter Oleander* Vol. 2, #2, 1977. pp. 53–70.

C268   "And Now?" "Barter," "Old Jewish Cemetary," "At the Tomb of Abigdor Kara," untitled: "This Doctor Urbanova . . . ," [On cover: "BE ZOA RRRRRRRR!"—Clayton Eshleman]. [Also on cover: ". . . for the point in talking about any poet / is not dates nor even his meanings, but his / meanings as crowbar to pry open more life." —C.E.]. *Bezoar* n.d. (c. 1977). np.

1978

C269   "A Climateric," untitled: "Unexpectedly this morning . . . ," "Still-Life, with Manson." pp. 100–102. César Vallejo: from: *Payroll Of Bones:* untitled: "For several days I have felt . . . ," "Clapping and Guitars," untitled: "A man walks by with a stick . . . ," (translated from the Spanish by C.E. and José Rubia Barcia). pp. 34–38. *Impact* Vol. 1, #4, February 1978.

C270   "Satanas." *Lettera* Vol. 15, Quanderno 3, Febbraio 1978. pp. 26–31. (An international magazine, published in England). [See: *Poetry In English Now,* B29].

C271   Michel Deguy: "Prose," (translated from the French by C.E.). *Text* 5, April 1978. np.

C272   César Vallejo: from: *Poemas Humanos:* untitled: "Until the day I will return . . . ," untitled: "It was Sunday in the clear ears of my jackass . . . ," untitled: "Life, this life . . . ," untitled: Today I would like to be happy . . . ," untitled: "Idle on a stone . . . ," "Telluric and Magnetic," untitled: "I stayed on to warm up the ink . . . ," untitled: "Mocked, acclimatized to goodness . . . ," untitled: "Alfonso, you keep looking at me . . . ," untitled: "I have a terrible fear of being an animal . . . ," (translated from the Spanish by C.E. and José Rubia Barcia, with an introduction by C.E.) *Ecuatorial* #1, Spring 1978. pp. 2–21. (Note: while Eshleman's introduction calls for 12 poems, I have checked these translations and there were only 10 printed in this journal).

C273   "Still-Life, with Manson," "1945." *Helicon* Spring 1978. pp. 30–31.

C274   "Joseph." *Tracks* Vol. 6, #2, Spring 1978. pp. 12–13.

C275   (Review by C.E. in P.J.'s column: "Getting Around Town":) "Sleeping Beauty" performance of the Royal Ballet Company in Los Angeles, California. *The Los Angeles Enterprise* June 2, 1978 (newspaper). p. 6.

C276   "At the Tomb of Abigdor Kara," "Hearing Betty Carter," Michel Deguy: "History of Relapses," (translated from the French by C.E.). *Text* 6, June 1978. np.

C277   "A Muscular Man with Gossamer Ways," "Angry Angel," "Century Village." *Text* 8, October 1978. pp. 47–52.

C278   (Essay) Doing *Caterpillar. TriQuarterly* 43, Fall 1978. pp. 450–471. (See B27).

C279   "This I Call Holding You." *Porch* Vol. 1, #3, Winter 1978. pp. 53–56.

C280   "Joseph." *Curtains* #18–21, 1978. pp. 131–132.

C281   (Essay) "Vallejo, 1978." pp. 260–273. Milan Exner: "Elegy on the Death of a Friend," (translated from the Czech by C.E. and Jan Benda). [Note: "Milan Exner is a Czech poet, born in Northern Bohemia in 1950, due to censorship problems with the state-controlled press, these poems, in English translation, are the first appearance in print of his work." (Also see: C285, C308)]. pp. 12–14. *Montemora* 4, 1978.

1979

C282   "A Muscular Man with Gossamer Ways." *Atropos* Vol. 1, #2, Spring 1979. [Includes an interview with C.E., a photograph of Eshleman by Al Vandenberg, and a revised manuscript page of "Santanas"]. pp. 11–34.

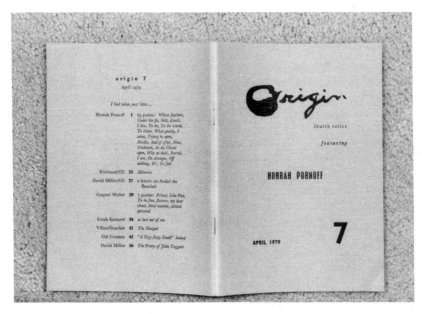

C284. Origin (fourth series) #7, April 1979

C283   "Fleuve encaissé d'un nom." (Traduction: Michel Deguy et Didier Permerle). *Art Press International* April 1979. p. 11. [Translation of "The Name Encanyoned River" from the original English into French].

C284   Horrah Pornoff [pseudonym for Clayton Eshlman:] (all untitled:) "Whose feathers do...," "Under the fly...," "Shit...," "d/eath...," "I live in the sky...," "To be an udder dripping in the lie...," "To the extent that I am injected...," "To listen to each menstrual...," "When poetry actually occurs...," "I came upon my mother, an unborn child...," "Trying to open the other...," "Needle, fabric and...," "And if after so many gods...," "Now never completes...," "Unchosen...," "As at the tee...," "Closed open...," "Why at dusk...," "Barred–Open...," "I am–said as a wave...," "On stronger, less...," "Off nothing...," "It? As if a stone...," "To feel the earth's curve...," *Origin* (fourth series) #7, April 1979. (Featuring Horrah Pornoff). pp. 1–24.

C285   "Frida Kahlo's Release." pp. 155–157. Milan Exner: "Elegy About a Postal Deliverer," (translated from the Czech by Jan Benda and C.E.); [see note, C281]; pp. 152–154. "The Poetry Business: 18 poets respond to a letter by Nathaniel Tarn," letter from C.E. pp. 106–110; letter from Michel Deguy, (translated by C.E. and Michel Deguy). pp. 110–112. Letter by C.E. to the editor (in response to a letter to the editor by Reginald Gibbons about

C.E.'s: "César Vallejo, 1978," in *Montemora* 4, 1977. See C281) "Eshleman Responds." pp. 276–277. *Montemora* 5, 1979.

C286   Aimé Césaire: "Notebook of a Return to the Native Land," (with an introduction by C.E., translated from the French by C.E. and Annette Smith). *Montemora* 6, Summer 1979. pp. 9–37.

C287   "Placements," "Statement for *New Wilderness Letter.*" *New Wilderness Letter* Vol. 2, #7, Summer 1979. pp. 21–22.

C288   "Preface to *What She Means,*" "Marelle Du Scorpion," "Meandre Souche," "Eternite," "Assassin," "Skeezix Agonistes," "Tous Les Blancs Sur Le Pont," (translated into French by Didier Pemerle, English and French versions given). pp. 11–27. Letter by C.E. (in English) to Louis Dalmas dated: 20 April, 1979 Les Eyzies de Tayac. p. 28. *PO&SIE* 10, Troisieme Trimestre 1979.

C289   "Variations Done for Jerry Rothenberg," "Century Village," *Kudos* Vol. 1, 1979. pp. 55–58.

C290   "Canso." *River Styx* 5, 1979. pp. 127–129.

C291   (Review) Ted Hughes: *Remains of Elmet. Los Angeles Times* (Book Review Section) December 9, 1979. p. 18.

1980

C292   (Review) "Ashberry Poetry—A Story Coldly Told." A review of: John Ashberry: *As We Know. Los Angeles Times* (Book Review Section) January 20, 1980. pp. 10, 11.

C293   "Cuauhxicalli." *New Wilderness Letter* Vol. 2, #8, Spring 1980. p. 42.

C294   (Review) "The Processual Poetry of Robert Kelly: Power and Perception." A review of: Robert Kelly: *Kill The Messenger. Los Angeles Times* (Book Review Section) April 27, 1980. p. 11.

C295   (Review) "The Lives and Works of 9 Poets." Reviews of: William H. Pritchard: *Lives Of The Modern Poets;* and Frank Doggett: *Wallace Stevens: The Making Of The Poem. Los Angeles Times* (Book Review Section) June 29, 1980. p. 4.

C296   "The Butterpillar," "Etruscan Vase." *Cedar Rock* Vol. 5, #3, Summer 1980. p. 10.

C297   "Poem Copied from Text Written in a Dream," and "A Note on the Poem." *Dreamworks* Vol. 1, #2, Summer 1980. pp. 150–151.

C298   (Review) "Hughes: As the 'Crow' Flies": A review of: Ekbert Faas: *Ted Hughes: The Unaccommodated Universe. Los Angeles Times* September 17, 1980. Part V. p. 10.

C299   (Review) "Dark Clouds Over the Isle of Skye." A review of: Richard Hugo: *The Right Madness On Skye. Los Angeles Times* (Book Review Section) September 21, 1980. p. 14.

C300   (Review) "Lawrence Durrell: Bitter Fruits Collected." A review of: *Lawrence Durrell: Collected Poems 1931–1974. Los Angeles Times* October 20, 1980. Part V. p. 10.

C301   "A Small Cave." p. 11. "In Fog." p. 68. *The Madison Review* Vol. 3, #1, Fall 1980.

C302   "Our Lady of the Three-Pronged Devil," "Tartaros," "Permanent Shadow." *Poetry L A* #1, Fall–Winter 1980. pp. 6–13.

C303   Aimé Césaire: "Magic," "The Oricous Have the Floor," "The Law Is Naked," "Velocity," "Among Other Massacres," "The Griffin," "Mississippi," "Blues of the Rain," To Africa," (translated from the French by C.E. and Annette Smith). *Ba Shiru* (A Journal of African Languages & Literature) Vol. 11, #2, 1980. pp. 106–113.

C304   "The Lich Gate," [with a note on "The Lich Gate"], "Mother's Comb," "Self-Portrait," "Ramapithecus." *Bachy* 17 1980. pp. 19–20.

C305   (Review) "The Not-So-Naked Nature Revealed in Whitman's Life." Review of: Justin Kaplan: *Walt Whitman, A Life. Los Angeles Times* (Book Review Section) December 7, 1980. pp. 1, 11.

C306   (Essay) "Narration Hanging from the Cusp of the Eighties." *The Difficulties* 1, 1980. np.

C307   "In Memory of Wallace." *Jazz* 6, 1980. pp. 26–27.

C308   "Hades in Manganese," pp. 63–69. Aimé Césaire: "Les Pur-Sang," (translated by C.E. and Annette Smith, with a note on Césaire's

"Miraculous Weapons" by C.E.). pp. 97–113. Milan Exner: "Elegy on the Eternal Bum in the Heart of Bohemia," (translated from the Czech by Jan Benda and C.E.). [Note: the original Czech is given, as well as the English translation. The first time an Exner poem has appeared anywhere in Czech, (also see: C281, C285)]; pp. 114–121. *Montemora* 7, 1980.

C309 Antonin Artaud: "The Theatre of Cruelty," "Postscriptum," (translated from the French, with a note, by C.E. and Norman Glass). *New Wilderness Letter* Vol. 2, #9, 1980. pp. 9–16.

C310 "Master Hanus to His Blindness," "The Tourist," "Silence Raving," "Cato's Altars." *Pequod* #11, 1980. pp. 78–84.

C311 "Variations Done for Jerry Rothenberg," "The Butterpillar," "Hermes Butts In." *River Styx* #6, 1980. pp. 37–43.

C312 "Permanent Shadow," "The Distance From St. -Circ to Caravaggio," "Sound Grottos," "Interior Deposition." pp. 69–77. Michel Deguy: from: *Jumelages Suivi De Made In USA:* "Voice of the Paleontologist," "Makeup," "To Forget the Image," (translated from the French by C.E.). pp. 79–85. *Seneca Review* Vol. IX, #2, 1980–1981.

C313 (Essay) "Proteus, Poetic Experiment and Apprenticeship." *Spring: An Annual Of Archetypal Psychology And Jungian Thought* 1980. pp. 63–77.

1981

C314 (Reviews) "Russian Collections That Lose Something in the Translation." A review of: *Selected Prose And Poetry By Mikhail Kuzmin.* Edited and translated by Michael Green, and *The Demesne Of The Swan By Marina Tsvetaeva.* Edited and translated by Robin Kemball. *Los Angeles Times* (Book Review Section) January 4, 1981. p. 5.

C315 (Reviews) "Laing Couched with a New Muse." A review of: R.D. Laing: *Sonnets.* p. 11. Review of: Mary Cheever: *The Need For Chocolate.* 'Notable' p. 10 *Los Angeles Times* (Book Review Section) February 8, 1981.

C316 (Review) "Jefferson Davis: A Portrait of Tragedy." A review of: Robert Penn Warren: *Jefferson Davis Gets His Citizenship Back. Los Angeles Times* Section V. March 19, 1981. p. 24.

C317 "The Shaft." *Text* 12, March 1981. pp. 133–134. [Not listed in Table of Contents].

C318   (Review) Leland Hickman: *Tiresis 1: 9: B Great Slave Lake Suite.* *Poetry News* #8, May 1981. p. 1.

C319   (Review) "Ashbery Poems: Welding of Voices." A review of: John Ashbery: *Shadow Train. Los Angeles Times* (Book Review Section) June 7, 1981. p. 10.

C320   (Reviews) "Poetry of a Christian Holocaust Survivor." A review of: Czeslaw Milosz: *Selected Poems.* p. 10. A review of: Leslie Marmon Silko: *Storyteller.* 'Notable' p. 6 *Los Angeles Times* (Book Review Section) July 5, 1981.

C321   (Review) "Poetry Carved Out of a Frostian Mold." A review of: Peter Davison: *Barn Fever And Other Poems. Los Angeles Times* Section V. July 6, 1981. p. 8.

C322   "Preface a 'Hades En Manganese,'" ("Preface to 'Hades in Manganese'"), "Notre Dame Du Trident Du Diable," ("Our Lady of the Three-Pronged Devil"), "Ombres Permanentes," ("Permanent Shadows"), "Reperages," ("Placements"), translated into French by Jacques Durras, English and French given). pp. 23-34. "Le Ramapitheque," ("Ramapithicus"), translated into French by Barnard Bador). pp. 35-37. *In'hui* #15, 1981.

C323   (Review) "Two Poets Talking at the Same Time." A review of: *Odysseus Elytis: Maria Nephele, A Poem In Two Voices.* Translated by Athan Anagnostopoulos. *Los Angeles Times* Section V. October 16, 1981. p. 36.

C324   Bernard Bador: "Anabasis." (Translated from the French by C.E.). *Kayak* #57, 1981. p. 34.

C325   (Review) Robert Phillips: *Running On Empty. Los Angeles Times* (Book Review Section) November 8 1981. p. 6.

C326   (Review) "A Poet Who Carries Coal to an Icy World." A review of: William Bronk: *Life Supports: New and Collected Poems. Los Angeles Times* (Book Review Section) November 15, 1981. p. 1.

C327   (Review) "The Unswaddler of American Poetry." A review of: Paul Mariani: *William Carlos Williams: A New World Naked. Los Angeles Times* Part V. December 30, 1981. p. 6.

C328   "The Eyes of Shostakovich," "Maladhara," "The Spiritual Hunt." pp. 11-12. Aimé Césaire: from: *The Miraculous Weapons* "Mythology," "Have

No Mercy," "Poem for the Dawn," "Serpent Sun," "Sentence," (translated from the French by C.E. and Annette Smith). pp. 100–102. Michel Deguy: from: *Quadratures: Selected Poetry:* "Beautiful Emphases," "The Eyes," "Who What," untitled: "When the world confines . . . ," (translated from the French by C.E.). pp. 103–104. [Note: *Quadratures* was the working title of what later became *Given Giving.*] *Bachy* 18, 1981.

C329   (Review) Leland Hickman: *Tiresis 1: 9: B: Great Slave Lake Suite.* *Montemora* 8, 1981. pp. 226–227.

C330   "Frida Kahlo's Release." *The Plaza Of Encounter* 1981. pp. 70–73.

C331   "Saturos," "A Small Cave," "The Death of Bill Evans." *Ploughshares* Vol. 7, #2, 1981. pp. 68–70.

C332   "The Loaded Sleeve of Hades." pp. 182–185. Aimé Césaire: from: *Les Armes Miraculeuses:* "Batoque," (translated from the French by C.E. and Annette Smith). *Sulfur* 1, 1981. pp. 212–218. (See D21).

C333   (Essay) "Seeds of Narrative in Paleolithic Art." *Sulfur* 2, 1981. pp. 39–52. (See D22).

C334   "The Joy of Persephone" *Conjunctions* Vol. 1, Winter 1981–82. pp. 225–226. (See B33.).

1982

C335   (Essay) "Modern Poetry: Some Relations and Reflections on Poetic Polarities." *Los Angeles Times* West View February 7, 1982. p. 3.

C336   "The Arcade's Discourse on Method," "Fracture," "The Language Orphan," "The Manticore," "Homage," "Walls for the Corpse of a Vortex." pp. 47–52. Aimé Césaire: from *Ferraments:* "Ferraments," "Nursery Rhyme," "Seism," "Hail to Guinea," "Kingdom," "Monsoon-Mansion," "For Ina," (translated from the French by C.E. and Annette Smith). pp. 1–8. *Butt* #5, June 1982.

C337   (Review) "Wakoski Poetry Aging with Concrete Realities." A review of: Diane Wakoski: *The Magician's Feastletters. Los Angeles Times* (Book Review Section) July 18, 1982. pp. 11.

C338   "Diana of Ephesus." pp. 66–67. (Essay) "Paleo-Spores." pp. 155–159. *Wch Way* 4, Summer 1982.

C339   (Review) "A Braggart, Boozer, Brute–And Poet." A review of: John Haffenden: *The Life Of John Berryman. Los Angeles Times* (Book Review Section) October 10, 1982. p. 2.

C340   (Photograoh of C.E.:) Becky Cohen: The Books As An Instrument Of Performance. (18 glossy photographs of contemporary poets reading from their work). *New Wilderness Letter* #11, December 1982. [6 pages, 3 fold-out, of a photographic insert between pages 32–33].

C341   "Too Medieval," "The Terrace at Le Centenaire," "Fracture," "The Kill." pp. 53–56. [Letter to the editor by C.E. dated July 1981 in response to the 'Perception material']. pp. 94–95. Michel Deguy: "Etc," (translated from the French by Michel Deguy and C.E.). pp. 102–105. *O.ARS* 2, 1982 (Perception).

C342   "The Diamonion Taxi Driver." p. 24. Aimé Césaire: "Howling," "Different Horizon," (translated from the French by C.E. and Annette Smith). pp. 25–26. *Oink* 16, 1982.

C343   "Voluntary Prayer." *Partisan Review* Vol. XLIX, #1, 1982. pp. 137–138.

C344   Bernard Bador: "Progress," "The Call of the Caverns," "Powerlessness," "End of the Walk," (translated from the French by C.E.). pp. 20–25. Michel Deguy: untitled: "I call Muse the seesaw of the sky . . . ," "To Forget the Image," (translated from the French by C.E.) pp. 65–70. *Sulfur* 3 1982. (See D23).

C345   "Terrestrial," pp. 73–76. Aimé Césaire: from: *The Miraculous Weapons:* "Visitation," "Debris," "Tom-Tom II," "The Oubliettes of the Sea and the Deluge," from: *Solar Throat Slashed:* "Tangible Disaster," "Redemption," "Your Hair," "Noon Knives," from *Lost Body:* "Lost Body," from: *Ferraments"* . . . But There Is This Hurt," "Corpse of a Frenzy," "I Perseus Centuplicating Myself," "Tomb of Paul Eluard," (translated from the French by C.E. and Annette Smith) pp. 33–49. *Sulfur* 5, 1982. (See D25).

C346   "Talking with My Death," "The Soul of Intercourse." *Kudos* issue ten. n.d. (c. 1982). pp. 37–42.

1983

C347   Aimé Césaire: "Automatic Crystal," "Samba," "Totem," "Interlude," "Calm," "The Wheel," "All the Way From Akkad, From Elam, From Summer," "At the Locks of the Void," "New Year," "Who Then, Who Then," "Your Portrait," "Nocturne of a Nostalgia," "Precept," "Indivisible," "Wifredo Lam." pp. 1–8. (Translated from the French by C.E. and Annette Smith, English and French versions given). (Essay by C.E. and Annette Smith:) "The Poetry of Aimé Césaire: Introductory Notes." (An excerpt, entitled "The Collections," from the authors' Introduction to *Aimé Césaire: The Collected Poetry 1939–1976*. (See: A66). pp. 104–110. *Callaloo* #17, Vol. 6, #1, February 1983.

C348   Aimé Césaire: "Marine Intimacy," (translated from the French by C.E.) *Exquisite Corpse* Vol. 1, #2, February–March 1983. p. 15.

C349   Aimé Césaire: from: *Soleil Cou Coupe:* "Ode to Guinea," "Lynch," "The Tornado," "I Hail You," "Sun and Water," "Barbarity," (translated from the French by C.E. and Annette Smith). *Network Africa* Vol. 2, #6, February–March 1983. pp. 21–22.

C350   "Tantrik X-ray," "Millenium." *Epoch* Vol. 32, #2, Winter–Spring 1983. pp. 117–118.

C351   "Niemonjima," (translated into French by Pierre Joris et M. Maire). *PO&SIE* #25, Deuxieme trimestre 1983. pp. 48–58.

C352   "The Language Orphan," "They," "The Arcade's Discourse on Method." *All Area* #2, Spring 1983. pp. 140–142.

C353   "Tiresias Drinking," "Cuitlacouche." *Wrld Wr* 4, Spring 1983. np.

C354   (Essay by C.E. and Caryl Eshleman:) "France: Buried Treasure: Prehistoric Art Meets Fine Cuisine in the Dordone." *Destinations: A Traveler's Guide To Special Places Around The World.* Vol. 4, #1, Spring 1983. pp. 28–35.

C355   (Review) "The Lines of a Poetic Lifetime." A review of: *Elizabeth Bishop: The Complete Poems 1927–1979*. *Los Angeles Times* (Book Review Section) April 17, 1983. pp. 3, 12.

C356   (Essay) "Court the Winds Eye." *Artweek* Vol. 14, #25, July 16 1983. p. 8. [A review of an art exhibit of Linda Jacobson].

C357   (Review) "A Poetry of Omens and Memories." A review of: John Yau: *Corpse And Mirror. Los Angeles Times* (Book Review Section) Sunday August 7, 1983. pp. 3, 9.

C358   "Nothing Follows." *Tendril* #16, Summer 1983. p. 30.

C359   (Review) "A Poetics to Re-embed Man in the World." A review of: Charles Olson: *The Maximus Poems.* Edited by George F. Butterick. *Los Angeles Times* (Book Review Section) September 4, 1983. p. 9.

C360   (Review) "A Poet Reports on Life in the Kibbutz." A review of: Susan Tichy: *The Hands in Exile. Los Angeles Times* Part V, October 4, 1983. p. 8.

C361   "Aids." *Sapiens* #1, Fall–Winter 1983. pp. 10–11.

C362   (Poetry column edited by C.E.:) "Ill Fate and Abundant Wine." *L.A. Weekly* Vol. 6, #3, December 16–22, 1983. p. 18. (See D52).

C363   "Certification." *L.A. Weekly* February 25–March 3, 1983. p. 29.

C364   "Tomb of Donald Duck." *Bomb* #6, 1983. pp. 34–35.

C365   Antonin Artaud: "Interjections," (translated from the French by C.E. and A. James Arnold). *Bomb* #7, 1983. pp. 42–44.

C366   Aimé Césaire: from *Les Armes Miraculeuses:* "High Noon," (translated from the French by C.E. and Annette Smith). *Conjunctions* Vol. 4, 1983. pp. 212–219. (See B38).

C367   "Tomb of Donald Duck." *Correspondances* #3, 1983. pp. 67–72.

C368   "Through Breuil's Eyes." *Cream City Review* Vol. 8, #1–2, 1983. pp. 164–165.

C369   "Possession," (extrait de *Coils [Torsions],* translated into French by Pierre Joris et M. Maire). *In'Hui* #18, 1983. pp. 123–130.

C370   Aimé Césaire: "Son of Thunder," "Ex-Voto for a Shipwreck," "Millibars of the Storm," "Night Swamp," (translated from the French by C.E. and Annette Smith). *O.ARS* #4, 1983. pp. 144–146.

C371   Aimé Césaire: "Debris," "The Virgin Forest," "Another Season," "Day and Night," (translated from the French by C.E. and Annette Smith).

(One People's Grief: A Special Issue of:) *Pacific Quarterly Moana* Vol. 8, #3, 1983. pp. 65–67.

C372   "The Color Rake of Time," "Elegy," "Manticore Vortex," "Certification." pp. 52–60. Robert Marteau: "Bread and Wine," (translated from the French by C.E. and Bernard Bador). pp. 40–43. Antonin Artaud: "Letter to Peter Watson," (translated from the French by C.E., Bernard Bador, and David Maclagan). pp. 91–99. *Sulfur* 7, 1983. (See D27).

C373   (Review) John Haffenden: *The Life of John Berryman*. pp. 178–180. Michel Deguy: "Etc," (translated from the French by C. E.). pp. 109–113. (Letter by C.E. to *American Poetry Review* (not published by them) regarding: Marjorie Perloff's essay on Lowell and Berryman in the May–June *American Poetry Review* 1983). *Sulfur* 8, 1983. pp. 186–189. (See D28).

C374   Aimé Césaire: from *Ferraments:* "Emmet Till," "Statue of Lafcadio Hearn," "...On the State of the Union," "From My Stud Farms," "It Is Myself, Terror, It Is Myself," (translated from the French by C.E. and Annette Smith). *Bomb* #8, 1983–1984. pp. 50–51.

1984

C375   (Review) "The Poetry of Central Wounds, Gaping." A review of: C.K. Williams: *Tar. Los Angeles Times* (Book Review Section) January 22, 1984. p. 3.

C376   (Letter by C.E.:) "Open Letter to George Butterick." [Regarding George Butterick's review of *Fracture* in *Exquisite Corpse* Vol. 1, #12, December 1983 p. 3]. *Exquisite Corpse* Vol. 2, #1, January–February 1984. p. 4–5.

C377   (Poetry column edited by C.E.:) "Ill Fate and Abundant Wine." *L.A. Weekly* Vol. 6, #13, February 24–March 1, 1984. p. 10. (See D53).

C378   (Review) "With Love for the Muse in Charlie Parker Tempo." A review of: Robert Creeley: *Mirrors. Los Angeles Times* (Book Review Section) March 4, 1984. pp. 3, 7.

C379   (Letter on *Fracture,* by C.E. regarding Susan Shafarzek: Small Press Roundup: Best Titles of 1983 in *Library Journal* December 15, 1983. pp. 2297–2302). *Library Journal* Vol. 109, #5, March 15 1984. p. 522. [There is also an unsigned letter on *Fracture* in this issue].

C380   (Poetry column by C.E.:) "Ill Fate and Abundant Wine." *L.A. Weekly* Vol. 6, #18, March 30–April 5, 1984. p. 16. (See D54).

C381   (Poetry Column by C.E.:) "Ill Fate and Abundant Wine." *L.A. Weekly* Vol. 6, #22 April 27–May 3, 1984. p. 8. (See D55).

C382   (Essay by C.E. and Caryl Eshleman:) "Ancient Cave Art of France." *Diversion: For Physicians at Leisure* April 1984. pp. 221–228.

C383   (Essay) "Translations as Transformational Reading: Vallejo, Artaud, Césaire." *American Poetry* Vol. 1, #3, Spring 1984. pp. 68–84.

C384   (Essay by C.E. and Caryl Eshleman:) "La Pescalerie: A Jewel of an Inn Sitting Atop Treasury of Ice Age Art." *Chicago Tribune* April 15, 1984. p. 9.

C385   (Poetry column by C.E.:) "Ill Fate and Abundant Wine." *L.A. Weekly* Vol. 6, #27, June 1–7, 1984. p. 126. (See D56).

C386   (Review) "Ashes and Fire in a Tender, Durable Poetics." A review of: Hayden Carruth: *If You Call This Cry A Song. Los Angeles Times* (Book Review Section) June 3, 1984. p. 16.

C387   (Letter by C.E. to the editor:) "Several More Erections." [Includes: "Scorpion Hopscotch."] *L.A. Weekly* Vol. 6, #28, June 8–14, 1984. p. 14. [Also includes a reply by editor, Michael Ventura]. (see: G153).

C388   (Poetry column by C.E.:) "Ill Fate and Abundant Wine." *L.A. Weekly* Vol. 6, #31, June 29–July 5, 1984. p. 8. (See D57).

C389   (Poetry column by C.E.:) "Ill Fate and Abundant Wine." *L.A. Weekly* Vol. 6, #37, August 10–16, 1984. p. 18. (See D58).

C390   (Untitled:) "At her funeral...," *Electrum* #34, Fall 1984. pp. 37–38.

C391   (Review) "Life as a Poetic Puzzlement." A review of: Charles Wright: *The Other Side Of The River. Los Angeles Times* (Book Review Section) August 19, 1984. p. 7.

C392   (Review) "Adam's Rib or Goddess: A perspective on the First Lady." A review of: J.A. Phillips: *Eve: The History Of An Idea. Los Angeles Times* (Book Review Section) September 9, 1984. p. 11.

C393   (Review) "Sobbing Worms and Screaming Shoes." A review of: *Phillip Levine: Selected Poems. Los Angeles Times* Part V, September 10, 1984. p. 6.

C394   (Review) "A Poet in Praise of Other Poets." A review of: Robert Hass: *Twentieth Century Pleasures. Los Angeles Times* (Book Review Section) November 18, 1984. p. 8.

C395   (Review) "From the Trenches: A Poetic Testimony to Risk." A review of: *Wilfred Owen: The Complete Poems and Fragments.* Edited by Jon Stallworthy. *Los Angeles Times* (Book Review Section) December 23, 1984. p. 4.

C396   Antonin Artaud: from *Suppots Et Supplications:* untitled: "This book is comprised of three parts...," (translated from the French by A. James Arnold and C.E.) pp. 15–16. from: *Interjections:* "Pounding and Gism," (translated from the French by A. James Arnold, C.E., and David Maclagan). pp. 38–42. "Civil Status," (translated from the French by A. James Arnold and C.E.). pp. 43–59. *Sulfur* 9, 1984. (See D29).

C397   Bernard Bador: from *Sea Urchin Harakiri:* "Progress," "Cadaver Cracks in the Lotus Pond," (translated from the French, with a Note on Bernard Bador's Poetry by C.E.), "A Cape of Wild Flies," (written in English by Bernard Bador and edited by C. E.). *Sulfur* 10, 1984. pp. 60–67. (See D30).

C398   Untitled: "The peak of the obsidian mountain swarms...," pp. 110–112. (Essay) "A Note on Paul Celan." pp. 85–88. *Sulfur* 11, 1984. (See D31).

C399   Bernard Bador: "Checkmate," "Irritations," "Archeology," "Cancer Dreams," (translated from the French by C.E.). *Conjunctions* 6, 1984. pp. 221–222. (See B39).

C400   "The Aurignacian Summation." *Cream City Review* Vol. 9, #1&2, 1984. pp. 103–104.

C401   Untitled: "In Munch's great canvas 'Angst' the passers-by...," untitled: "In Atget's sleep the road beside the apple trees...," pp. 116–117. Michel Deguy: "Advanced Study," "Sleeping Under the Star 'N'," "Ballad," "Iaculatio Tardiva," "Poetic Air 1966," (translated from the French by C.E.). pp. 61–65. *Bluefish* Vol. II, #3–4, Autumn 1984–Spring 1985.

C402   (Art review) "At Play in the Fields of Hades: Arthur Secunda's Recent Work." *SunStorm* December 15, 1984–January 15, 1985. p. 11.

1985

C403   (Review) "Poems as a Mirror Image of Self." A review of: Judy Grahn: *The Work Of A Common Woman*. *Los Angeles Times* (Book Review Section) January 20, 1985. p. 4.

C404   (Review) *Otherwise, Last And First Poems Of Eugenio Montale*. Translated by Jonathan Galassi. *Los Angeles Times* (Book Review Section) February 24, 1985. p. 2.

C405   (Review) *Selected Poems Of Kenneth Rexroth*. *Los Angeles Times* March 31, 1985. p. 1, 10.

C406   (Review) "Rilke in French." A review of: *Rainer Maria Rilke: The Roses & The Windows, The Astonishment Of Origins, Orchards,* and *The Migration Of Powers*. Translated by A. Poulin Jr. *Los Angeles Times* (Book Review Section) May 26, 1985. p. 7.

C407   "Reagan at Bitburg." *L.A. Weekly* June 21–27, 1985. p. 128.

C408   (Essay by C.E. and Caryl Eshleman:) "France Pâte and Prehistory: The Allure of Les Eyzies." *Pan Am Clipper* Vol. 25, #6, June 1985. pp. 51–67.

C409   (Interview with C.E.:) "Bookshop Survives Storm: Chatterton's Lovers Help Celebrate Its Reopening." [A brief interview with C.E. on his patronage of the bookstore, owned by William (Koki) Iwamoto). *Los Angeles Times* Part VI, September 22, 1985. pp. 1, 14, 15.

C410   "Deeds Done and Suffered by Light." *Exquisite Corpse* Vol. 3, #9–10, September–October 1985. p. 9.

C411   "Sienna." *Cafe Solo* Series 3, #4 & 5, Summer, Fall 1985. pp. 22–23.

C412   (Letter by C.E.:) "Response." [In response to an article by Diane Wakoski: "Neglected Poets: The Attempt to Break an Old Mold — Visionary Poetry of Clayton Eshleman." In *American Poetry* Vol. 1, #3, Spring 1984]. *American Poetry* Vol. 2, #2, Winter 1985. pp. 79–82.

C413 "At Forest Lawn," "The Oven of Apollo." *Another Chicago Magazine* #12, 1985. pp. 50–52.

C414 Milan Exner: "Elegy for a Friend in a Wheelchair," (translared from the Czech by Jan Benda and C.E.). *Another Chicago Magazine* #14, 1985. pp. 45–48.

C415 Untitled: "O-shock of a fresh deadman discovering...," untitled: "Turned off...," *Conjunctions* 7, 1985. p. 209. (See B41).

C416 (Essay written by C.E. and Caryl Eshleman:) "Les Eyzies: For the Homo Sapien Who's Had His Fill of the Champs Elysies." *Frequent Flyer* (Official Airline Guides) October 1985. pp. 108–111. [The article was written on arrangement with the magazine by Clayton and Caryl Eshleman and then rewritten, retitled, and author credit changed by the magazine without their knowledge or consent, so that it is signed by Clayton Eshleman and Donald Duncan].

C417 (Essay) "Dedication." *Pequod* #18, 1985. pp. 57–60.

C418 (Interview) "An Interview with Clayton Eshleman by Michael McLaughlin." *The Southern California Anthology* Vol. 3, 1985. pp. 144–155.

C419 Vladimir Holan: from *A Night With Hamlet:* (untitled section of the poem, part 1:) "When passing from nature to being...," (translated from the Czech by C.E. and Frantisek Galan). *Sulfur* 12, 1985. pp. 4–11. (See D32).

C420 "Tuxedoed Groom on Canvas Bride." pp. 21–27. (Essay) "Response to Mary Kinzie." pp. 153–157. (Essay) "A Seifert Translation." pp. 169–172. Vladimir Holan: from *A Night With Hamlet:* (untitled section of the poem, part 2:) "The wind blustered through the chimney...," pp. 129–134. *Sulfur* 13, 1985. (See D33).

C421 "The Excavation of Artaud." p. 105. Vladimir Holan: from *A Night With Hamlet:* (untitled section of the poem, part 3:) "Orpheus: Are you glad?...," pp. 74–80. *Sulfur* 14, 1985. (See D34).

C422 Untitled: "I so much want no meaning as part of...," "Auto---." *Temblor* #1, 1985. pp. 62–63.

C423 "Ariadne's Reunion" (complete:) "Scarlet Expériment," "Placements," "In a Grove of Hanged Saviors," "The Crone," "Ariadne's Re-union," "I Blended Rose," "Deeds Done and Suffered by Light," "A Man with a Beard of Roses." *Temblor* #2, 1985. pp. 3–15.

C424   "The Natal Daemon." *The Minetta Review.* n.d. (c. 1985). pp.
18–20.

1986

C425   (Interview) "Clayton Eshleman: An Interview/Gyula Kodolányi.
Poetry Flash #155, February 1986. pp. 3–5. [Published in Berkeley, California,
the Bay Area's Poetry Calendar & Review].

C426   "Still-Life, with Grapes and Pears." *Writing* 13 February 1986.
[Vancouver B.C. New Poetics Colloquium Issue]. pp. 14–15.

C427   "A Nyelv-Árva," ("The Language Orphan"), "A Sáfrányhajtás,"
("The Crocus Bud"), "Átlók," ("Diagonal"), (translated into Hungarian by
Gyula Kodolányi). pp. 85–88. (Interview by Gyula Kodolányi with C.E.,
part 1:) Kodolányi Gyula: Psziché és Groteszk Realizmus: Beszélgetés
Clayton Eshlemannel 1. pp. 89–99. *Új írás* #5, (XXVI) Majus 1986.

C428   "Another Way Into the Maze." [editor Andrei Codrescu's title for
the prose poem "Placements II"]. p. 9. (Essay) "Orgasm Stimulates Fantasy."
p. 2. [regarding Hakim Bey's "Pornography," in *Exquisite Corpse*
November–December 1985]. *Exquisite Corpse* Vol. 4, #3–4, March–April
1986.

C429   (Interview by Gyula Kodalányi with C.E. part II:) Psziché és
Groteszk Realizmus: Beszélgetés Clayton Eshlemannel II. (Translated into
Hungarian by Gyula Kodalányi). *Új írás* 6, (XXVI) (Janius) 1986. pp.
89–95.

C430   "Reagan at Bitberg." *Friendly Local Press* Vol. II, #1, Fall–Winter
1986. p. 16.

C431   from: "Our Journey Around the Drowned City of Is": untitled:
"Dolmens curved in luscious ways...," "Postcards From Carnac," untitled:
"Then I dreamed my way to Henry Miller...," *Another Chicago Magazine* #16,
1986. pp. 10–14.

C432   "Apotheosis." (Essay) "A Visit from Hart Crane." *Caliban* I, 1986.
pp. 118–121.

C433   "Galactite." *River Styx* 20, 1986. p. 36–37.

C434   (Essay) "The Meaning of Indigenous in Vallejo." *Sulfur* 15, 1986. pp. 164–168. (See D35).

C435   Vladimir Holan: from *A Night With Hamlet:* (untitled section of the poem part 4:) "And it does last...," (translated from the Czech by C.E. and Frantisek Galan). pp. 130–137. Juan Larrea: "Thorns in the Snow," (written in Spanish), "Risk Attraction," (written in French), "On Vacation Like a Stone," (written in French), "Anxiety of Signs," (written in French), (translated from the Spanish and French by José Rubia Barcia and C.E.). pp. 121–123. (Discussion: James Hillman and Clayton Eshleman:) "Part One of a Discussion on Psychology and Poetry." pp. 56–74. *Sulfur* 16, 1986. (See D36).

C436   "The Bill." *Sulfur* 17, 1986. pp. 56–61. (See D37).

C437   "Emplazamientos II." ("Placements," translated into Spanish by Carlos Dominguez). *Syntaxis* 11, (Primavera) 1986. pp. 26–29. [The last three sections of the work are missing—note by C.E.].

C438   "Emplazamientos II." ("Placements," the last three sections, translated into Spanish by Carlos Dominguez). *Syntaxis* #12–13, Ontono 1986–Invierno 1987. pp. 82–83.

C439   (Essay) "Addenda to a Note on Apprenticeship." *Translation Review* Number Twenty, 1986. pp. 4–5.

C440   "The Tower," "Spelunking the Skeleton." *Tyuonyi* 2, 1986. pp. 15–20.

1987

C441   (Essay) "Is There, Currently, An American Poetry? A Symposium." *American Poetry* Vol. 4, #2, Winter 1987. pp. 2–40.

C442   "Notas de una Visita a Le Tuc d'Andoubert (sic)," ("Notes on a Visit to Le Tuc D'Audoubert," translated into Spanish by Julio Ortega). *Crisis* Buenos Aires, Marso 1987. pp. 46–52.

C443   "Out of Graves' Greek Myths." *Panoply* Vol. 1, #1, Winter–Spring 1987. pp. 66–72.

C444   "Variations on Jesus and the Fly," "Brown Thrasher." pp. 55–58. (Interview) "An Interview with Clayton Eshleman by Gyula Kodolányi." pp. 51–55. *B-City* 4, Spring 1987.

C445   "Gisants." *Michigan Quarterly Review* Vol. XXVI, #2, Spring 1987. p. 355.

C446   "Outtakes," "Indiana in the Night Sky." *Notus: New Writing* Vol. 2, #1, Spring 1987.

C447   Untitled: "Not one of Rilke's 'early departed'. . .," [A Tribute to Porfirio Didonna (1942–1986)]. pp. 52–53. "Brown Thrasher," "Children of the Monosyllable." pp. 109–112. *Sulfur* 19, Spring 1987. (See D39).

C448   (Interview) "An Interview by Gyula Kodolányi with Clayton Eshleman." *Talus* #1, Spring 1987. pp. 7–30.

C449   "Mistress Spirit." *Talus* 2 Autumn 1987. pp. 21–31.

C450   from *Our Journey Around The Drowned City Of Is:* "Hyperbole Sur L'Ile De Re," "Kerlescan," "La Fin De Yorunomado," (translated into French by Eric Sarner). *PO&SIE* #40, 1987. pp. 21–29.

C451   "The Sprouting Skull," "Impotence Still-Life." *Temblor* #5, 1987. pp. 34–38.

C452   "The Night Against Its Lit Elastic." *Tsunami* #1, 1987. pp. 18–20.

C453   (Essay) "Golub the Axolotl." *Temblor* #6, 1987. pp. 109–113.

C454   from "Our Journey Around the Drowned City of Is": "Kerlescan." *Dirty Bum: A Magazine* #2, Winter 1987–1988. pp. 13–16.

C455   (Essay) "Introduction to: *The Parallel Voyages By Paul Blackburn. Jimmy & Lucy's House of "K"* #8, 1987–1988. pp. 75–86.

C456   "Lemons." *Borders Review Of Books* Vol. VII, #1, February 1987. p. 6.

C457   "Children of the Monosyllable." *New Directions* 51, 1987. pp. 54–57; (see B49).

D. Books and Periodicals Edited by

(I. Magazines Edited by Eshleman)

D1   *Folio* Vol. XXV, #1, Winter 1960. 36 leaves. Includes: William Carlos Williams, Mary Ellen Solt, Cid Corman, Clayton Eshleman, Robert Kelly, Allen Ginsberg, Gregory Corso, Robert Bly, Stu Michner, Ken Goodall, Pablo Neruda (translated by Walter Compton and Clayton Eshleman). Cover design: William Paden.

D2   *Folio* Vol. XXV, #2, Spring 1960. 40 leaves. Includes: Jack Hirschman, Robert Creeley, Louis Zukofsky, Maria Stranska, Seymor Gresser, Michael Rumaker, Vladimir Mayakofsky (translated by Victor Erlich and Jack Hirschman), Mary Ellen Solt, Jerome Rothenberg, Diana Henstell, David Wade, Cid Corman, A.K. Ramanujan, Michel Leiris (translated by Emile Snyder). Cover design: William Paden.

D3   *Folio* Vol. XXV, #3, Summer 1960. 36 leaves. Includes: Robert Duncan, Andre Breton (translated by Robert Champigney), Cesar Vallejo (translated by Clayton Eshleman and Maureen Lahey), Edward Dorn, Louis Gallo, David Antin, Larry Rubin, Ingeborg Bachmann (translated by Ulrich Weisstein), Karl Krolow (translated by Ulrich Weisstein), Sylvan Karchmer, Gene Frumkin, David Wang, Charles Farber, Constantine Cavafy (translated by Konstantinos Lardas). Cover design: William Paden. (Note: This literary magazine was published three times a year at Bloomington, Indiana by the Department of English, Indiana University. Eshleman was student editor for three issues, after first serving as associate editor in 1959. He expanded the magazine to include contemporary poets as well as students, made trips to New York to meet such important authors as Louis Zukofsky, Allen Ginsberg, Robert Kelly and Jerome Rothenberg, and obtained their poetry for the magazine. In the year he edited the magazine he changed it from a local "Academic" effort to a national publication featuring "open poetry" and an awareness of 20th Century European Modernism. However, problems arose after publication of the second issue, in the winter of 1960.

D3. Folio *vol. XXV, #3, Summer 1960*

Some of the professors of the English Department resented having *Folio* become what they perceived as a vehicle for the work of "Beat" and "Black Mountain" poets, and found some of the work submitted to be "pornographic" and *Folio* funds were removed from the following year's budget. After 27 years, the publication of *Folio* was ended.)

D4   *Caterpillar* 1, October 1967. (A magazine of the leaf, a gathering of the tribes). 70 leaves. Includes: Paul Blackburn, Robert Duncan, Gilbert Sorrentino, Gary Snyder, Nancy Spero, Leon Golub, Margaret Randall, Norman O. Brown, David Henderson, Cid Corman, Diane Wakoski, Frank

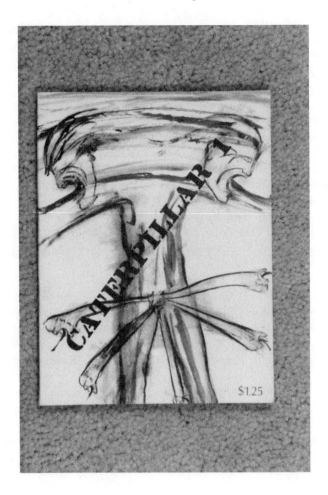

D4. Caterpillar *1, October 1967*

Samperi. Test of Translation I: Montale (translations by Robert Lowell and Cid Corman). Test of Translation II: César Vallejo (translations by Lillian Lowenfels & Nan Braymer, and by Clayton Eshleman). Cover: Nancy Spero: "The Bomb"

D5 *Caterpillar* 2, January 1968. 77 leaves. Includes: Cid Corman, César Vallejo (translated by Clayton Eshleman), Carolee Schneemann, Stan Brakhage, Clayton Eshleman, Andrei Codrescu, Michael Heller, Horst Benjamin (adapted by Rose Marie and Hayden Carruth), Armand Schwerner, Philip Corner, D. Alexander, Sam Abrams, Hugh Seidman, Ted

Enslin, Adrienne Rich, Nora Jaffe, Antonin Artaud (translated by Cid Corman), Robert Duncan. Test of Translation III: Constantin Cavafy (translations by Rea Dalven and by Dennis Kelly). Cover Carolee Schneemann: Still From "Fuses."

D6   *Caterpillar* 3/4 (double issue), April/July 1968. 136 leaves. Includes: Jack Hirschman, Sidney Chafetz, Akutagawa (English version by Will Petersen), Will Petersen, Frank Samperi, Sam Abrams, Jerome Rothenberg, Gilbert Sorrentino, Robert Kelly, Margaret Randall, E.D. Howe, D. Alexander, Stanley Nelson, Aimé Césaire (translated by Clayton Eshleman), Allen Ginsberg, George Ohsawa, Saul Gottlieb, Ted Enslin, Richard Grossinger, Michael Heller, Donald Gardner, Donald Phelps, Carolee Schneemann, Leon Golub, Gary Snyder, Lorine Neidecker, Clayton Eshleman. Test of Translation V: Catullus (translations by Louis Zukofsky, by Sam Abrams, by Peter Whigam, by Frank Copley, and by C.H. Sisson. Cover: stoneprint by Will Petersen.

D7   *Caterpillar* 5, October 1968. 80 leaves. (Contributing Editor: Robert Kelly: Assistant Editor: Hugh Seidman). Includes: Garcia Lorca versions by Paul Blackburn, Gerrit Lansing, Charles Olson, Christine La Belle, Clayton Eshleman, Jackson MacLow, Neil Meyers, Armand Schwerner, Vala, John McMaster, Helmut Heissenbuttel (translated by Rosmarie Waldrop), Yasuhiro Yoshioka, Theodore Enslin, Rilke (translated by George Quasha), David Bromige, Stephen Jonas, Jerome Rothenberg, Frank Samperi, Elaine Summers, Toby Olson, Robert Kelly, Gary Snyder, Hugh Seidman, Philip Corner. Test of Translation VII: Brecht (translations by Eric Bentley, and by Rosemarie Waldrop). Test of Translation VIII: Sappho (translations by Mary Barnard, by Robert Lowell, by Willis Barnstone, and by Guy Davenport, commentary by Tim Reynolds). Cover: Collage by Elly Antin.

D8   *Caterpillar* 6, January 1969. 80 leaves. (Contributing Editor: Robert Kelly). Includes: Charles Olson, Carl Thayer, Harvey Bialy, Jerome Rothenberg, Richard Johnny John, Bernard Forrest, Robert Duncan, Gerrit Lansing, Michael McClure, Joe Early, Stanley Nelson, René Daumal (translated by Cid Corman), Clayton Eshleman, Jack Hirschman, Larry Eigner, Greg Orr, D. Alexander, Jess, Kenneth Irby, Diane Wakoski, Adrienne Rich, Michael Heller, Armand Schwerner, Robert Kelly, David Antin, Richard Grossinger. Cover: Michael McClure.

D9   *Caterpillar* 7, April 1969 (Volume 2, #2) 128 leaves. (Contributing Editor: Robert Kelly). Includes: Cid Corman, Ed Dorn, Max Douglas, Eric Kiviat, Allen Ginsberg, Victor Coleman, Robert Duncan, Nelson Ball, Diane Wakoski, Jack Hirschman, Harvey Bialy, James Gill, Gerrit Lansing,

Clayton Eshleman, David Antin, Lynne Banker, Christine La Belle, John Shannon, George Stanley, Sue Rozen, Jess, Tom Meyer, Armand Schwerner, Michael McClure, Will Petersen, Dick Higgins, Robert Kelly, Ted Enslin, Kenneth Irby, Wilhelm Reich, Paul Blackburn, Richard Grossinger, Michael Heller, Mark Hedden, Lewis Warsh. Test of Translation IX: Nerval (translations by Garrit Lansing, and by Robert Duncan). Cover: Carolee Schneeman.

D10   *Caterpillar* 8/9 October 1969. (Volume II, 3, 4). 128 leaves. (Contributing Editor: Robert Kelly, Managing Editor: Brian McInerney). Includes: Paul Celan versions by Cid Corman, Garrit Lansing, David Meltzer, Carolee Schneemann, Charles Bukowski, Clayton Eshleman, Kenneth Irby, Joanne Kyger, Stephen Jonas, Peter Passuntino, Richard Grossinger, Frank Samperi, Rochelle Owens, Diane Wakoski, Charles Stein, Leon Golub, Nancy Spero, Jeanetta Jones, Cid Corman, Thomas Meyer, Robert Kelly, John Enright, Jerome Rothenberg, Robert Hogg, Samuel Charters, Larry Eigner, Ronald Silliman, Janine Pommy-Vega, Corinne Robins, Joe Early, Larry Goodell, Michael McClure, Jack Hirschman, Sue Wilkins, Robert Duncan. Cover: front and back cover Collage: Jess.

D11   *Caterpillar* 10, January 1970 (Vol. III, #2). 128 leaves. (Contributing Editor: Robert Kelly, Managing Editor: Brian McInerney). Includes: Ed Dorn, Robert Kelly, Ted Enslin, James Tenney, Jack Hirschman, Russell Edson, Charles Stein, Denise Levertov, Kenneth Irby, Jeanetta Jones, Joseph Kurhajec, Diane Wakoski, Garrit Lansing, David Bromige, Paul Blackburn, Wayne Oakes, Clayton Eshleman, Thomas Meyer, Cid Corman, George Economou, Heywood Haut, Philip Corner, Donald Phelps, Paul Malanga, Robert LaVigne, Sue Wilkins, Max Douglas, David Antin, J.D. Whitney, Gary Snyder, Joyce Benson, Richard Grossinger, Peter Quartermain, Julie Winter. Test of Translation X: Comte de Peitau (translations by George Economou, by Thomas G. Bergin, by Frederick Goldin, by Ezra Pound and by Paul Blackburn). Cover: Robert LaVigne.

D12   *Caterpillar* 11, April 1970 (Volume III, #3). 80 leaves. (Contributing Editor: Robert Kelly, Managing Editors: Caryl Rider (sic) & Brian McInerney. Includes: Stan Brakhage, George Stanley, Theodore Enslin, Clayton Eshleman, Irving Petlin, Armand Schwerner, Harold Dull, Stephen Jonas, Thomas Meyer, Hugh Seidman, Kenneth Irby, The Prajna-Paramita Heart Sutra (translated by Richard B. Clarke), Lindy Hough, Carl Rakosi, John Wieners, Stan Persky, James Tenney, David Bromige, Richard Grossinger, Donald Phelps, Harvey Bialy, Gary Snyder, Robert Kelly. Cover: Robert Kelly.

D13   *Caterpillar* 12, July 1970. Volume III, #4. 112 leaves. (Contributing Editor: Robert Kelly, Managing Editors: Caryl Rider (sic) and Brian

McInerney). Includes: Robin Blaser, Jack Spicer, Stan Persky. Cover: collage: Robin Blaser.

D14   *Caterpillar* 13, October 1970 (Volume IV, #1) 80 leaves. (Contributing Editor: Robert Kelly, Managing Editor Caryl Reiter). Includes: Allen Ginsberg, Billy McCune, Jackson MacLow, George Stanley, Michael Burkard, Nora Jaffe, Clayton Eshleman, Robert Kelly, Brian McInerney, Fielding Dawson, Larry Goodell, Leonore L. Schwartz Goodell, Jerome Rothenberg, Bradford Stark, Richard Grossinger, Norman O. Brown, Stan Brakhage, Daphne Marlatt, John Shannon. Cover: William Paden.

D15   *Caterpillar* 14, January 1971 (Volume IV, #2). 80 leaves. (Contributing Editor: Robert Kelly, Managing Editor: Caryl Eshleman). Includes: Robert Kelly, Kenneth Irby, Clayton Eshleman, Michael Palmer, Jack Hirschman, Elaine Edelman, Theodore Enslin, Brian McInerney, Fielding Dawson, David Bromige, Stan Brakhage, William Lane, Thomas Meyer, Wallace Berman, Diane Wakoski, Allen Ginsberg, Robert Creeley, Rochelle Nameroff, Carl Thayler. Cover: Walace Berman: "Topanga Seed".

D16   *Caterpillar* 15/16 April/July 1971 (Volume IV: 3/4). 152 leaves. (Contributing Editor: Robert Kelly, Managing Editor: Caryl Eshleman). Includes: Jonathan Williams, Stephen Jonas, Fielding Dawson, Clayton Eshleman, George Herms, Kenneth Irby, Rae Armantrout, Will Staple, Stan Brakhage, David Antin, Stan Persky, Hayden Carruth, Richard Grossinger, Thomas Meyer, Frank Samperi, George Stanley, Bruce McClelland, Edward Dorn, R.B. Kitaj, Larry Eigner, Robert Kelly, Charles Stein, Garret lansing, Paul Blackburn, Theodore Enslin. Cover: Leon Golub.

D17   *Caterpillar* 17, October 1971 (Volume V, #1). 64 leaves. (Contributing Editor: Robert Kelly, Managing Editor: Caryl Eshleman). Includes: Philip Lamantia, Robert Kelly, Theodore Enslin, David Bromige, Daphne Marlatt, Tenney Nathanson, Jerome Rothenberg, Laurence Weisberg, Thomas Meyer, Hugh Seidman, Brian McInerney, George Stanley, Diane Wakoski, Kenneth Irby, Clayton Eshleman, Gary Snyder. Cover: Berman.

D18   *Caterpillar* 18, April 1972 (Volume V, #2). 64 leaves. (Contributing Editor: Robert Kelly, Managing Editor: Caryl Eshleman). Includes: Gary Snyder, Robert Kelly, Will Staple, Gerrit Lansing, David Bromige, Brian McInerney, Antonin Artaud (translated by Clayton Eshleman), Clayton Eshleman, Nancy Spero, David Antin, Theodore Enslin, Howard McCord, John Felstiner, Carl Thayler, Daphne Marlatt, Bob Coffman. Cover: Jess.

D19   *Caterpillar* 19, October 1972 (Volume V, #3). 74 leaves. (Contributing Editor: Robert Kelly, Managing Editor Caryl Eshleman). Includes: Gary Snyder, Robert Kelly, Theodore Enslin, César Vallejo (translated by Clayton Eshleman), Thomas Meyer, Clayton Eshleman. Cover: Photograph by Gary Snyder, design by Caryl Eshleman.

D20   *Caterpillar* 20, June 1973 (Volume V, #4). The final issue. 87 leaves. (Contributing Editor: Robert Kelly, Managing Editor: Caryl Eshleman). Includes: Charles Baudelaire (translated by Oreste F. Pucciani), César Vallejo (translated by Clayton Eshleman and José Rubia Barcia), Paul Blackburn, Fielding Dawson, Theodore Enslin, Hayden Carruth, Carl Thayler, Gary Snyder, Jerome Rothenberg, David Antin, Clayton Eshleman, Robert Kelly, Kenneth Irby, Michael Heller, George Quasha, Robert Bertholf, Thomas Meyer, Spencer, George Bereshinsky, Norman Weinstein, Michael Palmer, Michael Davidson, Will Staple, Robert Gluck, Rae Armantrout, Tenney Nathanson, Bruce McClelland, Bill Mayer, Lauren Shakely. Cover: Spencer.

D21   *Sulfur* 1, 1981. A Literary Tri-Quarterly of the Whole Art. 128 leaves. Published tri-quarterly, by California Institute of Technology, Pasadena, California. Contributing Editor: Robert Kelly. Book Review Editor: Dennis Phillips. Assistant Editor: Caryl Eshleman, Design: Robin Palanker. Production Assistant: Rebecca Morales. Includes: Ezra Pound, Jerome Rothenberg, Gustaf Sobin, Bruce McClelland, Jacinto Cua Pospoy (translated from the Spanish by Martin Prechtel and Nathaniel Tarn), Kimberly Lyons, James Hillman, Charles Stein, John Ashbery, Karin Lessing, Hayden Carruth, Thomas Meyer, Lyn Hejinian, Robert Kelly, Ana Mendieta, Lynn Behrendt, Letters of Edward Dahlberg and Charles Olson, Paul Blackburn, Michael Palmer, Clayton Eshleman, Gerrit Lansing, Mary Caponegro, Jonathan Williams, Diane Wakoski, Jed Rasula, Rachel Blau DuPlessis, Billie Chernicoff, Aimé Césaire (translated from the French by Clayton Eshleman and Annette Smith), Alan Williamson, Eliot Weinberger, Michael Davidson, Donald Wesling, Dennis Phillips, Thomas Meyer, Martin Nakell, David R. Smith. Cover: photograph: "Silueta Series" 1980 (Earth & gunpowder) by Ana Mendieta. Logo: F.X. Feeney.

D22   *Sulfur* 2, 1981. (Volume I, #2). 135 leaves. Published tri-quarterly, by California Institute of Technology, Pasadena, California. Contributing Editor: Robert Kelly. Book Review Editor: Dennis Phillips. Design: Robin Palanker. Art Assistant: Rebecca Morales. Includes: Jerome Rothenberg, Ronald Johnson, Theodore Enslin, Clayton Eshleman. Pierre Joris, Will Alexander, Hector Manjarrez (translated from the Spanish by Nathaniel Tarn), The Letters of Edward Dahlberg and Charles Olson, Six

D21. Sulfur 1, 1981

photographers selected by Darryl J. Curran: (Ruth Thorne-Thomsen, Richard Gordon, Chuck Nicholson, Wayne R. Lazorik, Joe Jachna, Diana Schoenfeld), Garth Tschernisch, Hayden Carruth, Dennis Phillips, Antonin Artaud (translated from the French by Norman Glass), Michael Davidson, Hart Crane to Kenneth Burke (ten unpublished letters), Ron Padgett, Keith Waldrop, George F. Butterick, Jed Rasula, Eliot Weinberger, Robert N. Essick, Eric Gans, Don Byrd, Robert Peters, Donald Wesling, Barbara Einzig, Bill Zavatsky, Ed Dorn, David R. Smith. Cover: photograph by Elaine O'Neil from Self Portrait Series, 1980.

D23   *Sulfur* 3, 1982. (Volume I, #3). 128 leaves. Published tri-quarterly, California Institute of Technology, Pasadena, California. Contributing Editors: Michael Palmer, Jerome Rothenberg, Eliot Weinberger. Book

Review Editor: Dennis Phillips. Design Robin Palanker. Art Assistant: Laurel Burden. Copy Editor: Caryl Eshleman. Business Manager: Irene Baldon. Includes: Robert Duncan, Ron Silliman, Allen Fisher. Rachel Blau DuPlessis, Bernard Bador (translated from the French by Clayton Eshleman), Alison Watkins, Karin Lessing, Gerald Burns, José Lezama Lima (translated from the Spanish by James E. Irby), Gisele Celan-Lestrande, David Rattray, Susan Howe, Michel Deguy (translated from the French by Clayton Eshleman), Larry Eigner, Leonardo Sciascia (translated from the Italian by Bradford Morrow), Barbara Moraff. San Juan De La Cruz (translated from the Spanish by Eliot Weinberger), Holly Prado, Jerome Rothenberg, François Janicot, Hayden Carruth, Andrew Robbins, Mark Karlins, August Kleinzahler, The Letters of Edward Dahlberg and Charles Olson, Cid Corman, Jed Rasula, Craig Watson, Cornelia Emerson, Martin Nakell, Henry Weinfeld, Eliot Weinberger, Dick Shreve, Robert Peters. Cover: Arturo Secunda: "A Clear Space," 1980.

D24   *Sulfur* 4, 1982 (Volume II, #1). 88 leaves. Published tri-quarterly by California Institute of Technology, Pasadena, California. Contributing Editors: Michael Palmer, Jerome Rothenberg, Eliot Weinberger. Book Review Editor: Dennis Phillips. Design Robin Palanker. Art Assistant: Laurel Burden. Copy Editor: Caryl Eshleman. Business Manager: Irene Baldon. Includes: William Carlos Williams, Ed Kaplan, David Shapiro, Nora Jaffe, Jonathan Greene, Boris Pasternak (translated from the Russian by Mark Rudman), Sandra Braman, Paul Blackburnb, Karin Lessing, Jed Rasula, John Taggart, Irving Petlin, Michael Davidson, John Yau, Nathaniel Tarn, Ron Silliman, George F. Butterick, Michael Palmer, Pierre Joris, Eliot Weinberger. Cover: Irving Petlin: portrait study for "The Tidal Man," pastel, 1975. *[Note:* this issue contains twenty-two previously unpublished poems by Paul Blackburn, the first major selection of individual pieces based on a comprehensive survey of the recently established and indexed canon from the large cache of manuscripts located in the University of California, at San Diego Archive for New Poetry].

D25   *Sulfur* 5, 1982 (Volume II, #2). 88 leaves. Published tri-quarterly by California Institute of Technology, Pasadena, California. Contributing Editors: Michael Palmer, Jerome Rothenberg, Eliot Weinberger. Book Review Editor: Dennis Phillips. Design: Robin Palanker. Art Assistant: Laurel Burden. Copy Editor: Caryl Eshleman. Business Manager: Terry Atwell. Includes: Eliot Weinberger, Michel Leiris (translated from the French by A. James Arnold), Aimé Césaire (translated from the French by Clayton Eshleman and Annette Smith), Nora Jaffe, Bruce McClelland, Gustaf Sobin, Lauren Shakely, Michael Palmer, Clayton Eshleman, Peter Redgrove, Dennis Phillips, John Mandel, Carl Rakosi, John Ashbery,

Penelope Shuttle, George Economou, Jerome Rothenberg, Lyn Hejinian, Miroslav Valek (translated from the Czechoslovakian by Kaca Polakova), Charles Stein, Ron Silliman, Annette Smith, Jed Rasula, Norman Klein, Jerome McGann, Cornelia Emerson, Craig Watson, Robert Peters, Norman Weinstein, William Bronk. Cover: graphite drawing by John Mandel.

D26   *Sulfur* 6, 1983. (Volume II, #3). 96 leaves. Published tri-quarterly by California Institute of Technology, Pasadena, California. Contributing Editors: Michael Palmer, Jerome Rothenberg, Eliot Weinberger. Book Review Editor: Dennis Phillips. Design: Robin Palanker. Art Assistant: Laurel Burden. Copy Editor: Caryl Eshleman. Business Manager: Terry Atwell. Included: Jackson MacLow, Paul Hoover, Rosmarie Waldrop, Jerome Rothenberg, Clark Coolidge, Samuel Beckett, Richard H. Abrams, Raoul Hausmann, Kurt Schwitters, Madeleine Burnside, Ronald Johnson, Rochelle Owens, Marwan, Gene Frumkin, William Corbett, Claude Gauvreau, Lydia Davis, Todd Baron, Friedrich Holderlin, Bernard Heidsieck, Gerrit Lansing, John Taggart, Baroness Elsa Von Freytag-Loringhoven, Eliot Weinberger, Lori Chamberlain, Diane Wakoski, Jed Rasula, Marjorie Perloff, Norman Klein. Cover: Choreography-Costume from the dance "After Words," 1981 by Alice Farley, photograph by Ronald Kienhuis.

D27   *Sulfur* 7, 1983. (Volume III, #1). 96 leaves. Published tri-quarterly by California Institute of Technology, Pasadena, California. Contributing Editors: Michael Palmer, Jerome Rothenberg, Eliot Weinberger. Book Review Editor: Dennis Phillips. Design: Robin Palanker. Art Assistant: Laurel Burden. Editorial Assistant: Caryl Eshleman. Business Manager: Terry Atwell. Includes: Octavia Paz (translated from the Spanish by Eliot Weinberger), Stokes Howell, Bob Perleman, Diane Wakoski, Randy White, Robert Marteau (translated from the French by Clayton Eshleman and Bernard Bador), Jerome McGann, Timothy Washington, Clayton Eshleman, Martin Anderson, Gary Snyder, Antonin Artaud, (translated from the French by Norman Glass), Antonin Artaud (translated from the French by Clayton Eshleman, Bernard Bador, and David Maclagan), James Eric, Karin Lessing, Velimir Khlebnikov (translated from the Russian by Paul Schmidt), Bill Wilson, Angelyn Spignesi, Aaron Shurin, John Yau, August Kleinzahler, William Carlos Williams, Hayden Carruth, Jed Rasula, George F. Butterick, Paul Christensen, Craig Watson, Paul Blackburn. Cover: photograph of John Cassavetes by Steve Reisch.

D28   *Sulfur* 8, 1983. (Volume III, #2). 112 leaves. Published tri-quarterly by California Institute of Technology, Pasadena, California. Contributing Editors: Michael Palmer, Jerome Rothenberg, Eliot Weinberger.

Correspondents: James Clifford, Marjorie Perloff, John Yau. Book Review Editor: Dennis Phillips. Institute Advisors: Ronald Bush, Jenijoy LaBelle, Jerome McGann, Roger Noll, Robert Rosenstone, David Smith. Design: Haycock Kienberger. Editorial Assistant: Caryl Eshleman. Business Manager: Sue McCloud. Includes: William Everson, Ed Sanders, Charles Bernstein, Arpine Konyalian-Grenier, Geoffrey Young, Nina Subin, Theodore Enslin, Edmond Jabes (translations from the French by Rosmarie Waldrop and Keith Waldrop), Nathaniel Tarn, Dennis Phillips, John Norcross, Martha I. Moia (translated from the Spanish by Susan Pensak), Michel Deguy (translated from the French by Clayton Eshleman), John Yau, David True, Jerome Rothenberg, Rachel Blau DuPlessis, Gael Turnbull, Michael Palmer, Eliot Weinberger, William Corbet, Peter Redgrove, Penelope Shuttle, Octavia Paz (translated from the Spanish by Eliot Weinberger), James Clifford, August Kleinzahler, Michael Davidson, Clayton Eshleman, George J. Leonard, Don Byrd, Norman Weinstein, George F. Butterick, Diane Wakoski, Laura Riding Jackson. Cover: photograph by Nina Subin.

D29   *Sulfur* 9, 1984. (Volume III #3). 112 leaves. This issue published by Clayton Eshleman. *[Note:* Although as editor of *Sulfur,* Eshleman was the recipient of grants from California Arts Council, Los Angeles Department of Cultural Affairs, The National Endowment for the Arts, The Co-ordinating Council of Literary Magazines, Chevron USA, and the General Electric Foundation, the magazine was no longer to be published at Cal Tech. A trustee of the Weingart Foundation (some of whose discretionary funds were used by Cal Tech President Marvin Goldberger to underwrite *Sulfur)* was offended by one poem by Paul Blackburn in issue #4, (see D24), thus Eshleman was informed that the magazine could no longer be published under the auspices of Cal Tech and he published this issue himself]. Contributing Editors: Michael Palmer, Jerome Rothenberg, Eliot Weinberger. Correspondents: James Clifford, Marjorie Perloff, John Yau. Book Review Editor: Dennis Phillips. Design Haycock Kienberger. Editorial Assistant: Caryl Eshleman. Business Manager Sue McCloud. Includes: Antonin Artaud (translated from the French by A. James Arnold, Clayton Eshleman, David Rattray, and David Maclagan), Nancy Spero, Peter Redgrove, Diane Ward, Janet Rodney, Susan Howe, Pierre Joris, R.B. Kitaj, David Plante, Sandra Fisher, John Ashbery, Christopher Dewdney, Martha Lifson, Hans Magnus Enzensberger (translated from the German by Herbert Graf), Lyn Hejinian, Rafael Lorenzo, John Yau, Malcolm Morley, Jed Rasula, Barrett Watten, Eliot Weinberger, Marjorie Perloff, Rachael Blau DuPlessis, James Clifford, Michael Davidson, Martin Nakell, Lori Chamberlain, Andrew Schelling, Gerald Burns, Charles Bernstein. Cover: photograph of "Kitaj in Paris" (charcoal drawing by R.B. Kitaj).

D30   *Sulfur* 10, 1984. (Volume IV, #1). 112 leaves. Published by The Writer's Program, University of California at Los Angeles, Extension Program. Contributing Editors: Michael Palmer, Jerome Rothenberg, Eliot Weinberger. Correspondents: James Clifford, Marjorie Perloff, Jed Rasula, John Yau. Managing Editor: Caryl Eshleman. Business Manager: Sue McCloud. Includes: Laura Riding Jackson, Gerald Burns, Barrett Watten, John Yau, Anton van Dalen, Alejandra Pizarnik (translated from the Spanish by Susan Pensak), Clayton Eshleman, Robert Peters, Jerome Rothenberg, Leon Golub, Jackson MacLow, Stephen Rodefer, George Evans, Paul Christensen, Robert Morris, Fran O'Farrell, Robert Fitterman, Ray A. Young Bear, Michael Palmer, Ronald Johnson, Bruce Boone, Jack Spicer, Charles Bernstein, James Clifford, Jed Rasula, Marjorie Perloff, Hayden Carruth, Robert Peters, Norman M. Klein. Cover: Drawing by Anton van Dalen.

D31   *Sulfur* 11, 1984. (Volume IV, #2). 108 leaves. Published by The Writer's Program, University of California at Los Angeles, Extension Program. Contributing Editors: Michael Palmer, Jerome Rothenberg, Eliot Weinberger. Correspondents: James Clifford, Marjorie Perloff, Jed Rasula, John Yau. Managing Editor: Caryl Eshleman. Includes: A special section on Paul Celan edited by Jerry Glenn: Paul Celan (translations from the German by Beth Bjorklund, Esther Cameron, Katharine Washburn, Pierre Joris and Jerry Glenn), Milo Dor (translated by Joachim Herrmann and Rebecca S. Rogers), Hans-Jürgen Heise (translated by Linda Kraus Worley and Jeff Worley), Hans Richter (translated by Donald Hamilton, Daniel C. Nutzel, Carrie Ohst, and Susan O'Shaughnessy), John Felstiner, Gotz Wienold (translated by Joachim Herrmann and Rebecca S. Rogers), Esther Cameron, Richard Exner (translated by Suzanne Shipley Toliver), Jed Rasula, Clayton Eshleman, Erich Arendt (translated by Suzanne Shipley Toliver), Rose Auslander (translated by Carl Clifton Toliver), Heinz Czechowski (translated by Suzanne Shipley Toliver), Hans-Jürgen Heise (translated by Carl Clifton Toliver), Arno Reinfrank (translated by Suzanne Shipley Toliver), Annemarie Zornack (translated by Carl Clifton Toliver), Giséle Celan-Lestrange, Johannes Poethen (translated by James Phillips), John Yau, Porfirio DiDonna, George F. Butterick, Charles Olson, Eliot Weinberger, Don Byrd, Marjorie Perloff, Ron Silliman, Andrew Schelling, David Levi Strauss, August Kleinzahler, James Clifford, Nathaniel Mackey, Jean McGarry. Cover: "Untitled" (oil on canvas) by David True.

D32   *Sulfur* 12, 1985 (Volume IV, #2). 92 leaves. Published by The Writer's Program, University of California at Los Angeles, Extension Program. Contributing Editors: Michael Palmer, Jerome Rothenberg, Eliot Weinberger. Correspondents: James Clifford, Marjorie Perloff, Jed Rasula,

John Yau. Managing Editor: Caryl Eshleman. Includes: Vladimir Holan (translated from the Czech by Clayton Eshleman and Frantisek Galan), Leland Hickman, Mark Karlins, Marjorie Welish, Jean McGarry, Geoffrey Young, Linda Connor, Stephen Rodefer, Allen Fisher, Jed Rasula, Judith Gleason, Charles Olson, Jackson MacLow, Sandra Beall, Jerome Rothenberg, Brian Nissen, Dore Ashton, Eliot Weinberger, Michael Davidson, Benjamin Hollander, George F. Butterick, Barry Schwabsky, Jenny Penberthy, James Clifford, Albert Mobilio, Marjorie Perloff. Cover: "Virideon, 1984" (oil on canvas) by Ed Paschke.

D33 *Sulfur* 13, 1985. (Volume V, #1). 92 leaves. Published by The Writer's Program, University of California at Los Angeles, Extension Program. Contributing Editors: Michael Palmer, John Yau, Eliot Weinberger. Correspondents: Charles Bernstein, James Clifford, Marjorie Perloff, Jed Rasula, Jerome Rothenberg. Managing Editor: Caryl Eshleman. Includes: Charles Olson, Clayton Eshleman, John Yau, Robert Morris, Jed Rasula, Carl Rakosi, Thom Gunn, Hayden Carruth, Eliot Weinberger, Two Greenlandic Folktales (translated from the Greenlandic by Lawrence Millman), Karin Lessing, Sam Messer, Mike Newell, Benjamin Peret (translated from the French by Rachel Stella and John Yau), Geoffrey O'Brien, August Kleinzahler, Brent Mackay, Ron Padgett, Howard Buchwald, Charles Bernstein, Jackson MacLow, Michael Davidson, Lauren Shakely, Barbara Drake, Vladimir Holan (translated from the Czech by Clayton Eshleman and Frantisek Galan), John Taggart, Rachel Stella, A. James Arnold, James Clifford, Tafey Martin, Andrew Schelling, Peter Michelson, Benjamin Friedlander, Marilyn Kallet. Cover: Untitled (Anabasis 6) Pencil, crayon, oil on paper by Cy Twombly.

D34 *Sulfur* 14, 1985. (Volume V, #2). 96 leaves plus fold-out artwork on leaf of glossy stock. Published by The Writer's Program, University of California at Los Angeles, Extension Program. Contributing Editors: Michael Palmer, John Yau, Eliot Weinberger. Correspondents: Charles Bernstein, James Clifford, Marjorie Perloff, Jed Rasula, Jerome Rothenberg. Managing Editor: Caryl Eshleman. Includes: August Kleinzahler, Basil Bunting, Clark Coolidge, Jerome Rothenberg, Laurie Weeks, Rachel Blau DuPlessis, Diane Glancy, Larry Eigner, Gustaf Sobin, Jorge Peréz Román, Vladimir Holan (translated from the Czech by Clayton Eshleman and Frantisek Galan), Nancy Spero, George Evans, Paul Christensen, John Yau, Michael Kessler, Eliot Weinberger, Clayton Eshleman, Saul Yurkievich (translated from the Spanish by Cola Franzen), Honor Johnson, Barbara Moraff, Arkadii Dragomoshchenko (translated from the Russian by Lyn Hejinian and Michael Molnar), Marjorie Perloff, Laura Riding Jackson, Andrew Schelling, Alan Williamson, George Economou,

Mikhail Bakhtin. Cover: Untitled watercolor on paper by Henri Michaux.

D35   *Sulfur* 15, 1986. (Volume V, #3). 102 leaves. Published by The Writer's Program, University of California at Los Angeles, Extension Program. Contributing Editors: Michael Palmer, John Yau, Eliot Weinberger. Correspondents: Charles Bernstein, James Clifford, Marjorie Perloff, Jed Rasula, Jerome Rothenberg. Managing Editor: Caryl Eshleman. Includes: Michel Leiris (translations by James Clifford, Lydia Davis, Richard Sieburth, Paul Auster. Michael Haggerty), James Clifford, Michael Palmer, Peter Redgrove, Christopher Middleton, Bob Perelman, John Yau, Alan Cote, Charles Bernstein, Sven Birkerts, Jed Rasula, Clayton Eshleman, Nathaniel Tarn, Paul Christensen, Benjamin Hollander. Cover: "Portrait of Michel Leiris" (oil on canvas) by Francis Bacon.

D36   *Sulfur* 16, 1986. (Volume VI, #1). 90 leaves. Published by Clayton Eshleman in Los Angeles, California. Contributing Editors: Michael Palmer, John Yau, Eliot Weinberger. Correspondents: Charles Bernstein, James Clifford, Marjorie Perloff, Jed Rasula, Jerome Rothenberg. Managing Editor: Caryl Eshleman. Includes: Mark Karlins, Andrei Codrescu, Bill Wilson, James Gaver, R. Nemo Hill, William Corbett, Jean McGarry, Stephen Rodefer, Rae Armantrout, James Hillman, Clayton Eshleman, Bruce McClelland, Lyn Hejinian, Diane Wakoski, Clark Coolidge, Jerome Rothenberg, John Register, More Greenlandic Folktales (translated from the Greenlandic by Lawrence Millman), Charles Bernstein, Juan Larrea (translated from the Spanish and the French by José Rubia Barcia and Clayton Eshleman), Ron Silliman, Vladimir Holan (translated from the Czech by Clayton Eshleman and Frantisek Galan), José Miguel Oviedo, Sven Birkerts, Eliot Weinberger, Marjorie Perloff, Norman Weinstein, Christopher Middleton, Don Byrd. Cover: "Red Booths (oil on canvas) by John Register.

D37   *Sulfur* 17, 1986. (Volume VI, #2). 84 leaves. Published by East Michigan University, Ypsilanti, Michigan. Contributing Editors: Clark Coolidge, Michael Palmer, John Yau, Eliot Weinberger. Correspondents: Charles Bernstein, James Clifford, Marjorie Perloff, Jed Rasula, Jerome Rothenberg. Managing Editor: Caryl Eshleman. Includes: Jackson MacLow, Octavio Paz (translated from the Spanish by Eliot Weinberger), Arlena Gibson-Feller, Allen Ginsberg, Ronald Johnson, Christopher Middleton, Robert Gluck, Nick Piombino, John Yau, Clark Coolidge, Norma Cole, Clayton Eshleman, Leon Golub, Paul Laffoley, C.K. Williams, Eliot Weinberger, Paul Piper, Don Byrd, Christopher Middleton, Lawrence R. Smith, Edith Jarolim, Paul Metcalf, Robert Peters, James Clifford, George

F. Butterick. Cover: "I, Robur Master of the World" (oil and acrylic on canvas) by Paul Laffoley.

D38 *Sulfur* 18, Winter 1987. (Volume VI, #3) 100 leaves. Published by Eastern Michigan University, Ypsilanti, Michigan. Contributing Editors: Clark Coolidge, Michael Palmer, John Yau, Eliot Weinberger. Correspondents: Charles Bernstein, James Clifford, Marjorie Perloff, Jed Rasula, Jerome Rothenberg. Managing Editor: Caryl Eshleman. Includes: César Vallejo (translated from the Spanish by Sandra Ferdman), Irving Petlin, Michael Palmer, Marjorie Welish, Henri Michaux (translated from the French by Richard Sieburth), Steve Benson, Diane Glancy, Bob Perelman, Benjamin Hollander, Ammiel Alcalay, Antonio Lopez Garcia, Nicholas and Lisa Corrin, Charles Bernstein, Lorine Niedecker, Milo De Angeli (translated from the Italian by Lawrence Venuti), Sean Killian, Clark Coolidge, Ross Neher, John Yau, Jerome Rothenberg, Jerome McGann. Cover: "Skinned Rabbit 1972" (oil on board) by Antonio Lopez Garcia.

D39 *Sulfur* 19, Spring 1987. (Volume VII, #1). 96 leaves. Published by Eastern Michigan University, Ypsilanti, Michigan. Contributing Editors: Clark Coolidge, Michael Palmer, John Yau, Eliot Weinberger. Correspondents: Charles Bernstein, James Clifford, Marjorie Perloff, Jed Rasula, Jerome Rothenberg. Managing Editor: Caryl Eshleman. Includes: John Yau, Charles Simic, Norman O. Brown, John Taggart, Nancy Spero, Jon Bird, Pierre Joris, Linda Reinfeld, Douglas Lowell, Julio Ortega (translated from the Spanish by Clayton Eshleman), "A tribute to Porfirio DiDonna" (by: Anton van Dalen, Clayton Eshleman, Naoto Nakagawa, Medrie MacPhee, William Corbett, Jake Berthot, David True, Stephen Greene, David Reed, Lee Sherry, and John Yau, edited by John Yau), Porfirio DiDonna, John Ashbery, Diane Wakoski, George Butterick, Norma Cole, Gary Indiana, Francine A. Koslow, The Starn Twins, Susan Wheeler, Arkadii Dragomoshchenko (translated from the Russian by Lyn Hejinian and Elena Balashova), Clayton Eshleman, Georges Bataille (translated from the French by Daniel Tiffany), David Maclagan, Jed Rasula, Michael Davidson, Sven Birkerts, Eliot Weinberger, Clark Coolidge, Michael Palmer, Daniel Wolff, Gerald Burns, Andrew Schelling, Elizabeth Horan, Linda Reinfeld, Benjamin Hollander. Cover: Untitled (oil on linen) by Porfirio DiDonna.

D40 *Sulfur* 20, Fall 1987. (Volume VII, #2). 104 leaves. Published by Eastern Michigan University, Ypsilanti, Michigan. Contributing Editors: Rachel Blau DuPlessis, Michael Palmer, John Yau, Eliot Weinberger. Notes, Correspondence, Reviews Editor: Jed Rasula. Correspondents: Charles Bernstein, James Clifford, Clark Coolidge, Marjorie Perloff, Jerome

Rothenberg. Managing Editor: Caryl Eshleman. Includes: Michael Palmer, Rachel .Blau DuPlessis, August Kleinzahler, Philip Lamantia, Robert Avens, Gary Snyder, Rosanne Wasserman, Terry Yank, John Yau, Octavio Paz (translated from the Spanish by Eliot Weinberger), Tom Mandel, Robert Tejada, Thad Ziolkowski, Laura Riding Jackson, Gene Frumkin, Robert VanderMolen, Ron Padgett, Friederike Mayröcker (translated from the German by Rosmarie Waldrop), Jackson MacLow, Michael Helsem, Sven Birkerts, Marjorie Perloff, Eliot Weinberger, Gerald Burns, Charles Bernstein, Don Byrd, Robert Grenier, Garrit Lansing, Christopher Dewdney, Jed Rasula, Russell Fraser. Cover: "Song for Sarah ... Puzzle, 1985" (pastel on paper) by Irving Petlin.

[Note: Sulfur is an ongoing publication.

(II. Books Edited by Clayton Eshleman)

D41 *A Caterpillar Anthology: A Selection Of Poetry And Prose From Caterpillar Magazine.* Edited by Clayton Eshleman. Published by Anchor Books, Doubleday & Company, Inc. Garden City, New York, 1970. (See B9).

D42 CATERPILLAR I: *Aime Cesaire: State of the Union* (Translated from the French by Clayton Eshleman & Denis Kelly). Published by Clayton Eshleman of Caterpillar Books, Bloomington, Indiana, 1966. (See A5).

D43 CATERPILLAR II: *At: Bottom.* Cid Corman.

[Cover title, on yellow card stock, in black:] AT: BOTTOM / CID CORMAN.

35.6 × 21.7cm. 19 leaves; pp. [1] 2–36 text; p. [37] colophon; p. [38] blank.

[Stiff yellow wrappers, with three exposed staples; back cover:] CATER-PILLAR 1966 [Paper: wove; all edges trim with cover].
Publication: Published by Clayton Eshleman of Caterpillar Books in Bloom-ington, Indiana, May 1966. 150 copies priced at $1.00 a copy. Colophon: *AT: BOTTOM* is the second CATERPILLAR, / a series of publications edited by Clayton / Eshleman. The essay was mimeoed in Blooming- / ton, Indiana, May 1966. Copies may be obtained / through The ASPHODEL BOOKSHOP, 465 The Arcade, / Cleveland 44114 Ohio. All rights belong to / the author.

Contains: "At Bottom." An essay on Louis Zukofsky by Cid Corman.

D44   CATERPILLAR III. *Lachrymae Mateo.* Clayton Eshleman.

Publication: Published by Clayton Eshleman of Caterpillar Books in New York City, New York, December 1966 and February 1967. (See A6).

D45   CATERPILLAR IV. *sing-song.* Paul Blackburn.

a. First edition, first printing:
[On green in black:] SING-SONG PAUL BLACKBURN / *caterpillar IV*

28 × 21.5cm. 6 leaves, printed on rectos only; p. [1] title page as above; pp. [2–5] text, p. [6] colophon.

[Brown textured paper, with three exposed staples, on front cover printed in red:] SING-SONG / BLACKBURN [Paper: wove; all edges trim with the cover].

Publication: Published by Clayton Eshleman of Caterpillar Books in New York City, New York, December 1966. 100 mimeoed copies, priced at $1.00 a copy. Colophon: SING-SONG is the fourth *Caterpillar,* / a series of publications edited by / Clayton Eshleman. 100 copies of the / book were mimeoed in New York City, / December, 1966.

Contains: "The Concern," "Málaga: Port," "Sing-Song in Winter for the Lady & the Gent," "Rockhound," "Do that Medieval Thing Again, Baby," "And a Moxie New Year to You."

b. Second printing:
Same as a. except: 7 leaves (arrangement of poems on the pages is different from the first edition); title page printed on white; [blue paper cover stencilled in black outline:] SING-/ SONG / [in solid black:] BLACKBURN [back cover, stencilled in black outling:] CATERPILLAR / [the Caterpillar Glyph: "a small napalmed Vietnamese child"] / [stencilled in black outline:] IV [Mulitlithed in New York City, New York, March 1967. 300 copies, priced at $1.00 a copy]. Colophon: SING-SONG is the fourth *Caterpillar,* a series of publications / edited by Clayton Eshleman; 100 copies of this book were / mimeoed and 300 multilithed, New York City, December 1966 / and March 1967.

D46   CATERPILLAR V. *Crystals.* Frank Samperi.

CRYSTALS / Frank Samperi / caterpillar V

21.2 × 17.5cm.; 10 leaves; p. [1] title page as above; p. [2] blank; pp. [3–18] text; p. [19] colophon; p. [20] blank.

[Stiff blue wrappers, stapled twice through to the spine, front cover, stencilled in black outline:] FRANK / [stencilled in black:] SAMPERI / [stencilled in black outline:] CRYS / TALS [Back cover, stencilled in black outline:] CATER / PILLAR / V / [the Caterpillar Glyph: "a small napalmed Vietnamese child"]. [Paper: wove; all edges trimmed with the cover].

Publication: Published by Clayton Eshleman of Caterpillar Books in New York City, New York, March, 1967. 300 multilithed copies, priced at $1.00 a copy. Colophon: CRYSTALS is the 5th *Caterpillar,* a series of / publications edited by Clayton Eshleman; 300 / copies of this book were multilithed, New York / City, March, 1967.

Contains: "Crystals."

D47   CATERPILLAR VI. *Definitions.* David Antin. (Author's first book). [On graph paper in black:] DEFINITIONS / DAVID ANTIN / caterpillar

20.4 × 15.2cm.; 20 leaves; p. [1] title page as above; p. [2] copyright page; p. [3] contents; p. [4] blank; pp. 5–38 text; p. [39] blank; p. [40] publication and distribution information.

[Spiral-bound stiff tan boards, on front cover, printed in black]: definitions / david antin / Name [rule] / Address [rule] / [rule] [Back cover:] [the Caterpillar Glyth: "a napalmed Vietnamese child"] / caterpillar VI [Paper: blue lined graph paper; all edges trimmed with the cover].

Publication: Published by Clayton Eshleman of Caterpillar Books in New York City, New York, 1967. 500 copies priced at $2.00 a copy.

Contains: "Definitions for Mendy," "Trip Through a Landscape," "The Black Plague," parts I–IV.

D48   CATERPILLAR VII. *Terms of Articulation.* D. Alexander.

TERMS OF ARTICULATION / D Alexander / CATERPILLAR VII

21.6 × 18.3cm.; 14 leaves; p. [1] title page as above; p. [2] copyright page; pp. [3–4] blank; pp. [5–26] text; p. [27] blank; p. [28] colophon.

[Stiff red paper wrappers, stapled twice through to the spine, front cover, in black outline:] TERMS / OF / ARTIC / ULATION / [in black:] d. alexander [Back cover:] CATERPILLER (sic) / VII / [the Caterpillar Glyph: "a small Vietnamese child"]. [Paper: wove; top and bottom edges trim with cover].

Publication: Published by Clayton Eshleman of Caterpillar Books in New York City, New York, May 1967. 300 multilithed copies, priced at $1.00 a copy. Colophon: TERMS OF ARTICULATION is the 7th *Caterpillar,* / a series of publications edited by Clayton / Eshleman; 300 copies of this book were multi- / lithed, New York City, May 1967.

Contains: "Terms of Articulation."

D49 CATERPILLAR VIII: *The Counted.* Robert Vas Dias.
[On tan in black:] THE COUNTED / Robert Vas Dias / Caterpillar VIII

22.9 × 15.2cm.; 6 leaves; p. [1] title page as above; p. [2] copyright and contents; pp. 3–11 text; p. [12] colophon.

[Stiff textured green paper wrappers, in black:] THE COUNTED / Robert Vas Dias [back cover:] [the Caterpillar Glyph: "a small napalmed Vietnamese child"] / Caterpillar VIII [Paper: tan laid].

Publication: Published by Clayton Eshleman of Caterpillar Books in New York City, New York, May, 1967. 300 multilithed copies, priced at $1.00 a copy. Colophon: THE COUNTED is the 8th *Caterpillar,* a series / of publications edited by Clayton Eshleman; 300 / copies were multilithed, New York City, May, / 1967.

Contains: "The Greenness of the Burma Jade World," "Colorado Sijo," "Ceremony," "A Soft Landing," "While Waiting for His Birth," "The Counted," "At Four Months," "The Two Rivers."

D50 CATERPILLAR IX: *August Light Poems.* Jackson MacLow. (Author's first book).

AUGUST LIGHT POEMS / JACKSON MAC LOW / *Caterpillar IX* / Copyright c 1967 by Jackson Mac Low

27.9 × 21.7cm. 22 leaves, printed on rectos only; p. [1] title page as above; pp. [2–21] text; p. [22] colophon.

[Stiff yellow wrappers, three staples, (may have yellow tape covering staples and spine), within circles with narrow rediating black "petals":] LIGHT / AUGUST / POEMS / JACKSON / LOW / MAC [Back cover:] [circle with "petals"] / [circle with "petals"] / CATERPILLAR / [the Caterpillar Glyph: "a small napalmed Vietnamese child"] / IX [circle with "petals"] [Paper: wove; all edges trim with cover].

Publication: Published by Clayton Eshleman of Caterpillar Books in New York City, New York, September 1967. 300 multilithed copies, priced at $1.50 a copy. Colophon: cover design by Iris Lezak / AUGUST LIGHT POEMS by Jackson MacLow is the ninth *Caterpillar,* / a series of publications edited by Clayton Eshleman. 300 copies of / this book were multilithed in NYC September 1967.

Contains:"12th Light Poem," "13th Light Poem," "14th Light Poem," "15th Light Poem," "16th Light Poem."

D51   CATERPILLAR X. *Walks.* Clayton Eshleman.

Publication: Published by Clayton Eshleman of Caterpillar Books, New York City, New York, 1967. (See A8).

With CATERPILLAR X, the publication series became the quarterly, *Caterpillar* magazine beginning October 1967. An occasional CATERPILLAR book was planned. *Brother Stones* was published as such a CATERPILLAR book. (see A11).

(III. Poetry Column Edited by Clayton Eshleman)

D52   *L.A. Weekly* December 16–22, 1983. Vol. 6, #3. "Ill Fate and Abundant Wine," edited by Clayton Eshleman. Contains poems by: Jerome Rothenberg: "The Icon (2)," Jennifer Olds: "Narcissist Over the Edge," August Kleinzahler: "Where Souls Go." p. 18.

D53   *L.A. Weekly* February 24–March 1, 1984. Vol. 6, #13. "Ill Fate and Abundant Wine," edited by Clayton Eshleman. Contains poems by: Michelle T. Clinton: "Good People Know How to Grease," August Kleinzahler: "Shooting," Mark Karlins: (untitled) "I am amazed by lightness..." p. 10.

D54   *L.A. Weekly* March 30–April 5, 1984. Vol. 6, #18. "Ill Fate and Abundant Wine," edited by Clayton Eshleman. Contains poems by: Diane Wakoski: "On the Broadwalk in Atlantic City," Charles Olson: (untitled) "The proper soul in the proper body...," Paul Christensen: "Genoa." p. 16.

D55   *L.A. Weekly* April 27–May 3, 1984. Vol. 6, #22. "Ill Fate and Abundant Wine," edited by Clayton Eshleman. Contains a poem by: Jackson MacLow: "Central America." p. 8.

D56 *L.A. Weekly* June 1–7, 1984. Vol. 6, #27. "Ill Fate and Abundant Wine," edited by Clayton Eshleman. Contains poems by: Barbara Moraff: "Song of Witch," "Found Poem #3," "Now the Old Hills Unbend Into Spring," "Found Poem #11," (untitled:) "Dawn moon reeling...," "Found Poem #32." p. 126.

D57 *L.A. Weekly* June 29–July 5, 1984. Vol. 6, #31. "Ill Fate and Abundant Wine," edited by Clayton Eshleman. Contains poems by: Charles Olson (untitled:) "17th century men who founded this land...," Robert Harris: "Toblach Surrender, 1909." p. 8.

D58 *L.A. Weekly* August 10–16, 1984. Vol. 6, #37, "Ill Fate and Abundant Wine," edited by Clayton Eshleman. Contains poems by: August Kleinzahler: "Song," "Tenderloin: An Etymology," "A Birthday Bash for Thomas Nashe," "Friday Morning in the Haight," "Hot Night On East Fourth." p. 18.

[Note: The title of the column "Ill Fata and Abundant Wine" was selected by Eshleman from Ezra Pound's *Canto I,* (the response that Elpinor makes to Ulysses in Erebus)].

E. Tapes

E1   (ca. 1960). *An Introduction To Pablo Neruda.* Discussion of Pablo Neruda by Clayton Eshleman, David Ossman, Jerome Rothenberg, and Robert Kelly and readings by each from translations of Neruda's poetry. C.E. reads "Death," "Ritual of My Legs," "Unity," (from *Residencia,* translated from the Spanish by C.E.). BB2702. Pacifica Foundation Radio Archive, Los Angeles, California. Recorded and broadcast in Los Angeles in 1960.

E2   February 1962. *Clayton Eshleman In Tokyo, Japan.* (A tape sent to Paul Blackburn). C.E. reads from: Paul Blackburn: *The Nets.* C.E. reads: (from his translations from the Spanish of César Vallejo:) "The Spider," (from his translations from the Spanish of Pablo Neruda:) "Lone Gentleman," "Ritual of My Legs," "Walking Around." C.E. reads from the poems of Gary Snyder. C.E. reads his poems: "Inheritance," "Water Song," "A Very Old Woman," "Poco Tomado," "La Mujer," "Bloomington, October," "The Night Hawks," "The Minister as a Black Swan," "Little Song for a Departure," "Son of Lighting," "Chapala," "Prothalameon." (APN tape 21—4 Cassettes) University of California, San Diego, (UCSD) Library, The Mandeville Department of Special Collections, Archive for New Poetry. The Paul Blackburn Archive.

E3   (ca. 1962) *Clayton And Barbara Eshleman From Kyoto, Japan.* (A tape sent to Paul Blackburn). Includes a conversation between Gary Snyder, Cid Corman, Clayton Eshleman, Will and Ami Petersen. C.E. reads: "Phrases," "Tea," "After Love," "Rock I," "Rock II," "Grandma's Dance," "The Exorcism," "Spiders," "The Ascent," "Old Ladies," untitled: "Poke up path a dying fire...," "The Translation Done In February," "News from Kyoto," "The U.S. Army," untitled: "The Koreans she said get their power...," "Seppuku," "Recalling a Holy Fire, February 25th," "February 20th," "February 28th, the Rocks," "Cyclings," "The Bell-Shrine II," "Agitation at Night." Barbara and C.E. at the Petersens. C.E. reads: (from *Pablo Neruda: Residence On Earth.* Translated from the Spanish by C.E.) "Pecho de Pan." C.E. reads his essay on his stay with Jimmy George in Mexico. (APN tape 25) UCSD Library, The Mandeville Department of Special Collections, Archive for New Poetry. The Paul Blackburn Archive.

E4   (ca. 1963) *Clayton Eshleman Reads From: César Vallejo: Poemas Humanos.* (Translated from the Spanish by C.E.) Side I. (ANP tape 57) UCSD Library, The Mandeville Department of Special Collections, Archive for New Poetry. The Paul Blackburn Archive.

E5   July 24, 1964. *Poemas: Clayton Eshleman, 1964.* C.E. reads: "One Morning," untitled: "I am taking a walk and holding Barbara's hand...," "The Koreans she said...," "After Love," untitled: "Walking Omea...," untitled: "The stillness of magenta azaleas...," untitled: "Night and the possibility of fulfillment...," "The Kitchen." C.E. reads from: "The Tsuruginomiya Regeneration": "The Book of Niemonjima," from: "The Book of Yorunomado," from: "The Book of Coatlicue, Section V)," *(Note:* much of this seems to remain still unpublished, I find only some of the sections read, in print). BB5113 Pacifica Foundation Radio Archive, Los Angeles, California. Recorded July 24, 1964, broadcast September 11, 1964.

E6   July 1964. *César Vallejo: Human Poems, Parts I & II.* Clayton Eshleman gives an introduction to César Vallejo; reads from: *César Vallejo: Poemas Humanos;* (translated from the Spanish by C.E.:) untitled: "It's here today I greet you...," untitled: "Confidence in the eyeglass...," untitled: "A column supporting solace...," untitled: "My chest wants and doesn't want its color...," "The Hungry Man's Rack," untitled: "It was Sunday in the pale ears of my burro...," untitled: "The miners came out of the mine," untitled: "Today I love life much less...," untitled: "The fact is the place where I pull on my pants...," "Death Sermon," untitled: "Alfonzo you are looking at me, I know...," untitled: "Considering coldly, impartially...," "Black Stone on a White Stone," "Two Gasping Children," untitled: "Walks stripped naked the millionaire...," untitled: "Contrary to the birds of the mountain...," "Palms and Guitar," untitled: "There comes to me, there are days...," "Those Out of Grace," untitled: "What gets into me...," "Guitar." (End of Part I). Part II. David Ossman reads an introduction by William Paden, Clayton Eshleman reads from: *César Vallejo: Poemas Humanos;* (translated from the Spanish by Clayton Eshleman:) "The Gravest Moment," untitled: "Something identifies you...," untitled: "No one now lives in the house...," untitled: "In sum, I've got it in me...," untitled: "Exists a man mutilated...," "I Am Going to Speak of Hope," "Common Sense," "Violence of the Hours," untitled: "The windows have been shaken...," A concluding statement by C.E. BB5018a and BB5018b. (Two cassettes). Pacifica Founda-

ation Radio Archive, Los Angeles, California. Recorded July 1964 and
broadcast in Los Angeles September 24, 1964.

E7   February 26, 1965. *Contemporary Poetry.* (Paul Blackburn's program
on WBAI, N.Y.C.). Paul Blackburn introduction to Clayton Eshleman.
C.E. reads: "The Shore," "The Orange Gate," "Violent Sunset," "Menstrous,"
"The Sense of Beauty in New Ireland," "For William Paden," "Centers of
Praise," "The Mercies," "Walking Out of the Chagall Exhibition," "What Is
The Period?" "Boughs and Christmas Berries," "The Pan of the Hot Water
in the Dish Trough Making Cookies," "The Stones of Sanjusangendo," "The
Heavens Over Tsuruginomiya," "A Little Essay," "Rhythms," "The Fox
Hunt," "The Creation." (APN tape 167) UCSD Library, The Mandeville
Department of Special Collections, Archive for New Poetry. The Paul
Blackburn Archive.

E8   November 23, 1966. *Benefit Reading At St. Mark's In The Bowery
(N.Y.C.) For Indian Poet, Malay Roy Choudhury.* Readings by: Carol Berge,
David Antin, Jerome Rothenberg, Ted Berrigan, Paul Blackburn (Side I).
Side II: (continues) Gary Yuri, Clayton Eshleman, Allen Planz, Bob
Nichols, Jackson MacLow. Eshleman reads: "Sogipo," César Vallejo: "The
Starving Man's Rack," (translated from the Spanish by C.E.) (APN tape 123)
UCSD Library, The Mandeville Department of Special Collections, Archive
for New Poetry. The Paul Blackburn Archive.

E9   December 14, 1966. *Reading At St. Mark's In The Bowery (N.Y.C.).*
C.E. reads: "Chestnuts," "The Fox Hunt," "Sensing Duncan," "Eulogy for
Bud Powell," "Bull," "Friends," "Rembrandt's Family," "The Dreyer St.
Joan," "Lines for Barbara Beddoe," "Mate," "Ancient Idol," "Prayer," "After
Issa," "The Burden," "Slowly We Learn," "Holding Duncan's Hand,"
"Transmutation," "The Night in the Okumura House," "A Woman Whose
Open Eyes," "Lachrymae Mateo," "Red Armor Plated Chakra Numbers 6 &
8." (ANP tape 126) UCSD Library, The Mandeville Department of Special
Collections, Archive for New Poetry. Paul Blackburn Archive.

E10   March 4, 1968. *Benefit Reading For Andrei Codrescu.* Side I. C.E.
reads: "Marie Valentine," untitled: "When I was born...," "Lilacs and
Roses," untitled: "Was sympathetic, a doctor to me...," Side II. Ted
Berrigan. (ANP tape 277) UCSD Library, The Mandeville Department
of Special Collections, Archive for New Poetry. The Paul Blackburn
Archive.

E11   (ca. 1969) *Clayton Eshleman Reads: César Vallejo: Poemas Humanos-
Human Poems;* (translated from the Spanish by Clayton Eshleman). An
unidentified reader gives the original Spanish. (ANP tape 108) UCSD

Library, The Mandeville Department of Special Collections, Archive for New Poetry. The Paul Blackburn Archive.

E12   1969. *Reading At San Francisco State College* (now University of California, San Francisco). (Two tapes, three sides.) Side I: C.E. reads: from "Tsuruginomiya Regeneration:" "The Book of Niemonjima," from a journal notation: The Shelf, an essay: "The Red Mantle," two poems: "Giant Forms," "Waiting." Side I also includes Robert Kelly reading from his poetry. Side II includes Robert Kelly, Paul Blackburn. Side III: Paul Blackburn. Clayton Eshleman personal archive.

E13   December 1969 *Clayton Eshleman Reading At Dr. Generosity's, New York City*. C.E. reads: from a series titled: "Altars": "The King." An untitled Christmas poem. "6th Set." "Walk 12," "Walk 14," "Walk 15," "Walk 16," "Walk 17," "Walk 18," "Walk 19." Poems titled after astrological signe: "Virgo," "Libra," "Scorpio," "Sagittarius." (ANP tape 179) UCSD Library, The Mandeville Department of Special Collections, Archive for New Poetry. The Paul Blackburn Archive.

E14   February 4, 1970. *Memorial Reading For Charles Olson At St. Mark's In The Bowery (N.Y.C.)*. Side II: C.E. Speaking about Charles Olson; reads: "The Gates of Capricorn." Also includes (in order of appearance): Ed Sanders, Ted Berrigan, Harvey Brown, John Wieners, Robert Hellman, Gerald Malanga, Vincent Ferrini, Clayton Eshleman, John Clark, Fielding Dawson, Ray Bremser, Diane Wakoski, Jackson MacLow, Paul Blackburn. Side I: Paul Blackburn reading. (ANP tape 186) UCSD Library, The Mandeville Department of Special Collections, Archive for New Poetry. Paul Blackburn Archive.

E15   May 10, 1970. *Caterpillar Benefit*. C.E. reads: from a poem with astrological structure, "The Brothers," and "Ode to Reich." Also includes readings by Diane Wakoski, Jackson MacLow, Carolee Schneemann, Paul Blackburn. (ANP C14) UCSD Library, The Mandeville Department of Special Collections, Archive for New Poetry. The Paul Blackburn Archive.

E16   (ca. 1971). *Paul Blackburn Memorial Reading*. N.Y.C. (Poets reading in tribute following Paul Blackburn's death September 13, 1971). C.E. (unidentified) reads: "A Memorial: For Paul Blackburn," also C.E. reads Paul Blackburn's "El Camino Verde" at Robert Kelly's request, (who was in California at the time of this memorial reading and unable to attend). Other poets reading include: David Antin, George Economou, Allen De Loach, Fielding Dawson. Ted Enslin, Steve Barbash, Al Bellows, Allen Ginsberg,

Harry Lewis, Howard Lynn, etc. (ANP tape 236) UCSD Library, The
Mandeville Department of Special Collections, Archive for New Poetry. Paul
Blackburn Archive.

E17   October 19, 1971. *Clayton Eshleman Reads:* "For Caryl," Introductory
talk about Paul Blackburn, "A Memorial: For Paul Blackburn," from *Altars,*
from *Bearings.* (ANP tape 238) UCSD Library, The Mandeville Department
of Special Collections, Archive for New Poetry. Paul Blackburn Archive.

E18   January 17, 1979. *Clayton Eshleman: The Dragon Rat Tail.* Number
47. (C.E. reading at Dusseldorf-Munchen). Side I: Introduction by Clayton
Eshleman. C.E. reads: "Portrait of Vincent Van Gogh," commentary, C.E.
reads: "Portrait of Charlie Parker," commentary, C.E. reads: "A Climacteric,"
commentary, C.E. reads: "Ira," commentary, C.E. reads: "The Dragon Rat
Tail." Side II: C.E. reads: "The 9 Poem of Metro Vavin." C.E. reads: from
César Vallejo: The Complete Posthumous Poetry; (translated by C.E. and José
Rubia Barcia): untitled: "Mocked aclimitized to goodness...," untitled:
"Chances are I am another...," "The Book of Nature," untitled: "I have a
terrible fear of being...," "Intensity and Height," "The Soul That Suffered
from Being Its Body." C.E. reads: "The Name Encanyoned River." Recorded
by Nikolaus Einhorn. AUSLIEFERUNG: WOLFGANG MOHRHENN,
TALSPERRENSTR. 21, D-56 WUPPERTAL.

E19   February 13, 1980. *Clayton Eshleman Reading At UCSD.* (Recorded by
Michael Davidson). Side I: C.E. reads untitled: "I passed Soutine's rock...,"
Side II blank. [tape appears to be incomplete]. (ANP L-521) UCSD Library,
The Mandeville Department of Special Collections, Archive for New Poetry.
Paul Blackburn Archive.

E20   February 1981. *Reichian Therapy And The Orgone Accumulator.* C.E.
discusses his experience with Reichian therapy. C.E. reads: "Ode to Reich,"
"Lustral Waters from the Spring of Aires," "The Cogollo." Also includes
David Boadella, Eva Reich, Mark Abraham, John Beaulieu. Barhatch Farm
Cranleigh, Surrey, England. Revealer Cassettes III-1.

E21   (ca. 1981-82) *New Letters On The Air.* (A production of *New Letters*
magazine, University of Missouri, K.C., Kansas. Side II: Introduction to
C.E. by Rich Miller, producer. C.E. reads: from *Hades In Manganese:*
"Placements" (prose poem in 7 sections), "Turnstiles," "Initial," "Meditation
on Marwan's Faces," "The Woman," "Master Hanus to His Blindness," "The
American Sublime," "Blues," "Cimmera." Side I: Charles G. Bell. Clayton
Eshleman personal archive.

E22   March 18-20, 1983. *Symposium Of The Whole: Toward A Human
Poetics.* (A program on non-Western traditions in poetry and culture,

presented by the University of Southern California Center for the Humanities and departments of English, French and Italian, and Spanish and Portugese. Side 19: C.E. reads from *Fracture:* "Tomb of Donald Duck," (4 sections). USC (On-site Taping Services) Program #712–83.

E23 May 16, 1984. *Clayton Eshleman At UCSD Formal Lounge.* C.E. reads Aimé Césaire, (translated by C.E. and Annette Smith): "Perdition," "Barbarity," "Elegy," "Nursery Rhyme," untitled: "If my thought borrows the wings...," "My Profound Days Clear Passage," "Corpse of a Frenzy." C.E. discusses his translations of the poetry of Aimé Césaire and his reasons for doing the translations. C.E. reads from his own work: "For Aimé Césaire," "Strange Lemons," "A Recently Discovered Poem by César Vallejo," "Auto...," "Navel Intelligence Is Periscopic," (prose), "Japanese Garden," untitled: "And because I am human...," "A Piece on the Photographer Atget," untitled: "The challenge of wholeness...," (ANP L–794?, presently uncatalogued) UCSD Library, The Mandeville Department of Special Collections, Archive For New Poetry. Clayton Eshleman Archive.

E24 January 30, 1985. *C.C.S. (Center For Creative Studies) Literature Symposium.* (Three day event) University of California at Santa Barbara, English Department, Santa Barbara, California. C.E. reads: "Ira," "Dragon Rat Tail," "Still-Life with Fraternity," C.E. reads from César Vallejo: "Intensity and Height," untitled: "For several days I felt a need...," (translated from the Spanish by C.E. and José Rubia Barcia). C.E. reads: "Lemons," "On Atget's Road." C.E. reads from Aimé Césaire: "Barbarity," "Your Hair." (translated from the French by C.E. and Annette Smith). C.E. reads: "Placements," "Silence Raving," "The Aurignacians Have the Floor," "Notes on a Visit to Le Tuc D'Audoubert." (The tape runs out, the last stanza is missing). Color video tape. Clayton Eshleman personal archive.

E25 June 8, 1985. *Clayton Eshleman At U.C. DAVIS.* Introduction by Alan Williamson. C.E. reads: "Auto...," "Junk Mail," "Lemons," "Nora Jaffe," "Man and Bottle," "The Crone," "Reagan at Bitberg," "Tuxedoed Groom on Canvas Bride," "The Oven of Apollo," "The Man with a Beard of Roses." Clayton Eshleman personal archive.

E26 November 13, 1985. *Clayton Eshleman Reading At UCSD.* Introduction by Donald Wesling. C.E. reads: "The Natal Daemon," "On Atget's Road," "Junk Mail," "The Man with a Beard of Roses," "Outtakes," "Variations on Jesus and the Fly," "Reagan at Bitberg," "On a Photograph of Gaul," "Night Against It's Lit Elastic," "Deeds Done and Suffered by Light." (ANP SP TC 307) UCSD Library, The Mandeville Department of Special Collections. Clayton Eshleman Archive.

E27   January 29, 1986. *Ruth Stephan Poetry Reading.* Peter T. Flawn
Academic Center, University of Texas at Austin. C.E. reads: "Placements,"
"Silence Raving," "The Aurignacians Have the Floor," "Permanent Shadow,"
"Fracture," "Notes on a Visit to Le Tuc D'Audoubert." Clayton Eshleman
personal archive.

E28   Winter 1986. *Winter Poetry Series, 1986 U.C. Berkeley.* C.E. reads:
"Placements I," (prose poem); "Silence Raving," "The Aurignacians Have the
Floor," "Permanent Shadow," "Fracture," "Notes on a Visit to Le Tuc
D'Audoubert," "The Tomb of Donald Duck," "The Language Orphan," "The
Color Rake of Time." SA 1610 12II86 Language Laboratory, U.C. Berkeley.
Clayton Eshleman personal archive.

E29   March 11, 1986. *César Vallejo: Conferencia Y Lectura De Su Poesía, Por
Clayton Eshleman.* Wellesley College, Massachusetts. C.E. gives an introduction to César Vallejo, discusses the translator's job, and reads: César Vallejo:
untitled: "Considering coldly . . . ," untitled: "A man walks by with a stick of
bread . . . ," untitled: "For several days, I have felt an exuberant . . . ," "The
Soul That Suffered From Being Its Body," "Mass," (translated from the
Spanish by C.E. and José Rubia Barcia). C.E. discusses translating and
answers questions from the audience. Clayton Eshleman personal archive.

F. Unpublished Manuscripts and Ephemera

F1 *For This You've Been Born?* Artists and Writers Protest The War in Vietnam. New York, Angry Arts, 1967. 4to. Pictorial black and white cover and 3 mimeographed leaves, stapled, given out to people in New York who came to see and hear the protest by actors and poets touring the city from a flat-bed truck, during the week of January 29 to February 5, 1967.

Contains: "Goya."

F2 Kelly, Robert. *Statement.* Los Angeles, Black Sparrow Press, 1968. Small 12mo. orange printed cover, 4 leaves.

Contains: a prose poem by Robert Kelly with recollections of Clayton Eshleman and seven other poets.

F3 *The New American Poetry Circuit.* First Season 1970–71. San Francisco, The New American Poetry Circuit, (n.d. ca. 1970–71). Printed in Santa Barbara by Noel Young. 4to. Glossy white wrappers printed in blue and red, stapled twice through to the spine, 14 leaves, blue endpapers. A brochure designed and published by Eshleman and Robert Kelly, for an organization designed by them to assist poets in making lecture arrangements with universities.

Contains: statement of concerns by Eshleman, brief biography and bibliography, with photograph of Eshleman and his young son Matthew.

F4 Eshleman, Clayton (editor). *Living, I Want To Depart To Where I Am:* An Anthology of African, European, Latin-American and North American Poetry done especially for students at Manual Arts High School and in the USC Writing Workshop. Edited by Clayton Eshleman. Los Angeles, 1977. 4to. Bound with an unprinted acetate front cover and stiff blue back cover.

190 mimeographed leaves printed on rectos only.

Contains: Introduction, brief biographical statement, "The night in the Okumura house...," from the Introduction to *Coils,* "The House of Okumura VI (a tale)," Dedication to *The Gull Wall.* César Vallejo: "A man walks by...," "Considering coldly...," "Stumble Between Two Stars," "Intensity and Height," (translated from the Spanish by Clayton Eshleman and José Rubia Barcia). Aimé Césaire: "First Problem," "The Wheel," "Mississippi," "Beat It Night Dog," (translated from the French by Clayton Eshleman and Denis Kelly).

A second printing of this anthology was mimeographed and bound with two screw-staples in stiff green printed wrappers by Michigan Document Services, Ypsilanti, 1986. 98 leaves, printed on rectos and versos. Used as a course pack for Eshleman's East Michigan University English and Creative Writing students.

F5   *American Writers: At German Universities 1979.* 4to. Pictorial blue wrappers printed in white. 12 stapled leaves.

Contains: brief biographical note, list of publications, note on Eshleman by Diane Wakoski, photograph of Eshleman by Al Vandenberg, Preface from *What She Means;* reproduces *Sparrow 57: Core Meander.*

F6   *Sunset Canyon Poster.* Los Angeles, George Fuller of the Jazz Press, April 30, 1980. 53.4 × 44.5cm. Glossy white poster paper. Printed for a reading at the Sunset Canyon Recreation Center, University of California at Los Angeles by Clayton Eshleman, Jerome Rothenberg and Diane Wakoski. 200 copies signed by each poet below their printed poem, given gratis to those who attended the reading.

Contains: "For Aimé Césaire."

F7   Mervin Lane and Arthur Secunda. *The Beverly Hills Birdbook.* Santa Monica, California, Arthur Secunda. 1981. Square 8vo. Stiff color pictorial wrappers. 16 leaves.

Contains: photographs of Clayton and Caryl Eshleman by Arthur Secunda.

F8   (Catalogue). *Am Here Books.* Richard Aaron. 2740 Willams Way, Santa Barbara, California. Catalogue Five 1981–82: A Collection of Post-Modern Poetry Books, Manuscripts & Letters. 4to. Glossy white printed wrappers. 75 leaves. Published in a trade edition, and special edition with e.p. record, etc.

Contains: "A Note on Cid Corman," "A Note on Theodore Enslin," "A Note on Robert Kelly." Also: 16 descriptive catalogued items of Eshleman's publications, with a note on the poet by Alan Williamson. Editor's note: "The signed comments in this catalogue were edited by Tom Clark and Richard Aaron, except for those on the work of Clayton Eshleman, in which case Mr. Clark's comments were excised (at the request of Mr. Eshleman) & replaced by those of another critic."

F9   (Catalogue). *Pharos Books.* Matthew & Sheila Jennett. Post Office Box 17, Fair Haven Station, New Haven, Connecticut. Spring 1984. 8vo. Black and white pictorial wrappers.

Contains: "Regarding Our So-Called 'Letter to the World'." (This talk was given at the first Los Angeles Poets on Poetry: A Celebration, sponsored by the UCLA Extension Department of the Arts on May 21, 1983, as part of a panel: ". . . My Letter to the World: Getting the Word Out.")

F10   *Sophomore Literary Festival 1986.* University of Notre Dame, Notre Dame, Indiana. 4to. Glossy grey pictorial wrappers printed in black, stapled through to the spine. 8 leaves.

Contains: brief biographical note, photograph of Eshleman by Al Vandenberg, and "Foo to the Infinite."

F11   *The Book of Coatlicue.* Date Kyoto — Bloomington 1964. 6 mimeographed leaves. 10 copies printed by the author to pass around among friends.

Contains: "The Book of Coatlicue." This poem was later published in *El Corno Emplumado* #14 April #11, 1965.

F12   *Composition For Caryl.* December 20, 1971. 4to. Xeroxed and bound in a red morocco type leatherette folder by the author; 5 leaves (3 leaves of text) printed on rectos only. Two copies, one a gift for Caryl Eshleman and the other a present for the author's friend John Martin.

F13   ("T" Shirt). Issued by Richard Levasseur of Ellsworth, Maine. 1977. Tan cotton "T" shirt printed in brown, on front: Feb. 3, 1874– / July 27, 1946 [on back, a 36 line poem: "For Gertrude's Birthday." dated 12 Dec 1978 Paris.] 10 copies.

F14   (Dust Jacket Blurb). Olson, Charles. *The Collected Poems Of Charles Olson: Excluding The Maximus Poems.* Edited by George F. Butterick. Berkeley,

University of California Press, 1987. Quote on back of dust jacket from a review by C.E.: "A Poetics to Re-embed Man in the World." *Los Angeles Times,* Sunday Book Review Section. September 4 1983. (See C359).

(Books Contracted For But Never Published)

F15 *Gatetime.* A collection of shorter poems written over 1964–65. A contract was given to the author by Fulcrum Press, (c. 1967), but a book was never issued.

F16 *Tlazolteotl-Ixcuina.* To have been published by Harvey Tucker of the Pierrepont Press. 70 Pierrepont Street, Brooklyn, New York. Announced in *Caterpillar* 6 January 1969, in a list of eight titles for Winter–Spring 1969. Was to have been published in an edition of 300 signed and numbered copies bound in cloth or fine paper. A frontispiece and about ¼ of the leaves were typeset, when the project was aborted.

F17 *The Atour Gates.* 1978. Santa Susana Press, California State University, Northridge Libraries. 4to. The book was to have been published by Norman Tanis in a limited edition to be signed by the author. After giving the manuscript to Norman Tanis, the Eshlemans left for Europe while the project was being completed. Upon their return, and seeing the extent to which the production was at variance with what had been proposed (the work had been written by a student calligrapher and line breaks had been arbitrarily altered, other changes were also made such as the size of the edition, as well as the edition of a new title and a fake publisher citation: ["Poems published for the / inauguration of the Collection / on Sex and Sexuality, / California State University, / Northridge, Libraries."] by Norman Tanis), Eshleman refused to sign the colophon and the project was aborted. Some sets with four black and white vignettes and three full page color linoprints by Irving Block, were completed but never bound.

Contains: "A Muscular Man with Gossamer Ways," "Angry Angel," "Century Village," "This I Call Holding You."

F18 *Our Journey Around The Drowned City Of Is.* "Poems and Notations based on a first visit to Brittany . . . ," To have been published by Clint Colby of Sun-Gemini Press, P.O. Box 42170 Tucson, Arizona in 1986–87. Announced in *Sulfur* 17, November, 1986. To have been published in hardcover and wrappers. Clint Colby broke the contract in the spring of 1987.

G. Books Partially About C.E., Criticism and Reviews

(I. Books Partially About C.E.)

G1   Ahearn, Allen. *Book Collecting: The Book of First Books.* Rockville, Maryland, Quill & Brush, 1975.

Contains: Mexico & North. pp. 88. (See A1).

G2   Buccoli, Mathew & C.E. Frazer Clark, Jr. *First Printings Of American Authors: Contributions Toward Descriptive Checklists.* Vol. 3. Detroit, Gale Research Company, 1977.

Contains: A brief description of books and translations published by C.E. through 1977, written by Herb Yellin; illustrated. pp. 103–108.

G3   Cooney, Seamus. *A Checklist Of The First One Hundred Publications Of The Black Sparrow Press.* Los Angeles, Black Sparrow Press, 1971.

Contains: Item #40: *Cantaloups & Splendor.* p. 24. (See A10). Item #64: *Indiana* p. 29. (See A13).

G4   Greiner, Donald J. (editor). *Dictionary Of Literary Biography. Vol. 5: American Poets Since World War II.* Part 1: A–K. Detroit, Gale Research Company, 1980. pp. 234–242.

Contains: List of the publications of Clayton Eshleman through 1978. Biographical notes and evaluation written by Walter Freed. Lists translations by Clayton Eshleman through *Aimé Césaire: A Notebook Of A Return To The Native Land* published in *Montemora* 6 Summer 1979. Also lists reviews of C.E.'s work, and reproduces a "corrected typescript" of "The Distance from Caravaggio to St. -Cirq." Photograph of Clayton Eshleman. pp. 234–242.

G5   Katz, Bill and Linda Sternberg Katz (editors). *Magazines For Libraries.* (Fifth Edition). New York, Bowker, 1986.

Contains: A review of *Sulfur.* pp. 624–625.

G6   Lepper, Gary M. *A Bibliographical Introduction To Seventy-Five Modern American Authors.* Berkeley, Serendipity Books, 1976.

Contains: A brief description of books and translations published by C.E. through 1975. pp. 181–185.

G7   Morrow, Bradford and Seamus Cooney. *A Bibliography Of The Black Sparrow Press 1966–1978.* Santa Barbara, Black Sparrow, 1981.

Contains: All publications of C.E. done by the Black Sparrow Press through *What She Means* and *Sparrow 61–72.* (1978).

G8   Murphy, Rosalie (editor). *Contemporary Poets Of The English Language.* Chicago London, St. James Press, 1970.

Contains: A brief biography of C.E.; lists publications: includes a statement by C.E. pp. 344.

G9   Peters, Robert. *The Great American Poetry Bake-Off.* Metuchen, New Jersey & London, The Scarecrow Press, 1979.

Contains: "Angeles with Genitals: Clayton Eshleman's *Coils.*" (A review by Robert Peters, reprinted from *Margins* #24–25–26 Fall 1975). pp. 52–57.

G10   Peters, Robert. *The Great American Poetry Bake-Off Second Series.* Metuchen, New Jersey & London, The Scarecrow Press, 1982.

Contains: Clayton Eshleman: *Hades In Manganese.* (A review by Robert Peters, reprinted from *Los Angeles Times* Book Review Section Sunday May 10, 1981. pp. 153–154.

G11   Peters, Robert. *The Peters Second Black And Blue Guide To Current Literary Journals.* Silver Spring, Maryland, Beach & Company (Cherry Valley Editions) 1985.

Contains: Sulfur. (A review of C.E.'s *Sulfur* #10 A Literary Tri-Quarterly of the Whole Art, 1984. pp. 92–101.

G12   Peters, Robert. *The Peters Third Black And Blue Guide To Current Literary Journals.* Paradise, California, Dustbooks, 1987.

Contains: A review by Robert Peters of two poems published in *Temblor* #2 1985, "Ariadne's Reunion," and "Deeds Done and Suffered by Light." pp. 116-117.

G13   Vinson, James (editor). *Contemporary Poets Second Edition.* London, New York, St. James Press, St. Martins Press, 1975.

Contains: A brief biography of C.E.; lists publications, editorship, Manuscript collections; includes a note on C.E. by Diane Wakoski. pp. 450-451.

G14   Vinson, James (editor). *Contemporary Poets Third Edition* New York, St. Martins Press [1980].

Contains: A brief biography of C.E.; lists publications, editorship; includes comments by C.E. and a note by Diane Wakoski: "Clayton Eshleman is unusual among his contemporaries..." pp. 449-452.

G15   Weinberger, Eliot. *Works On Paper: Essays By Eliot Weinberger 1980-1986.* New York, New Directions, 1986.

Contains: "The Spider" & "The Caterpillar." pp. 128-136.

G16   *Who's Who In America 1976-77.* (Volume 1). Chicago, Marquis, 1977. p. 939.

G17   *Who's Who In America 40th Edition 1978-1979.* (Volume 1). Chicago, Marquis [1978]. p. 981.

(II. Criticism and Reviews)

(In order to give some idea of the many reviews of the work of C.E. I have included reviews listed in *Book Review Index: 1965-1984.* Volume 2, and in *An Index To Reviews In The Humanities.* I have indicated those reviews not seen by me with an *. If no author was indicated in these source books, I have used the word "anonymous").

Mexico & North
G18   A review by J. Langland. *Poetry* Vol. 103 #4 January 1964. p. 256.

Pablo Neruda: Residence On Earth.
G19   Sorrentino, Gilbert *Kulchur* 12 Vol. 3 Winter 1963. pp. 90-92.

Lachrymae Mateo
G20   A review by Gilbert Sorrentino. *Poetry* Vol. 112 #1 April 1968. p. 56.

César Vallejo: Poemas Humanos-Human Poems. Translated by C.E.
G21   Anonymous. *Books And Bookmen* Vol. 15 October 1969. p. 32. *

G22   Anonymous. *Choice* Vol. 6 #3 May 1969. p. 375.

G23   Anonymous. *New York Times Book Review* June 8 1969. p. 60.

G24   Anonymous. *Times Literary Supplement* (London) September 25 1969. p. 1098.

G25   Knoepfle, John. "Literal & Free." *The Nation* October 28 1968. pp. 439–440.

G26   Moramarcco, Fred. *Western Humanities Review* Vol. 23 Winter 1969. p. 94.

G27   Rosenthal, M.L. *New York Times Book Review* March 23, 1969. p. 8.

Cantaloups & Splendor
G28   Brotherson, Robert. *Works* Vol. 11 #2 Fall–Winter 1969. p. 105. Also dicusses *Indiana*.

Indiana
(Also see G28)
G29   Carruth, Hayden. *Hudson Review* Vol. 23 #1 Spring 1970. p. 184.

G30   Harrison, J. "Eshleman's *Indiana.*" *Sumac* Vol. 2 # II & III Winter–Spring 1970. p. 231–233.

G31   Neiswender, Rosemary. *Library Journal* Vol. 95 February 1 1970. p. 502.

G32   Quasha, George. *Stony Brook* 3–4 1969. pp. 389–390.

G33   Teele, Roy E. "Two Poets and Japan." *Poetry* Vol. 118 June 1971. pp. 174–177.

House Of Ibuki
G34   Cushman, Jerome. *Library Journal* Vol. 95 July 1970. p. 2488.

G35   Warner, Jon. *Library Journal* Vol. 96 August 1971. p. 2508. (See G39).

A Caterpillar Anthology and Caterpillar magazine
G36   Carruth, Hayden. *New York Times Book Review* Sunday February 13 1972. p. 7. Also discusses *Altars.*

G37   Sommers, Jeanne. Index to *Caterpillar. Credences* New Series Vol. 3 #2 Spring 1985. pp. 113–152.

G38   Wakoski, Diane. "The Craft of Carpenters, Plumbers, & Mechanics." *American Poetry Review* Vol. 2 #5 September–October 1973. pp. 55–56.

G39   Warner, Jon M. *Library Journal* Vol. 96 August 1971. p. 2508.

Altars
(Also see G36)
G40   Dillingham, Thomas. *Open Places* #14 Winter 1973. pp. 58–60.

G41   Pritchard, William H. "Youngsters, Middlesters, and Some Old Boys." *Hudson Review* April 1972. pp. 119–134.

G42   Wagoner, David. *Virginia Quarterly Review* Vol. 49 #1 Winter 1973. p. xii.

Coils
G43   Dollard, Peter. *Library Journal* Vol. 98 July 1973. p. 2113.

G44   Mottram, Eric. "The Poetics of Rebirth and Confidence: An Introduction to Clayton Eshleman's *Coils.*" *Poetry Information* #11 Autumn 1974. pp. 36–44.

G44a   Mottram, Eric. "The Poetics of Rebirth and Confidence: An Introduction to Clayton Eshleman's *Coils.*" *Margins* #27, December 1975. pp. 28–32.

G45   Perloff, Marjorie G. *Contemporary Literature* Vol. 16 #1 Winter 1975. p. 84.

G46   Peters, Robert. "Angels with Genitals." *Margins* #24-25-26 September-October-November 1975. p. 40-51, 193.

G47   Shannon, John. *Margins* December-January 1973-74. p. 46.

G48   Wakoski, Diane. "Birthing the Myth of Himself." *Iowa Review* Vol. 6 #1 Winter 1975. pp. 132-138.

Realignment
G49   Katz, Bill. *Library Journal* Vol. 101 #21 December 15 1976. p. 2541.

G50   Ratner, Rochelle. *Margins* #28-29-30 1976. pp. 140-141.

César Vallejo: Spain Take This Cup From Me
D51   Anonymous. *Choice* Vol. 12 #2 April 1975. p. 228.

G52   Anonymous. *Kirkus Review* Vol. 42 August 1 1974. p. 866.

G53   Christ, Ronald. *Commonweal* Vol. 102 August 29 1975. p. 375.

G54   Neiswender, Rosemary. *Library Journal* Vol. 99 October 15 1974. p. 2607.

G55   Slater, Candace. "The Water That Runs to Its Burning." *Review* Spring 1976. pp. 96-100.

G56   Young, Vernon. *Hudson Review* Vol. XXVIII #4 Winter 1975-76. p. 590.

The Gull Wall
G57   Anonymous. *Choice* Vol. 13 #2 April 1976. p. 222.

G58   Scrimgeour, James. "Carrying the Spirit of Blackburn." *Contact II* Vol. 2 #10 September-October 1978. pp 29-30.

G59   Zweig, Paul. *New York Times Book Review* February 1, 1976. Sec. VII. p. 27.

New Poems And Translations
G60   Wheale, N. *Poetry Review* (London) Vol. 69 #2 December 1979. p. 43. (See: G76).

The Gospel Of Celine Arnauld
G61   Olson, Tobby. *New Letters* Winter 1981–82. p. 108.

The Name Encanyoned River
G62   Anonymous. *Booklist* Vol. 75 February 15, 1979. p. 907.

César Vallejo: The Complete Posthumous Poetry
G63   Bary, David. *Hispanic Review* Autumn 1980. p. 509.

G64   Cluysenaar, Anne. *Stand* (Newcastle Upon Tyne) Vol. 21 #4 1980. p. 66.

G65   Gonzalez-Cruz, Luis F. *Hispania* Vol 63 #3 September 1980. p. 618.

G66   MacAdam, Alfred J. *Virginia Quarterly Review* Vol. 56 Winter 1980. p. 185.

G67   Rebassa, Gregory. "Cow My Stomach." *Parnassus* Vol. 8 #1 Fall–Winter 1979. pp. 221–226.

G68   Simon, J. *Poetry* Vol. 137 #4 January 1981. p. 220.

G69   Thomas, D.M. *Times Literary Supplement* January 18 1980. p. 67.

What She Means
G70   Carruth, Hayden. *The Nation* Vol. 227 December 23 1978. p. 713.

G71   Kahn, Paul. *The American Book Review* Vol. II #1 Summer 1979. pp. 8–9.

G72   Jacobson, Dale. Letter to the editor (re: Paul Kahn review. See: G71). *The American Book Review* Vol II #5 July–August 1980. p. 16.

G73   Robbins, Doren. "Nadir Points, Storms From the Zenith." *Third Rail* #5 1982. pp. 117–121.

G74   Thayler, Carl. Letter to the editor (re: Paul Kahn review. See: G71). *The American Book Review* Vol. II #4 May–June 1980. p. 21.

G75   Wakoski, Diane. Letter to the editor (re: Paul Kahn review: See: G71). *The American Book Review* Vol. II #3 February 1980. p. 15.

G76   Wheale, N. *Poetry Review* (London) Vol. 69 #2 December 1979. p. 43. (See G60).

G77   Williamson, Alan. "Of Sexual Metaphysics." *Parnassus* Vol. 8 #1 Fall 1979. p. 187–191.

Sulfur Magazine edited by C.E. (See D21).
G78   Anonymous. "Not Just A Pretty Cover." *Los Angeles: The Magazine of Southern California* June 1983. p. 189.

G79   Centing, Richard. *Choice* Vol. 20 #6 1983. p. 802.

G80   Feeney, F.X. "Clayton Eshleman's Gorgeously Blunt Little Quarterly." (Includes an interview with C.E.). *L.A. Weekly* August 13–19 1982. p. 14.

G81   (Signed:) "G.W.L." *New Magazine Review* Vol. 3 #6 September–October 1981. p. 5.

G82   Tasini, Jonathan. "Literary Magazine Finds a Home Among the Slide Rules at Caltech." *Los Angeles Times* Part V Wednesday June 22 1983. pp. 1, 8.

G83   Warga, Wayne. "Emission of Sulfur from Caltech." *Los Angeles Times* Part V Thursday June 25 1981. pp. 22. (Includes a photograph of C.E. by Con Keyes).

Hades In Manganese
G84   Arnold, A. James. "Inscribing the Fall." *The Virginia Quarterly Review* Vol. 59 #1 Winter 1983. pp. 172–179.

G85   Drachler, Rose. *Small Press Review* December 1981. p. 5.

G86   Funsten, Kenneth. *Poetry News* #16 January 1982. pp. 1-2.

G87　Peters, Robert. "Gargantuan Scope in Poetry." *Los Angeles Times* Book Review Section Sunday May 10 1981. p. 15.

G88　(Poetry Nomination). "Nominations, Los Angeles Times 1981 Book Awards." Poetry nomination for: Clayton Eshleman: *Hades In Manganese,* Black Sparrow Press, 1981. *Los Angeles Times* Book Review Section Sunday September 27 1981. p. 1.

G89　Shafarzek, Susan. *Library Journal* Vol. 106 #22 December 15 1981. p. 2356.

G90　Wesling, Donald. *American Book Review* Vol. 4 #4 June 1982. pp. 2-3.

G91　Zweig, Paul. *The New York Times Book Review* October 11, 1981. pp. 32-33.

Aimé Césaire: Some African Poems In English.
G92　Hale, Thomas A. *Research In African Literature* Spring 1984. pp. 83.

Antonin Artaud: 4 Texts.
G93　Rattray, David. *Bluefish* Vol. 1 #2 Spring 1984. pp. 105-114.

G94　Soloman, Carl. "Artaud In the Age of Tranquilizers." *Exquisite Corpse* Vol. 1 #8-9 August-September 1983. p. 1.

Fracture
G95　Bertolino, James. Letter to the editor: *Fracture* defended. *Exquisite Corpse* Vol. 2 #1 January-February 1984. p. 4.

G96　Butterick, George. "Spelunking For Eshleman." *Exquisite Corpse* Vol. 1 #12 December 1983. p. 3.

G97　Christensen, Paul. "Back to the Mind Cradles." *Bluefish* Vol. 1 #2 Spring 1984. pp. 94-104.

G98　McCord, Howard. "Hard Pecker Letter." *Exquisite Corpse* Vol. 2 #1 January-February 1984. p. 4.

G99   Prado, Holly. In Verse. *Los Angeles Times* Book Review Section Sunday August 21 1983. p. 9.

G100   Shafarzek, Susan. *Library Journal's* Small Press Roundup: "Best Titles of 1983." *Library Journal* December 15 1983. pp. 2297–2302. (C.E. p. 2298).

G101   Vinge, Joyce. Letter to the editor: "Poetry at Issue," (re: Holly Prado review of *Fracture. Los Angeles Times* Book Review Section Sunday September 4 1983. p. 10.

Aimé Césaire: The Collected Poetry.
G102   Anonymous. *Virginia Quarterly Review* Vol. 60 #2 Spring 1984. p. 62.

G103   Arnold, A. James. "Twentieth Century Stepchild." *American Book Review* Vol. 7 #5 July–August 1985. p. 3.

G104   Burton, Richard D.E. *Modern Language Review* (London) Vol. 80 Part 2 April 1985. p. 474.

G105   Gavronsky, Serge. "Black Themes in Surreal Guise." *The New York Times Book Review* February 19 1984. p. 14.

G106   Jones, Rosemarie. *French Studies* (London) Vol. XXXIX #2 April 1985. p. 232.

G107   McDuff, David. *Stand* (Newcastle Upon Tyne) Summer 1985. p. 72.

G108   Miller, Christopher. "Render Unto Césaire." *Washington Post* Book World Sunday February 1984. pp. 11, 14.

G109   (Poetry Nomination) Poetry nomination for: *Aimé Césaire: The Collected Poetry* Translated by C.E. & Annette Smith. University of California Press, 1983. *Los Angeles Times* Book Review Section Sunday September 23 1984. p. 1.

G110   Perloff, Marjorie G. *American Poetry Review* Vol. 13 #1 January–February 1984. p. 40.

G111   Rasula, Jed. "Miraculous Weapons." *Hambone* #4 Fall 1984. pp. 188–192.

G112   Snyder, Emile. *Research In African Literature* Vol. 15 #4 Winter 1984. pp. 602–606.

G113   Wake, Clive. *Times Literary Supplement* (London) July 19 1985. p. 792.

The Name Encanyoned River: Selected Poems 1960–1985.
G114   Guillory, Daniel L. *Small Press Review* Vol. 4 #1 September–October 1986. p. 85.

G115   Mohr, Bill. *Los Angeles Times* Book Review Section Sunday April 27 1986. p. 3.

G116   Ratner, Rochelle. *Library Journal* April 15, 1986. p. 84.

G117   Silsky, Barry. *Another Chicago Magazine* #16 1986. pp. 200–202

G118   Wakoski, Diane. "Testimony and Leap." *Borders Review Of Books* Vol. VII #1 February 1987. p. 6.

G119   Weinstein, Norman. "Diving Into Dark Archetypal Waters." *The Bloomsbury Review* Vol. 7 #1 January–February 1987. pp. 13, 15.

(III. General Criticism and Reviews)

G120   Anonymous. "It's Happening in Grand Rapids." *Poetry Newsletter and Calendar* (Resource Center of Michigan) April 1987. p. 2.

G121   Anonymous. "Grapevine." *Poetry Newsletter And Calendar* (Resource Center of Michigan) May 1987. p. 2.

G122   Anonymous. "Hollywood, California 2/15/63." (re: Eshleman's translation of Pablo Neruda). *El Corno Emplumado* #7 July 1963. p. 175.

G123   Brasier, Virginia. Letter to the editor: "Bishop in a Corner." (re: Eshleman's review of *Elizabeth Bishop: The Complete Poems 1927–1979.* see C355). *Los Angeles Times* Book Review Section Sunday May 8 1983. p. 7.

G129 Clark, Tom. Letter to editor. *Exquisite Corpse* Vol. 2 #3-4 March–April 1984. p. 3.

G130 Dahl, Barding. Letter to editor. (re: Eshleman essay: "Modern Poetry: Some Relations and Reflections on Poetic Polarity." See C335). *Los Angeles Times* Book Review Section Sunday March 6 1982. p. 2.

G131 DuPlessis, Rachel Blau. "The Sisters' Secret [Interfering] Child." *Temblor* #6 1987. pp. 94–97.

G132 Durras, Jacques. "Clayton Eshleman Dans La Caverne, Jerome Rothenberg Castor." *Revue Francaise D'Etudes Americans* #15 November 82. pp. 357–359.

G133 Gibbons, Reginald. Letter to the editor re: Eshleman's essay (in *Montemora* 4, called: "Vallejo, 1978") on Gibbons' translation of César Vallejo. *Montemora* 5 1979. pp. 276–277.

G134 Gilam, Abraham. "Poet Eshleman's Work Is Inspired By Cave Drawings." *St. Louis Jewish Light* March 26 1986. p. 7.

G135 Hillman, James. "Behind the Iron Grillwork." *Temblor* #6 1987. p. 100.

G136 Kirsch, Jonathan. Paperback Originals column. Mention of C.E. as "figure of established reputation," in review of *Temblor*. *Los Angeles Times* Book Review Section Sunday February 8 1987. p. 6.

G137 Lampert, Morton. Letter to the editor: "Lost in Translation," (re: Eshleman review of the poetry of Rainer Maria Rilke. See: C406). *Los Angeles Times* Book Review Section Sunday July 7, 1985. p. 10.

G138 Leonard, George. Letter to the editor. (re: Eshleman review of *Elizabeth Bishop: The Complete Poems 1927-1979.* see C355). *Los Angeles Times* Book Review Section Sunday May 8 1983. p. 7.

G139 Lessing, Karin. "The Bill: A Review of Clayton Eshleman's poem 'The Bill'." *Temblor* #6 1987. pp. 101–102.

G140 McCloud, Mac. Letter to the editor: Congratulations. (re: Eshleman's essay "Modern Poetry: Some Relations and Reflections on Poetic Polarities." See C335). *Los Angeles Times* Book Review Section Sunday March 6 1982. p. 2.

G141   Morris, Richard. "Precious Poets." *The Smith (Nada O)* #22–23 July 4 1973. pp. 38–46.

G142   Morrow, Bradford. Letter to the editor: "In His Own Defense." (re: Eshleman review of *The Selected Poems of Kenneth Rexroth*. See: C405). *Los Angeles Times* Book Review Section Sunday May 5 1985. p. 13.

G143   Müller, Bertram. "Der Lyriker C. Eshleman: Eruptionen der Selle." *Rheinische Post Düsseldorfer Feuilleton* #16 Freitag 19 January 1979. n.p.

G144   Ortega, Julio. "Vallejo y Artaud: en un poema de eshelman" (sic). *Casa del Tiempo* Vol. 5 #55 y 56 Agosto–Septiembre de 1985. pp. 23–27.

G145   Ortega, Julio. "Vallejo y Artaud: en un poema de Eshleman." *Culturas* Suplemento semanal de Diario 16 #13 7 de julio de 1985. pp. 3–4.

G146   Perry, Jo Anne. Letter to editor, (re: Eshleman essay: "Modern Poetry: Some Relations and Reflections on Poetic Polarities." See: C335). *Los Angeles Times* Book Review Section Sunday March 6 1982. p. 2.

G147   Quartermain, Peter. Letter to Clayton Eshleman. *Caterpillar* 10 January 1970. pp. 233–236.

G148   Rasula, Jed. "To Moisten the Atmosphere: Notes on Clayton Eshleman." *Temblor* #6 1987. pp. 103–108.

G149   Reis, Jemi. "J E P's Resident Poet Teaches Art Reflecting Direct Human Experience." *Daily Trojan* Friday February 17 1978. p. 5.

G150   Ridland, John. Letter to editor: "Bishop in a Corner." (re: Eshleman review of *Elizabeth Bishop: The Complete Poems 1927–1979*. See: C355). *Los Angeles Times* Book Review Section Sunday May 8 1983. p. 7.

G151   Rothenberg, Jerome. Letter to the editor, (re: Eshleman's review of John Ashbery: *As We Know*. See: C292). *Los Angeles Times* Book Review Section Sunday February 3 1980. p. 2.

G152   Shiffrin, Nancy. "Playing Politics in the Poetry Game." (Mentions C.E. as poet known in the East). *Los Angeles Times* Calendar. Sunday February 23 1986. pp. 3, 4.

G153   Ventura, Michael. *L.A. Weekly* Vol. 6 #28 June 8–14 1984. p. 14.

G154   Wakoski, Diane. "Neglected Poets 1: The Attempt to Break An Old Mold — Visionary Poetry of Clayton Eshleman." *American Poetry* Vol. 1 #3 Spring 1984. pp. 38–46.

G155   Wray, Ronald E. "Clayton" a letter to Clayton Eshleman. *Primer* 1 December 1975. p. 1.

Appendix 1: Pseudonyms of Clayton Eshleman

Metro Vavin. Appeared in *The Gull Wall*. Black Sparrow Press, 1975. (A32): "The 9 Poems of Metro Vavin," pages 68–73, were written by Clayton Eshleman in the persona of Metro Vavin, a 64 year old Russian dwarf who does odd-jobs around a Paris cafe. "The Red Snow in *Grotesca* (A40) was also ascribed to Metro Vavin.

Celine Arnauld. Appeared in *The Gospel Of Celine Arnauld*. Tuumba Press, 1977. (A43). These poems were written in the spirit of Celine Arnauld, a French poet who lived in Paris and who published a dozen or so books in the 1920's and 30's. The publisher, John Martin, had given Eshleman Arnauld material to look at for a possible translation project, but Eshleman did not feel it was strong enough to warrant translating. Instead he imagines Arnauld's gradual release from the bourgeois Catholic mind of her era, through her encounters with other imagined personalities, and writes a serial poem in the spirit of Celine Arnauld.

Horrah Pornoff. Appeared in: *Fag Rag* 20, Summer 1977, (see C254); in *Momentum* #9-10, Fall 1977, pp. 3–29, (see C256). "Her" work was also featured in *Origin* (fourth series) #7, April 1979, 24 poems, pp. 1–24, (see C284). These poems were written by Clayton Eshleman in the persona of Horrah Pornoff, a disfigured reclusive woman poet whose only known address was a West Los Angeles post office box.

Appendix 2: Library Holdings of the Work of C.E.

Lilly Library, Indiana University, Bloomington, Indiana.

The Eshleman mss., 1953-1973. Writings of Clayton Eshleman given by him to Black Sparrow Press publisher John Martin during the early 1970's with two letters to Martin from Eshleman. (15 items, includes: "On the Horrors of Getting Up in the Morning," [typed at bottom: "written by Clayton for advanced composition senior year 1953"]. "Through a Window," [Inscribed on bottom verso: "for John Martin — my first piece of 'creative' writing — 1953 Bloomington Clayton Eshleman. (Oct. 10, 1972)"]; *Composition For Caryl Christmas 1971,* (see F12); *A Bringing Of Rilke Into My Own Road And Thought,* (see A21); *Eshleman Literary Materials,* (the author's description of his

219

life, writings and archive); and *Adhesive Love,* (see A28, A32, A71, C203, D20). *[Note:* these last three titles were xeroxed or photocopied by the author from his typescript in a printing of a few copies each].

The Eshleman mss., 1960-1965. [1960-62:] *Mexico & North.* (Drafts. A. & T.D.S. 1143p. 102 items). [1961-65:] The Gatetime. (Drafts. A. & T.D. 2752p. 300 items. [n.d.:] Eshleman translation of *Pablo Neruda: Residence In The Earth.* (Drafts, page proof, rejected poems. A. & T.D. 365p. 157 items.

Additional Eshleman writings and letters are found in the following collections: (Samuel) Yellen mss.; (Jack) Hirschman mss. II; American Literature mss.; "Poetry" mss. (William Henry) Wroth mss.; (Willis) Barnstone mss.; (Henry) Rago mss.; (Ralph Bruno Sipper, Antiquarian Book Dealer) Joseph the Provider mss.

Fales Library, Elmer Holmes Bobst Library, New York University, New York.

Eshleman literary materials from 1959-. *Caterpillar* Archive, 1967-1973, acquired from C.E. in 1973, including all received correspondence, and material relating to the publication of *Caterpillar* magazine, such as all submissions, manuscripts, proofs, etc. Copies of most book publications of Eshleman. Well organized and preserved copies of most periodicals with contributions by C.E.

Additional Eshleman material including diaries, correspondence and photographs can be found in the following files: Angel Hair; Paul Blackburn; Burning Water; Camels Coming; Cid Corman; El Corno Emplumado; Theodore Enslin; Ghost Dancer; Harry Lewis; Second Aeon. In some instances, the files include letters sent to Eshleman, in others, letters received from him.

Mandeville Department of Special Collections. University of California, San Diego.

Sulfur Archive 1981-1985. Including material relating to the publication of *Sulfur* magazine: manuscripts, submissions, proofs, etc. all correspondence received, from 1971-1985; the personal notebooks of C.E.; worksheets and typescripts for most of the published and unpublished poetry of C.E. from 1962 to 1985 including material relating to the following books: *The Name Encanyoned River: Selected Poems 1960-*1985: *Altars: Hades In Manganese;* Michel Deguy: *Given Giving; Coils; The Gull Wall;* and relating to the translations of the following poets: César Vallejo, Bernard Bador, Antonin Artaud, Aimé Césaire; and material relating to "Horrah Pornoff."

Additional Eshleman material including phono-tapes can be found in the Paul Blackburn archive.

Appendix 3: Manuscript Facsimile of "Dragon Rat Tail"

There must be a way to graph   *course*
the dodges and curves of the ~~passage~~
between the non-existent " rites of passage"
and ~~a~~ place where poetry is made,   *the*
I want to telegraph it in one word,
it is still so Satanic and raw
and se present ~~even tho it has been resolved,~~   *but has never*
it is so-much the ~~point~~ *juncture*   *it cannot as a word*
where the young man goes off to war,   *he said,*
where preoccupation with sex   *overconsumes*
~~unseats occupation,~~ *a belief* that
another can be fully lived with,
~~I see~~ this ~~point~~ all-around-me, *every when*
in the elderly as well as the young,
candles brought forth, a procession
coming into conversation where suddenly
a quick funereal rite is observed
done with and then the media talk continues,
a burial has occured, quickly, the seed
that would fuse the generational to
something else has not occured,
~~every person always feels this point,~~
" the moment of desire" Blake calls it
~~with its sexual hub, but-with-its-spokes-too,~~
~~its-sexual-nut,-to~~ break the judge
in highchair, ~~to~~ bring that Jack Horner
~~down,~~ that " Good boy" ~~sufficientkkx~~ satisfied with
his plum-rubbed-thumb, ~~down~~! *Into*
~~but-with-its-spokes too,~~
~~beloved threshold-but-loved only~~
~~for the spokes~~ I loved for its streamings off
~~into-rainbow-but-hated~~
~~for its generous human gates of physical~~
~~yearning-wherein-the-hub~~
~~is-hoop,-neck-to-another,~~
~~the-only-through-the-sulphur~~
~~digested,~~ the savage truth of this world
~~is-that~~ people want love
only as a passive given,
~~sponge-love,~~ they hate and actively
oppose love as active opposition,
~~how-few-actually-trade-ideas~~
~~how-few-allow-another-being-and—~~
~~and-remain-active-before-that-reception.~~
In Kyoto, faced with my dragon
rat tail I understood ~~that~~ the world
was adamant, that there was no way through it.
Gates, philosophies, arts, all ways
confronted orange mud running down
a twilit road on Sunday afternoon.
One way to get anything out: haul up
and sieve, ~~and~~ engage the haul,
make the rat tail big, ~~a~~ dragon tail,
make the dragon tail bigger than Jung,

~~make it~~ bigger than all my ideas, ~~try~~
~~to let it~~ ~~llllllllll~~
~~to~~ let it engorge the house, ~~up through the floorboards,~~
let it split the tatami! Ride
it! Not the moon, not
the nostalgia for that other place,
but the funk that struck inside me
on the way home from the public bath.
Not to remember or realize the bath.
Be in the bath. And if there, then deal
with this other thing, art does not have to
lip the natural, live the natural,
jack off on her fender if I have to but
live the natural and confront
this other thing, sieve out
the little performer,

break ~~toss~~ the piano bench you were to become
an alcoholic upon, "Blue Moon"
"White Christmas" a chain of command,
break the chain, open it up and discover
the seed-chum she and he and all of them,
the whole atavistic octopus,
pumped into your wine-cup, be
paranoic, splay out, feel spiderlike
throughout the realm that paranoia
seeks to feel, understand that the rigidty
pit is ~~deth, in your own marrow,~~
~~is~~ social, where you do not have to be,
where you are forever, as long as you
are alive, packed in with
who you are born with, ~~play by~~ alone or
brothered, essentially with the ghosts of
the fathering mothering powers you
can transform to aid you, ~~where?~~
~~Be over the pit which can flow~~
~~with colors, which I see now~~
~~In flood, treetops, housepeaks,~~
My mother's dead eyes float out
bald in raving love for me,
how she knew what she wanted me to be
so confused was she in what I should be,   *butt*
under every egg, every Boy Scout knot,
under the Betty Grable, allowed on my closet door,
under the ghost games, under my being allowed
to dress up in her girdle and twirl
the family safe, was ~~the person,~~ Liberace, *The person*
she hoped I would be, fully middleglass,
artistic, gay, fully in command, a hero,
wrapped ~~in her heroine, mediocre,~~ in a 146
pound floor-lengh black
mink c͜oat, *lined with Austrian rhinestones,*
a ghastly Virgil,

            confidence,
I pray, at 40
to lead this doppelganger out to pasture,
he cannot be done with,
~~he is tied up into~~
~~my shield, and my doubt,~~

[handwritten right margin, upper:] armor, ≠ something, you can get rid of, yet it is bone, what you stand in, armorless armor, your marrow, your very scent, is

[handwritten right margin, lower, partly illegible:] both of us must let him graze! I am no more American than... I am his sheep herd linked... I am American? They... within (them) them Hell my... is ... my doubt.

[handwritten date:] 21/22 Jan 76.

Afterword

no one has written me about my size.
— Metro Vavin

All poets have a sense of an experience of their size, often goofy relative to the ways others regard them, but probably ultimately somehow consistent with the extent to which they can inflate the cobra hood of their imaginations and in that way outsize themselves.

César Vallejo, facing his death in Paris, 1937, wrote that his size exceeded him and that the cruelist size was that of prayer. In pondering his demise, he seems to have added his death to his life, and found that he was engaging a projective size larger and more complex than his previous sense of identity. While Vallejo's European poetic output is modest pagewise (150 pages of poetry in 15 years) it has had for some of us an extraordinary imaginative size. Recently, Ernesto Cardenal, in an interview, remarked: "Vallejo is such a deeply personal, original poet, that almost no one can be really influenced by him without becoming his imitator."[1] While I would question that word "original,"[2] I understand what Cardenal is getting at. Leafing through the entries in Martha Sattler's conscientiously researched bibliography, I became more aware than ever before of the amount of time I had spent with Vallejo, and of the extent to which he had not only tested me as a translator, but charged me as a poetic apprentice to assimilate but not to imitate him. This struggle — to represent Vallejo as a translator and to learn from him but not be carried by him as a poet — is part of my shape and size.

I think that size also has to do with the felt density or porousness of a body of work. The sublimative poem, which tends to be procedural and planned, and more often than not a discrete lyric object, makes for a smaller body of work than what I would call the processual poem, a kind of poem that has constellational identity with poems before and after it. Blake's body of work, like Charles Olson's and Antonin Artaud's seems to cover an immense amount of ground, and part of this effect is the size that the exploratory nature of the work evokes. To directly engage one's desires (vs. sublimative procedures) allows the unconscious to not only present itself but to organize, as a coherent being, within the field or space of the poem.

Size, then, is an image of force, and may actually be at odds, literally speaking, with the amount of art produced. The ego as well as the unconscious is capable of going on ad infinitum about its sensitivities etc., without realizing, or becoming responsible for, its size.

*   *   *

At the point that I moved to Kyoto in 1962, in spite of my awareness of experimental European and Latin-American poetries, I was writing a set, lyrical-object poem, which attempted to close over, in closure, and present itself as a tiny but very self-sufficient declaration. The poetry of James Wright is a good example of what I mean here, even if in slow motion. Cid Corman's poetry is a better example. Dickinson and Celan may be the ultimate.

In 1962 I did not know how to crack the lid of the abyss of which my unconscious, my fantasy life etc., was a part. By 1964 I had begun to realize that everything should be material, and that through the "unpoetic" I had a better chance at discovering my own material than in sticking with what had become acceptably "poetic." I recall working several months, fulltime, on a Prothalamion for Paul Blackburn's second marriage, and discovering that I could not write it because there was an anti-marriage at stake (my marriage, my unmarried life) that was subtextually quicksanding my Ode. Against my wishes, I began to probe what I was doing in Kyoto, in my poetry, and to consider the Indiana memories that now ran forth in long, sad rivulets. My anguish in Kyoto consisted of not knowing how to convert the seemingly huge sizelessness of my past into images that I could respect.

After moving to NYC in 1966, the combination of Reichian therapy and Robert Duncan's advice against revision freed me from the endless rounds of doing/undoing — but the immediate consequence of starting a new poem each time I sat down to write was that the writing seemed superficial. By the mid-1970s, when I started to discuss everything I wrote with Caryl Eshleman, her suggestions sent me into a new phase of rewriting which seemed to represent a "middle way" between coagulated corrections and unreflective impulsiveness. I think that finding a satisfactory way of working (moreorless 15 years after I started writing poetry) also had to do with defusing various Protestant time-bombs that seemed "set" to go off at intervals throughout my life. With Indiana temporarily out of the way, I was able to turn to the utterly impersonal realm of the Upper Paleolithic decorated caves and begin to discover an otherness that I could affirm and work into my base. I now realize that Indiana will never be eliminated as a provocation; rather, I would like to think that it has become part of my underworld that I visit from time to time and continue to learn from.

While editing *The Name Encanyoned River* in 1985, I re-read all of my work published in books, and was struck by the extent to which I had not looked back before. Not looking back can be seen as a blessing or a curse. Regardless of its consequences for my own poetry, I think I have not done so, in terms of re-reading myself (is this what Spicer meant when he referred to sleeping with his poems?), because in the work itself there is a good deal of looking back, since the mid–1970's to fantasies and visions of the origin of art. One of the risks of constantly re-reading oneself is to become overwhelmed by the extent to which one crosses over the same ground again and again, and I imagine for certain poets such awareness could become paralyzing. On the other hand, there is something about remembering oneself that seems essential to me in building a coherent body of art.

I suppose that the onslaught of information, the extent to which the abyss of the deep past has opened up, and the truly terrible awareness, via technological communications, of what appears to be happening to everyone everywhere, have forced many poets of my generation into of of two very different paths: of closing off before the onslaught and working a plot with definite boundaries, or attempting to orchestrate as much of what seems to define contemporary reality as is possible. Northrop Frye, in honoring Blake, argues that the significant poet works out of a perspective that envisions reality as created, while lesser poets adopt a perspective that accepts reality as observed. It is a powerful and useful distinction, but I suspect that both creation and observation are embedded in the art that has moved me and that I have attempted to produce myself. All oppositional distinctions have become inadequate to define the responsibilities of art in the 20th century. At the point that one votes for Dionysus, one may very well realize to what extent Apollo is necessary in shaping the so-called Dionysian materials!

Notes

[1] "Interview with Ernesto Cardenal," from Kent Johnson's *A Nation of Poets,* West End Press, 1985, p. 23.

[2] In "Dedication," which ends *The Name Encanyoned River,* I wrote: "Blake's authors in eternity are also secretaries, for the origin of archetypal address, if there is one, is closer to 30,000 BC than to early Greek Gods." In this sense we are all derivative, and "originality" has more to do with the particular way we assemble and voice the collage in which our poetic identity is performed, than it does with priority or nondependence of thought.

Clayton Eshleman
Ypsilanti
March 11, 1988

Index

A

S